SPINNING WOOL

Beyond the Basics

SPINNING WOOL

Beyond the Basics

SUFFOLK

Anne Field

SHOAL BAY PRESS

ACKNOWLEDGMENTS

Many people contributed to this book. First, my thanks are due to the small group of spinners who met monthly to 'spin' their way through the manuscript: Cecily Adams, the late Pat Atwell, Jean Esquilant, Melva Finney, Beth Halliburton, Hans Opsomer and Nancy Reynolds.

I am grateful to all the wool producers who gave me samples, information and advice: Elspeth and David Wilkinson, Vince van den Dorpe, Rotocard, Hands Ashford, Wrightson NMA, Helen Heddle, Jenny Williams, Anne Paterson, Margaret Stewart, Ethel Stephenson, Shirley Caldwell, Fran Regan and Wendy Dennis (Australia), Joyce Chance and Judith Lange (USA) and Ann Mulley (England).

Roger Lundie was very informative and helpful about the section on black and coloured sheep, and the spinning wheel manufacturers, Timbertops Spinning Wheels, Ashfords, Louet, Schacht and Majacraft, gave me great support. Margaret Stove, Margaret Stewart and Mabel Ross helped me with advice and spinning samples. Helen Stephenson, with her talent for drawing sheep, Anita Bree and Edith Thwaites, who modelled the garments so well, are also due my thanks. To those who laboured over projects for this book, Alison Graham, Ann Mulley, Pat Atwell, Alice McElroy, Beth Halliburton, Jennifer Lineham, Joy Bryant, Meg Anderson and Marion Valentine, my thanks for all your work.

Once again, my husband Edward took most of the photos in this book, and spent long hours in his darkroom developing and printing, and achieving the impossible. We are a good team.

First published in 1995 by Shoal Bay Press Ltd,
Box 2151, Christchurch, New Zealand

ISBN 0 908704 27 5

Cover photograph by Jon Hunter, Standish & Preece
Title page drawings by Helen Stephenson

Production and design by Orca Publishing Services Ltd
Printed in Hong Kong through Bookprint Consultants Ltd, Wellington.

Contents

Introduction

This book is intended for spinners who have mastered the basic spinning techniques I explored in my *Ashford Book of Spinning*. It will build on those basics to further extend spinning techniques.

Spinning has changed since its upsurge in popularity some 15 or 20 years ago. Spinners want to know more than how to spin an adequate yarn; they are becoming more technical and interested in yarn design. They want to know how to extend the range of yarns they can produce, what is happening as they spin, and something about the raw materials they turn into yarn.

Spinning wheel manufacturers are responding to the more inquiring spinner by making wheels that can spin a wider range of yarns. But spinning books have not fully catered to this need for more detailed information. Spinners still rely on farming manuals and books by wool-classers for knowledge about wool, because little has been written from a spinner's point of view.

As I have conducted more and more spinning workshops both in New Zealand and further afield, I have gradually stopped looking at wool purely from the sheep-breed angle, as I have found that the breeds vary so much from country to country. A New Zealand Romney is very different from an English Romney and should be spun differently. A different approach was needed and I began to teach spinners to analyse each fleece on its own merits. We need to know the size of the fibres, the crimp and the handling qualities of each fleece we intend to spin. The first two chapters of this book cover wool in detail, with many examples of fleece types from all over the world.

After an analytical look at wool it is helpful to know about the spinning wheel. There are so many types now, that spinners are often confused about what they all do, and which is best for them. The functions of bobbin and flyer wheels are discussed in detail, and how to make the most of each wheel type.

The yarn design section of the book begins with Chapter Five. Spinners are taken step-by-step through the process of spinning yarns of a pre-determined size and twist count, and this knowledge is related back to the raw wool so we see that the size of the fibre in the fleece determines the size and twist count in the finished yarn. This proves a very satisfactory starting point for yarn design.

We then look at explanations of different spinning methods. A wide range of yarns can be spun, from solid hard-wearing worsted to a soft, fluffy woollen yarn. The aim of yarn design is to make a yarn suitable for the finished project.

Yarn on its own cannot achieve much; it needs to be knitted or woven into garments, rugs or fabrics. At the end of this book I have included woven and knitted projects that suggest suitable end uses for handspun yarn. These projects are only the beginning, of course, as the range is endless, but I hope they will solve the problem of many spinners who, when asked what they do with their handspun yarn, say, 'Hang it on the wall and admire it.' I cannot think of anything nicer to look at than hanks of handspun yarn as a wall-hanging but there comes a time when spinners are driven to progress further.

Anne Field

Part One

WOOL

COOPWORTH

1 Wool and the Care of Fleeces

In New Zealand we have many sheep – 60 million or thereabouts. Luckily, sheep have not progressed in intelligence to the stage where they have thought of staging a coup and taking over the country. With their sheer numbers such a takeover would be easy! They seem to be happy just eating grass and getting regular haircuts. Sheep are very good at eating: they do it all the time, converting food into meat and wool for human benefit.

Wool is so much a part of our daily lives that we take it for granted. We wear wool, walk on it, sit on it, and sleep in or on it. We wrap our babies in wool, and eat the meat and cheeses that are also sheep products. But spinners look at wool with different eyes. We see it as a raw product which, by our skill, can be turned into unique yarns for garments, coverings and artistic statements. So, spinners need to know about wool and have an understanding about the fibre and the animal it came from.

Many spinners use other fibres, such as cotton, silk or mohair, to make yarn but in this book I will concentrate on wool. In many parts of the world it is the main fibre handspinners work with and it certainly has the greatest variety of fibre characteristics. (My *Pocket Oxford Dictionary* says wool also comes from goats but as I do not have the necessary expertise to cover this fibre I will conveniently ignore it.)

Much of our information has been obtained from wool growers or manufacturers, but spinners have different needs from farmers and large-scale operators. With bulk-buying and manufacturing processes the wool industry can standardise large quantities of wool to make uniform yarns, but spinners do not usually want to spin large amounts of uniform yarn. Most take one individual fleece and turn it into a specialised yarn for a particular project.

Handspinners aim for original yarns that they can control, and the easiest way to control the finished yarn is to know the properties of the individual fleeces they are working with. Spinners can then make informed choices about which type of wool is best for their project. Even Rumplestiltskin probably asked what his raw material was before he turned it into gold! So we need to know what wool is made of, how it reacts under different circumstances, and its strengths and weaknesses. This knowledge will not only improve the yarn we spin, but will also widen the range of projects we can tackle.

WOOL STRUCTURE

It is helpful for spinners to understand the complex structure of a single wool fibre. It is in fact a protein, composed of many cells. The main parts of the wool fibre are the cortex, which forms the bulk of the fibre, and a thin outer cuticle that provides a surface covering. A very thin membrane called an epicuticle covers the cuticle. In addition, coarser fibres often have a medulla, a central core that contains empty spaces. The cuticle or scale layer consists of very tough, flat, overlapping cells.The upper edge of each cell is exposed

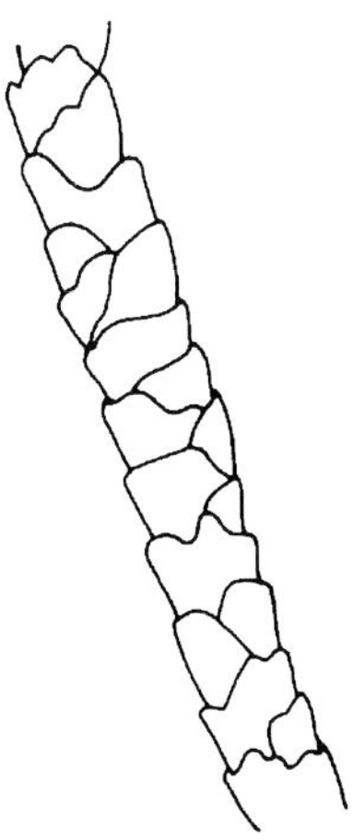

Fig. 1.A Magnified wool scales

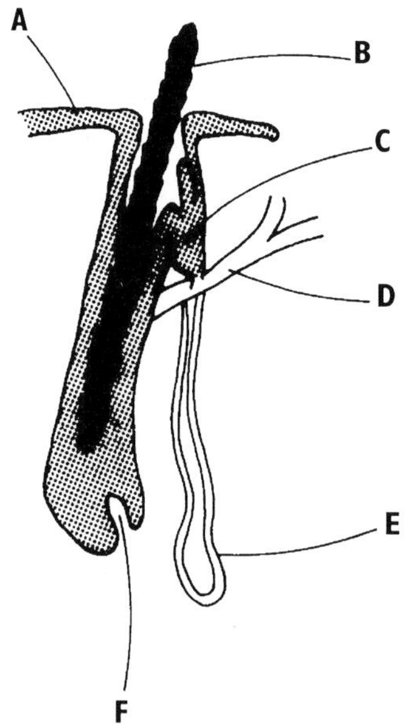

Fig. 1.B Primary wool follicle

A Epidermis
B Wool fibre
C Sebaceous gland
D Follicle muscle
E. Sweat gland
F Papilla

and points towards the tip of the fibre. This scale arrangement means that when the fibre is moved, it travels towards its root or base end. It is these scales that make wool so easy to spin, compared to many other fibres, because they catch on each other as the fibres are pulled out (drafted).

Each fibre grows from a shaft in the sheep's skin called a wool follicle. There are two types of follicle, primary and secondary. The primary follicle develops first and is equipped with a large sebaceous (fat) gland, a sweat gland and a follicle muscle. The secondary follicle is similar in structure but does not have a sweat gland or muscle, and has only a small sebaceous gland.

By the time the lamb is born there are millions of follicles. In a coarse-wool sheep there may be 1000 to every 2.5cm^2 (1sq in) of skin; in a fine-wool breed there may be more than 60,000.

The purpose of the sweat and sebaceous glands is to provide a protective film over each fibre as it emerges from the follicle and is exposed to the weather. The sebaceous gland produces wool wax, or grease,which when recovered and purified is known as lanolin. Spinners are sometimes confused by the two terms wax and grease, which in fact refer to the same substance. In the wool trade the term wax is more common, but spinners talk more about grease, so I will do likewise.

Yolk

The grease and sweat from these glands are collectively called yolk. Yolk is a complex substance. The sweat component in yolk is named suint and can be pale yellow in colour. It is water-soluble so some will have been washed from the back of the sheep towards the lower portions of the fleece, or it may have been washed out of the fleece completely, particularly in high-rainfall areas.

Suint can absorb a lot of moisture when humidity is high, and in these conditions wool feels 'greasy'. Do not confuse this feel with the grease content of wool. A washing test will determine the grease content of a fleece. Just run a staple or two from different sections of the fleece under cold water for a minute or two. The suint will wash out but not the grease. Fine-wool breeds, such as the Merino, produce less suint than coarse-wool breeds.

Grease is the second component of yolk. It is almost colourless and there are a number of different greases in each fleece. Each type will have a different melting point, ranging from 5°–36°C (31°–97°F). In higher temperatures, more of the greases are fluid and the wool will feel greasy, so if you buy a fleece on a hot humid day you will think it is more greasy than if you bought the same fleece on a cold day with low humidity.

The actual amount of grease varies considerably from breed to breed, from 10 per cent to 25 per cent of fleece weight. Coarse breeds usually produce less grease than fine-wooled breeds. In the Merino, which in New Zealand can produce about 1kg (2-3lb) of grease in a

PROPERTIES OF WOOL

Throughout the centuries, wool has been used more than any other fibre as a body covering, particularly in colder climates. It has been used as yarn for knitting and weaving, made into felt, and used as skins or pelts. This wide range of uses is made possible by some of its unique properties.

Warmth

Wool, and the air trapped within it, are poor conductors of heat, so do not readily carry away the natural body warmth. Up to 68 per cent of wool fabric is air, which is trapped by the individual fibres in the yarn and by the weave structure. Wool packs uniformly into yarn, and the finer the fibres, the greater the surface area. Because wool is so elastic, there is a constant loosening and opening up of the fibres, which helps maintain the air content.

The other reason for wool's warmth is that it generates heat when it absorbs water vapour from the air. When you go from a warm room into the colder outside air, the wool in your garment combines with the water vapour in the air and the complex reaction begins so your temperature falls slowly instead of quickly. Wool can also absorb up to 35 per cent of its weight in perspiration before it feels wet.

Water-resistance

Wool resists wetting, from rain for instance, and even when completely wet it does not feel cold. The wool industry scours and treats the wool chemically during processing, but handspinners are much more gentle with their wool and this helps retain its natural resistance. Handspun wool frequently appears to retain some of its grease content, even with repeated washing. Wool's ability to retain warmth even when wet is the main reason why woollen garments continue to compete so well with synthetics.

Static electricity

Because wool takes up water vapour it does not hold static electricity. This means wool garments will not cling and crackle, and they also attract less dirt than other fabrics.

Fire-resistance

Wool's moisture absorbtion also helps it to resist burning. It will burn in the flame but not out of it, and leaves a black crushable bead.

Affinity to dyes

Wool dyes well with natural plant dyes and also the synthetic dyes listed below. (I have included some brand names for easy identification, but this is certainly not an exhaustive list.)

Basic dyes

Brilliant colours but poor light- and wash-fastness.

Direct dyes

Cellulosic dyes, used for dyeing cotton, but many also dye wool and silk. Poor wash-fastness.

Reactive dyes

A new class of dye that reacts chemically with the fibre. There are two types: the cold dyeing (M) and the hot dyeing (H). Bright colours with high light- and wash-fastness are a feature of these dyes, which are mainly used in dyeing cotton, linen and viscose rayon. However, some have been modified to dye wool, such as the Earth Palette dyes used in Projects 2 and 8, and Hostalan and Lanasol.

Acid dyes

Used to dye wool from an acid dye bath. There are three types:

a. Level dyeing acid dyes, producing bright colours, with good levelling (evenness) properties, but poor wash- and light-fastness.
b. Acid milling dyes with high wash- and light-fastness, used extensively in dyeing fabrics that are later milled (similar to the felting process but taking place after the fabric is woven). Uneven dyeing can result if care is not taken in the dyeing process.
c. Pre-metallised dyes, an extension of the mordant dyes mentioned below (Cibalan, Irgalan, Isolan).

Mordant dyes

Dyes that use a mordant, i.e. metallic salts that form a bond between the dyestuff and the fibre. This group also includes many of the natural plant dyes. Mordants may be applied before, during or after dyeing.

When dyeing wool, take care to follow the manufacturer's instructions, take note of all the safety procedures, and thoroughly wash the wool free of all grease first. Any grease left in will cause uneven dyeing. Wool dyed in the fleece will also give an uneven colour because the weathered tips absorb more dye than the rest of the staple, which can be used to great effect in some articles. Washing information is given on page 26.

Coloured fleeces also dye very satisfactorily, as the overlaying of a colour on to a grey or light-brown fleece can produce very subtle end results. If the coloured fleece has different depths of natural colour, the dyeing will also produce various colour depths. The jersey or sweater in Photo 1.12, page 25, was spun from one fleece, with the colours sorted carefully before spinning. The green is light grey over-dyed with chemical dyes.

Susceptibility to damage

Wool is prone to attacks by moths and other insects because some larvae actually eat the wool. Mothproofing agents can be added to the rinsing water when washing wool, or added while dyeing. Wool can also be stored with some type of moth repellent. Remedies that have proved effective in New Zealand are storing wool with slivers of bar soap or spraying with pennyroyal oil.

Wool will yellow and weaken with exposure to boiling water, sunlight and alkalis. Chlorine bleaches will dissolve wool and this can be used as a test to determine if a yarn is wool or a synthetic fibre.

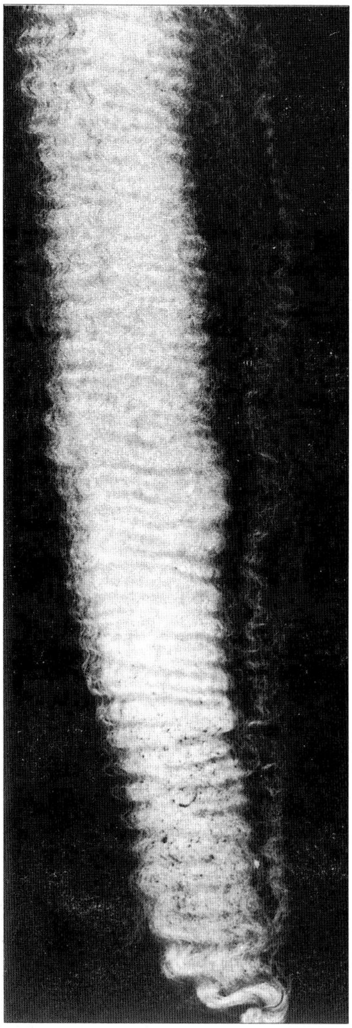

1.1 Even crimp

year, the grease will accumulate in the tips of the fleece, where it collects dust and dirt.

Grease is not water-soluble and cannot be washed out of the fleece by rain.

Normal growth pattern

With the normal growth pattern of a healthy sheep, the fibre will continue to grow out from the follicle and be uniform in size and crimp right to the tip. The crimp is the waves in a wool fibre. The tip of a fibre, which has been exposed to the weather, will be dirtier than the other end. The fibres grow together in groups called staples and in a good spinning fleece these staples will be well defined and free from each other.

CHOOSING A GOOD FLEECE FOR SPINNING

How can a spinner tell the difference between a fleece with a normal wool growth and one with faults?

Cleanliness is usually a good indicator. First, it shows good sheep management. A farmer who keeps his pastures clean and his sheep well cared for, up to and including shearing, will usually have healthy strong sheep and the wool will reflect this.

Secondly, if a fleece is clean it indicates that there will be no cotting or matting. A cotted fleece holds in dirt and the individual staples do not open up to allow proper ventilation.

An even crimp pattern, from tip to base, is also a guide when choosing a good fleece. A staple with an even crimp shows an even growth pattern and also aids in giving each fibre the same amount of elasticity along its length.

To test for a good spinning fleece I pull apart the tips of a fleece before buying it. If it parts easily, I know it will be easy to prepare.

REMOVING STAPLES FROM A FLEECE

There is a correct way to remove one staple from a fleece without disturbing the rest. Grasp the tip of the staple with the forefinger and thumb of one hand. Place the other hand with the thumb and forefinger forming a circle around the base of that staple. This hand will keep the rest of the fleece in place while you firmly tug the staple out by the tip.

If you just tug staples out without holding down the rest of the fleece you drag other fibres out with the staple and leave the fleece in a mess. It is much easier to have clear staples to comb, card or spin.

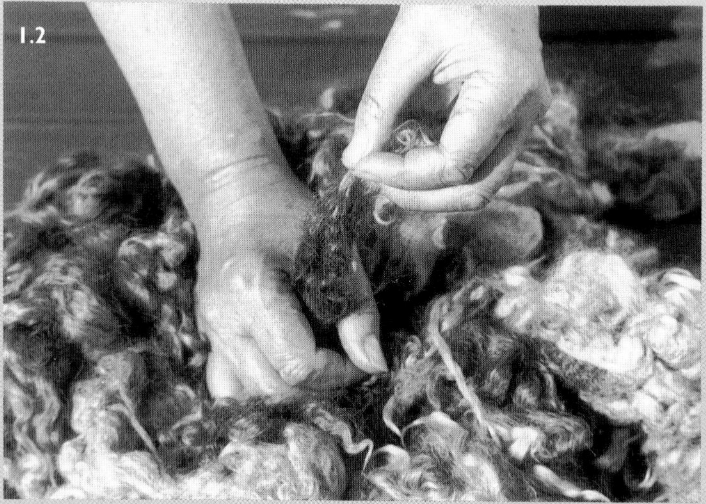

1.2

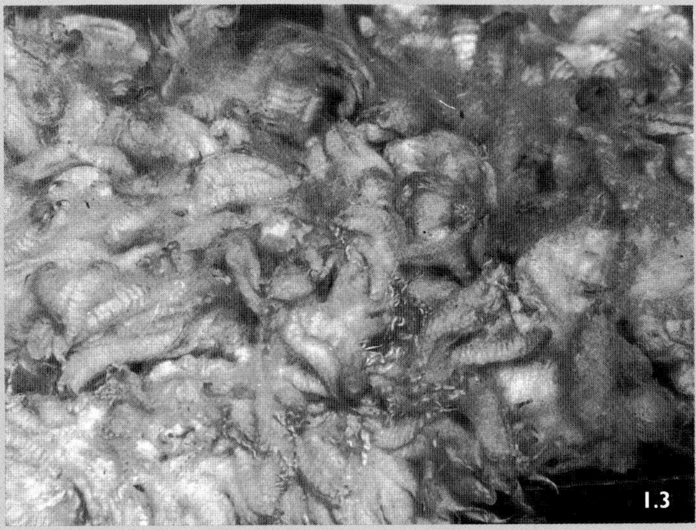

1.3

CHECKLIST FOR A GOOD SPINNING FLEECE

1. The fleece should be even; i.e. the wool should be the same over most of the fleece. This means an even crimp pattern and fibres of the same length and thickness.
2. The fleece should have no permanent discolouration.
3. The wool should be clean and free from vegetable matter, dust and dirt.
4. Fibres should be structurally sound.
5. Staples should be compact and clearly separated.
6. Staples should not be too pointed or tippy. The shape of the staple varies with different breeds, but this is a sound general guideline.

FAULTS AFFECTING SPINNERS

Breaks and tenderness

Wool growth is controlled by a combination of two factors: daylight hours and feed. The wool growth in New Zealand Romney-type sheep in particular is sensitive to daylight. In winter, with fewer daylight hours, wool growth in such sheep drops to about a third of the summer growth level. Wool growth in Merinos is mainly a matter of feeding, and with Corriedales and Halfbreds it is a little of each.

An unsound fleece is caused by a sudden drop in the rate of wool growth which in turn causes a reduction in the fibre diameter and length. This decrease can be brought about by many factors, such as drought, illness, dietary deficiencies or birthing problems.

A break in a staple is usually in a well-defined area, although occasionally there are two such areas. If most of the staple is unsound, the wool is defined as 'tender' and is unsuitable for spinning. If a break is severe, some fibres may temporarily stop growing and be shed from the follicles, leading to cotting or matting. In the break area there will therefore be fewer and thinner fibres than in the rest of the staple.

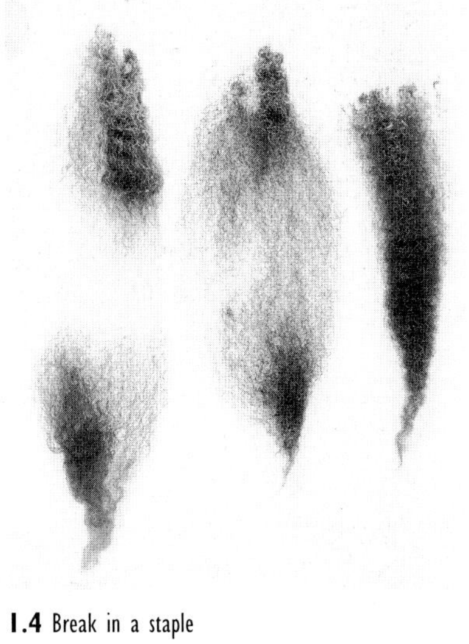

1.4 Break in a staple

The time of the year when the sheep is shorn can make a difference in the placement of the break, particularly with Romney-type sheep, who tend towards a break in the winter months. If these sheep are shorn as close to the break time as possible, the effect will be much less, as with pre-lamb shearing in the spring. However, shearing is also governed by climate and the farmer must balance all these factors to decide on the best shearing time.

To test a staple for soundness, take a staple, stretch it between your two hands and flick it with one finger. The staple should 'ping' with

WORSTED AND WOOLLEN YARNS

A short description of worsted and woollen yarn will be useful at this stage. (See Photo 5.1 on page 88.)

Worsted yarn
This is made from long-staple wool that has been combed to remove all the short fibres. The fibres are kept parallel by both the combing and the spinning process.

Woollen yarn
This is made from shorter-staple wools that are carded in such a way that the fibres are not parallel and fibres of varying lengths remain in the wool, which is then spun to produce a light airy yarn.

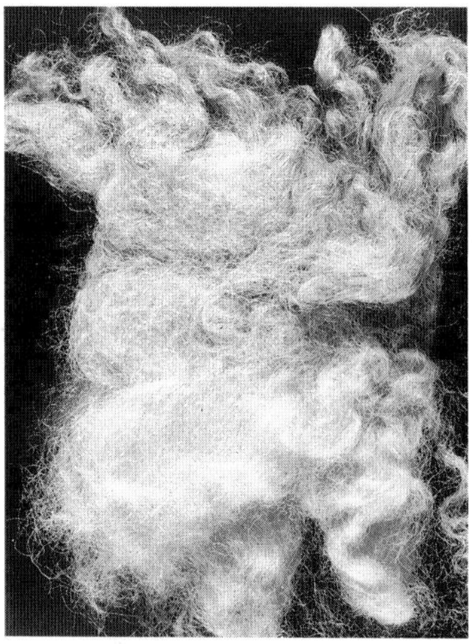

1.5 Cotted staple

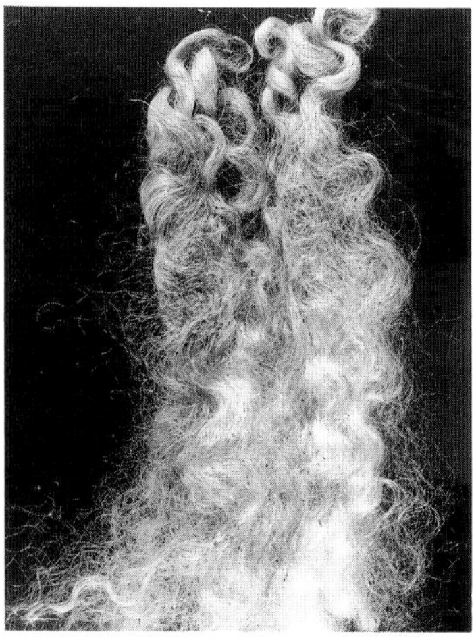

1.6 Dirty staple

a distinctive sound, which I cannot reproduce in a book, but after 'pinging' several sound fleeces you will soon recognise the sound. You can also test for soundness by taking hold of a staple at both ends and trying to pull it apart. If there is a break, the fibres will part at that point. If you do this up by your ear you will hear the damaged fibres breaking with a crackling sound. It may appear rather odd to be listening to wool, but it is sensible to test fleeces before you buy them! Holding a staple up to the light may also show up a break but it is surprisingly hard to detect one just by looking.

Wool with a break is not suitable for worsted spinning, but as long as the break is slight, it can be used for woollen spinning. Of course, this depends on the position of the break and the resulting fibre length. If you have a severe break halfway up an 8cm (3in) staple you will be left with fibres of 4cm (1.5in), which may be too short for easy spinning.

Cotting or matting

This fault is quite obvious in a fleece and can be seen as a matted area in the staple. It is caused by wool fibres being shed from the skin and becoming entangled in the rest of the fleece. The reasons for this shedding are many and varied. Cotted fleeces are more common from older and lower-producing sheep. Rainy seasons do not help, and all the factors that can produce a break – such as bad feeding, pregnancy and disease – can cause cotting if they are severe enough. Long-wool breeds are more prone to shedding than other varieties.

Usually cotting is found only in one part of a fleece. It first appears in the region of the lower hind legs, followed by the belly area, the lower forelegs and then the sides.

A cotted area interferes with the distribution of yolk, the mixture of wax and sweat that protects the fleece, and this causes the outside of the fleece to become badly weathered.

In the woollen industry these fleeces can be opened by mechanical means prior to preparation and spinning. This causes considerable fibre breakage and reduces the average fibre length. Handspinners can use pickers to open a fleece, but if the fleece is cotted and the fibres break during this preparation, the wool will not be suitable for worsted spinning. You would be wise to avoid buying a cotted fleece.

Foreign matter

All fleeces contain some dirt, dust and vegetable matter. I guess we would too if we wore the same clothes for up to 12 months! Opinions vary between spinners as to what level of extraneous matter makes a fleece unsuitable for spinning. I must admit I am a fussy spinner and choose clean fleeces only: it saves me so much time in the long run. If I do buy a dirty fleece, because the colour is exceptional or for some other reason, I will expect to pay less for it to compensate for the weight of the dirt and the extra time involved in preparation and spinning.

Dust and dirt will wash out of most fleeces with cold water. However, do watch out for earth or clay that leaves stains on the wool. Once I was given a fleece that came from an area of red soil and the finished yarn had a decidedly pinkish tinge. Also remember that you are paying for wool by weight, and fleeces that carry a lot of dirt may not be value for money.

Some seeds and vegetable matter will wash or fall out as you prepare the wool for spinning, but test for this before you buy a fleece. Some burrs are impossible to remove from the fleece because they are attached with fine hooks.

To test for cleanliness I take a couple of staples from different parts of the fleece and run them under cold water *before* I buy. If they emerge relatively clean I buy the fleece. One of my students once bought what she thought was a lovely pale grey fleece, only to find when it was washed that it was a white fleece. Colour changes when you wash coloured fleeces can be quite dramatic.

YIELD

When the fleece comes off the sheep we now know it contains more than just wool. Varying amounts of moisture, yolk, dirt, dust and vegetable matter are also in the wool. 'Yield' is the clean weight of wool expressed as a percentage of the greasy weight.

The amount of fleece waste varies according to breed, climatic conditions, sheep care, feeding and so on. The proportions of these waste products also vary by breed: for example, the New Zealand Merino has less suint (on average) than New Zealand Romney, but more grease.

It is practical to assume that at least 25 per cent in weight of the raw wool will be lost as you prepare the wool for spinning and after washing. Therefore, if a project needs 750g (1.6lb) of finished spun wool, it is wise to buy 1kg (2.2lb) of raw wool. If the wool has been carefully skirted for spinning before you buy it, the wastage will be less than 25 per cent, but it is always better to err on the safe side and buy more rather than less. No two fleeces will be exactly the same, and if you underestimate the amount you buy it will be difficult to match the wool if you need more later on.

Ageing

As some sheep grow older the wool changes, just as human hair changes with age. Most fleeces tend to become coarser and, if they are coloured fleeces, also lose some of their colour.

Stains and discolourations

Canary stain is very annoying to spinners. It is caused by heavy rainfall, heat and humidity, is bright yellow and will not wash out. Because of the colour, some spinners confuse it with yolk. The washing test described above will isolate this stain and help you avoid it.

Many other stains can make wool unsuitable for spinning. Do not buy any wool that has unwashable stains of any kind. They may be caused by fungi or disease, and some of the more common are pink tip, green and brown banded stains, black fungus tip, pink rot and apricot stain. You can also get dip stain, branding and dung stain.

Cakey yolk

This is also called 'dry' or 'hard' yolk, yellow banding or fleece rot. Cakey yolk, which is not in fact yolk at all, is caused by prolonged wetness of the skin resulting in a superficial inflammation that produces a yellow exudate. This exudate dries and becomes brittle foreign matter found in horizontal, yellow-coloured bands on the staple. It is also claimed that bacteria could be responsible for the yellow colour. Sometimes canary stain will accompany cakey yolk.

Fine-wool sheep are more susceptible to cakey yolk and the discolouration is usually confined to wool from the back of the sheep. It will wash out, so wash a staple first in hot or cold water to check that it is indeed this type of discolouration.

A fleece that has good ventilation and dries quickly will be less likely to contain cakey yolk. A well-ventilated fleece is one where the staples are neatly arranged and well-defined, allowing air movement.

Hairy wool

Hairy wool is coarse, straight and chalky in appearance. The fibres are heavily medullated, which means they contain a large proportion of medulla cells. Hairy wool, when dyed, comes out a different shade altogether from the rest of the fleece. Medullation seems to be due mainly to genetic characteristics in the sheep. Try to avoid grossly medullated fleece, which is easily recognisable as all the fleece is coarse, lacking in crimp and has a very harsh feel.

Hairy wool does have its uses, as a strong, hard fibre for use in carpets, and sheep such as the Drysdale and Tukidale have been bred specifically for this purpose.

Some fleeces have this characteristic in the tips of the staples only, and this is called 'hairy tip'. The tip of the staples will be very pointed, harsh, coarse and unpleasant to touch. Again, this type of fleece should be avoided.

Some fleeces have a hairy britch only. This means the hairy portion is limited to the hind region of the sheep, which is not a problem for the spinner because as long as the rest of the fleece is of good quality the britch portion can be removed.

Kemp

Kemp fibres are typical in some breeds, such as the Scottish Blackface, but as they are harsh and stiff to touch and do not dye satisfactorily they are a nuisance to spinners. The kemp fibre has a different structure to other wool fibres. The tip is sharp and not medullated, but the rest of the fibre is mainly medulla cells. These fibres are very short and have no crimp.

Kemp fibres are often spread throughout the normal staples in a fleece and, as they are very short, many will fall out during spinning. However, it is best to avoid a fleece that contains a lot of these fibres.

BLACK AND COLOURED SHEEP

Until recent years, in most countries, black and coloured sheep were not desirable in a flock and farmers aimed at a completely white wool clip. This was because manufacturers needed white wool for white yarn or cloth that they could then dye any colour. Even a few coloured fibres could change the dye colours or cause uneven dyeing and this was to be avoided at any cost.

Thirty years ago farmers gave me their coloured fleeces as a way of getting rid of them, and I am sure those sheep made a quick trip to the freezing works, truly the black sheep of the family. Farmers still shear their coloured sheep separately, because manufacturers still require uncontaminated white wool. However, handspinners can claim to have played a big part in the growing popularity of coloured wool, and many black and coloured flocks with a wide range of breeds are now being expanded, with great care taken to produce clean, sound good-quality fleeces just for spinners.

> Black and coloured sheep breeders' associations are rapidly growing in number. The address of the New Zealand Association of Black and Coloured Sheep Breeders is included in Appendix A. They can give you the addresses of equivalent associations in other countries.

Much study has also gone into the genetics of coloured sheep. Because colour is carried by only one pair of genes it is relatively easy to control, and coloured flocks producing coloured lambs are the result of careful breeding.

Pigmentation of the fleece, which causes the grey to black colouring, is an inherited trait and is caused by melanin, which can occur in the cuticle, cortex and medulla of the fibre, more commonly in the cortex. Inherited factors like pigmentation are passed on by genes that occur in pairs. Each pair of genes occurs at a specific location, termed a 'locus'. One of a pair is inherited from one parent, and one from the other. Many pairs of genes may govern a character while other characters, such as the one that controls the presence of white colour, is determined by a single pair of genes.

Genes at the *agouti* locus (it is sometimes called the pattern locus) control which pattern is present on the sheep by controlling the type of pigment present and its positioning. There are two types of pigment: phaeomelanin, which produces white or tan fibres; and eumelanin, which produces black or brown fibres.

At the *agouti* locus white (correctly known as *white/tan*) is the dominant gene and *nonagouti* (giving a completely black or brown animal) the recessive.

- If a sheep receives a *white/tan* gene from each parent it will be white.
- If a sheep receives a *nonagouti* from each parent it will be black.
- If a sheep inherits one *nonagouti* and one white gene, the white will dominate and the fleece will be white, but the hidden *nonagouti* gene will be carried on. Sheep that inherit a *nonagouti* (black) gene and a white gene are called heterozygous. If mating occurs between two such sheep, the genes will be passed on in such a way that there can be three possible kinds of offspring. One lamb could carry both the white genes and will be pure white (homozygous). One could carry one of each but will be white, because that is the dominant gene, and one could carry two *nonagouti* genes and therefore be black (which is why white sheep can produce black lambs).
- If a white heterozygous sheep mates with a black homozygous sheep, the result will either be a white sheep (one white, one *nonagouti* gene) or a black sheep (two *nonagouti* genes).

Many other patterns can occur at the *agouti* locus. Common examples are *badgerface* (black belly and white or tan on the rest of the body, *black and tan* (white belly and black on the rest of the body), and *blue* (black with a lighter saddle on the sides of the body and across the rear at the back).

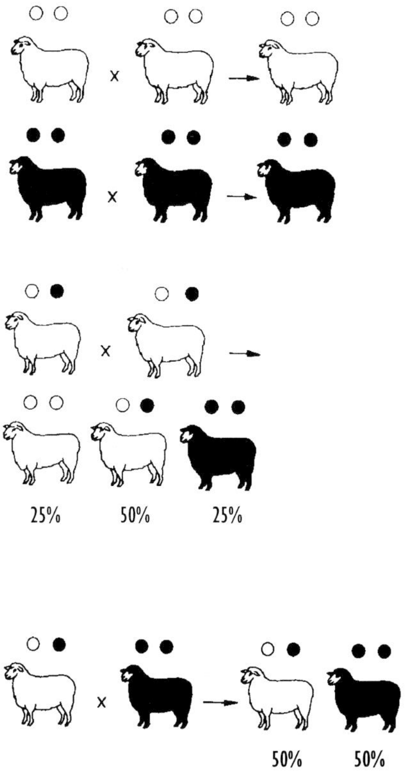

Fig. 1.C Genetic factors

In Britain the *black and tan* is common in the Soay breed, and the *badgerface* is a strain of the Welsh Mountain breed. In New Zealand and Australia coloured flocks are derived from the white breeds: the *badgerface* and *black and tan* patterns are common in the Merino, and all three patterns occur in the English woolled breeds, *blue* being particularly common on the English Leicester (see Photo 1.8).

It is thought that breeds such as the Suffolk, Hampshire, Dorset Down (the Down breeds), which are white-woolled with a dark head and leg, have the *white/tan* gene and that the darker points are caused by the selection of modifying genes.

The genes occurring at the *agouti* locus determine the pattern the sheep displays. For example, the black on the belly of a *badgerface* or on all the body of a *nonagouti* is an eumelanin type of pigment. Eumelanin can be black or brown, and another locus, the *brown* locus determines which occurs.

The colour produced by the *brown* gene is often referred to as moorit, and it is a colour that is increasing in popularity among spinners. Some spinners think this is a breed name but it is a specific genotype found in many breeds. A genotype is the term used for the entire array of genes carried by an individual. The term 'moorit' comes from the Icelandic 'moorut', meaning 'as red as the moors', and indeed the colour has a reddish tinge in many cases, but it can vary greatly. As with other coloured sheep, the colour will fade with age.

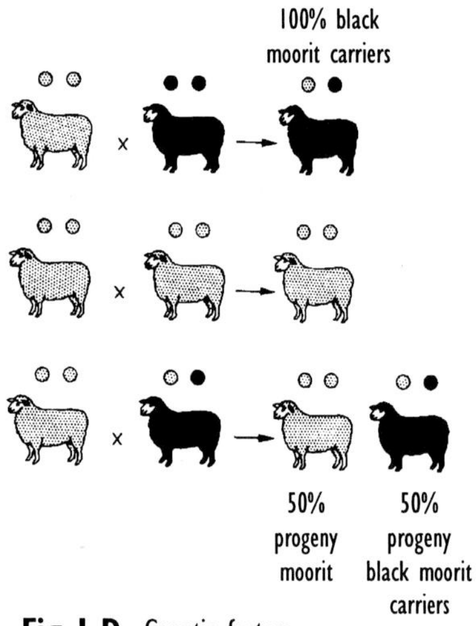

Fig 1.D Genetic factors

Black (wild) is dominant and *brown* recessive. If, for example, a badgerface sheep is homozygous for *brown* then it will be brown rather than black on the belly. The *agouti* locus determines the pattern and the *brown* locus, determines the colour of any eumelanin occurring. The mating of a black and a brown sheep produces all black offspring, while matings of brown and brown give brown offspring.

Moorit sheep can be recognised by the red-brown nose, eye-socket and lip tissue, and the facial hair is also red-brown. Some coloured sheep that are of a different genotype from the moorit also have some of this red-brown hair, but on the moorit it covers the entire area of pigmented skin. There is little fading of this facial hair with age. The hooves of moorit sheep are brown, not black.

Another locus that can alter coloured sheep is the spotting locus, where the recessive spotted gene when homozygous produces varying amounts of white on an otherwise coloured sheep. In New Zealand and Australia this is commonly seen in the Merino and Dorset Horn breeds.

The Jacob sheep is a well-known spotted sheep found mainly in Britain. The wool characteristics can vary greatly in a Jacob fleece, with the black wool being coarser and having less crimp than the grey or white wool. An average Jacob fleece will weigh about 2kg (4-5lb). The wool from older sheep can be quite coarse, and younger sheep will probably produce the best wool for spinners. Wool from these

1.7 Black and coloured sheep, English Leicester and Romneys (David and Elspeth Wilkinson's farm).

1.8 English Leicester sheep with the *blue* pattern (David and Elspeth Wilkinson's farm).

1.9 Moorit sheep (David and Elspeth Wilkinson's farm).

spotted sheep can be sorted into the different colour groups and spun separately, or it can be carded to produce a blended yarn with random flecks.

Changes in colour density

It is unusual to find a coloured fleece with even colour throughout and from tip to cut end. With all coloured sheep the colour will fade with age, but factors other than age can also affect the colour density of the fleece. The tips of the staple, for instance, will fade with constant exposure to the sun and weather. This bleaching effect gives handspun wool one of its most distinctive effects: the random colour changes when spinning black and coloured wool. When spun, the bleached tip of a dark brown fleece gives a delightful golden fleck to the yarn, but remember that this tip is weaker than the rest of the fibre and can break with wear, causing pilling. This bleaching and weakening of the tip also occurs in white wool but the colour change will not be so noticeable.

The fibres can continue to fade after the yarn is spun and knitted or woven. I have a seat-cover woven from handspun wool that started off dark brown and is now a pale orange/brown. It took several years of constant exposure to sun to fade this fabric to such an extent. Yet a pile rug I wove from a dark brown handspun yarn has never faded, despite almost the same exposure.

Change in colour density in the fleece can also result from a copper deficiency in the sheep's diet. As soon as the required copper intake is restored, the original pigmentation returns. These colour changes can be seen as horizontal bands in the staple. The hanging shown on p.25 was woven from such a fleece and the colour changes can clearly be seen in the fringe at the lower edge.

CARE OF FLEECES

Sheep coats

One way to take care of fleeces is to cover and protect the wool while it is still on the sheep's back. Coating or rugging of sheep has been done for some years in a small way, but with the growing number of small flocks of sheep bred specifically for spinners, more and more sheep are being covered.

Sheep do not have to wear the coats all year around. It has been found that short-term covering, for four to six weeks after shearing, can reduce sheep deaths by up to 50 per cent. After this time the wool is long enough to afford protection from the cold and wet.

It does seem that there are advantages in coating small, specialised flocks for spinners, particularly black and coloured flocks, where farming conditions are such that a lot of dirt, dust and sand contaminate the wool. Regular checking and maintenance are important. If farming conditions are clean, sheep coats are not so

ADVANTAGES AND DISADVANTAGES OF SHEEP COATS	
Advantages	**Disadvantages**
1. A sheep coat protects the sheep (particularly older sheep) from cold and wind, especially after early shearing and in winter. The sheep will suffer less from stress so the wool will be sound with fewer breaks.	1. The coats can tear on fences and need adjustment every six months, and replacing when damaged, outgrown or worn out.
2. The more even body temperature under the coat produces wool that is well grown and nourished.	2. The coats must be checked regularly for chafing, disintegration or damage.
3. It improves the appearance of the wool, with less weathering, especially along the back. The wool is softer-handling as there is no burnt tip.	3. The coats and their upkeep can be expensive. The increased price of the wool may not compensate for the cost of coating.
4. The colour is more even with no fading, which is important in black and coloured sheep.	4. Wool around the neck can become compressed.
5. The natural grease in the wool will not be washed out by rain.	5. White wool can become yellow in appearance (though this will wash out).
6. The fleece is cleaner, with fewer burrs and less dirt.	6. The uncoated portion (about 20 per cent) of the fleece needs heavy skirting.
7. The staple is longer and more blocky.	7. Wool faults can be hidden under the coats and not noticed.
8. The wool is less likely to snag on bushes, trees, fences etc.	8. Fine wool occasionally has a greenish tip after long periods of wet weather.
9. For show sheep, a coat will improve the appearance of the wool.	9. If regular and careful checking of young sheep is not possible, coats are not practicable as the growth rate in these sheep is rapid.
10. The sheep is less affected by fly strike.	10. The wool tends to mat on coated, strong-wool sheep.

important, and for large commercial flocks the cost and effort may not be reflected in the final wool price.

1.10 Wool from uncoated (top) and coated sheep (Tarndwarncoort, Australia)

Preparation time

Spinners have their own favourite way of caring for fleeces, according to the type of wool, the climate, the amount of space available and just plain personal preferences. Some spinners are impatient to begin the actual spinning and think of preparation time as time wasted. Others spend hours lovingly skirting, sorting and washing wool because they enjoy that part just as much as the actual spinning.

Because I learnt to spin when I had small children underfoot (and under wheel), time has always been an important factor in my life and I have usually chosen fleeces that were very clean and well skirted, and required no washing. If a fleece was full of gorse prickles or it was dirty and matted I did not buy it. I still had plenty of choice, as New Zealand wool was, and still is, plentiful and clean.

However, other spinners may not be so fortunate and may have to choose from a very narrow range of wool from sheep bred for meat. When a farmer is concerned only with meat production the wool can be very dirty, matted and unsound. Of course you will pay almost nothing for this wool but such a fleece may take days to get to a state suitable for carding or combing. Even then, a poor fleece makes a poor yarn, no matter how good a spinner you are.

If your local wool is like this, ask yourself whether you would be better to look elsewhere. A poor fleece may cost you only a few dollars, but think of the effort involved, and the end result. Would it not be better to spend twice as much money on a better fleece,

Most spinning magazines carry advertisements for mail-order wool and Chapter Two includes addresses of reputable wool suppliers. Send a supplier a stamped, addressed envelope with a request for some samples, telling them the type of fleece you usually spin. For example, you may like spinning fine wool from fine fleeces. If the supplier knows this and cannot supply this type of wool, they can often give you a contact who can. If you build up a good rapport with your wool suppliers they will get to know your needs and can keep special fleeces for you. Do not hesitate to return wool that is unsound or unsuitable with a polite note saying what is wrong with it.

Spinners' and weavers' guild spinning days are another useful source of wool, and local associations of black and coloured sheep breeders will give you names of wool suppliers. They can also be found through your Wool Board, if you have one, or by writing to the New Zealand Association of Black and Coloured Sheep Breeders. (Appendix A).

have less preparation time and end up with a better product? Spinners are fortunate that the raw materials are not expensive, and money spent here will be reflected in the finished product. It takes many hours to spin wool into yarn, and we should be making it as easy and enjoyable for ourselves as possible.

Skirting a fleece

Before a fleece is washed or stored it should be skirted, i.e. all the dirty and inferior pieces should be removed. This may have been done before you acquired the wool, but you need to check. If the wool is stored with dung, dead beetles, dirt, vegetable matter or other nasties still embedded in it, not only will it smell unpleasant but it may be impossible to remove this extraneous matter later.

Spread the fleece out with the tips uppermost. A slotted table is ideal as this allows small pieces and second cuts to fall through. Second cuts are caused by the shearer taking two passes with the blade instead of one, and the short pieces of wool fall out quite easily.

First, remove all foreign matter and stained and discoloured pieces. Then remove any wool that is distinctly different in character from the rest of the fleece. This may include harsh, hairy wool, usually found at the britch (the lower thighs). Lastly, check the centre back section. Because this wool is exposed to the weather, this portion may be mushy and tender. Test areas of this back wool for breaks and if you find any, remove this wool. If wool is left in a fleece that is very different from the rest, the yarn spun from it will also differ, and this could spoil a project.

If the wool is black or coloured it may be necessary to sort the fleece into separate light and dark portions. Even if you intend to blend the colours together when carding or spinning, it is helpful to have the colours separated first.

1.11 Skirting a fleece

When I first began spinning, I spun straight from the fleece – just pulled the wool out of the bag and spun it as it came. I got some interesting effects but found, if I knitted up as I spun, a jersey or sweater that may have started out grey ended up black at the neck edge. This certainly made my spinning and knitting an adventure as I never knew what would happen next! These days I prefer to plan.

1.12 (left) A sweater handspun by Anne Field, machine-knitted by Jenny Lineham. Exciting effects can be achieved when a garment using coloured wool from one fleece is planned carefully. The different greys used here are all from one Romney fleece, and the green areas are grey wool chemically dyed.

1.13 (right) Wall-hanging woven by Anne Field.

WASHING A FLEECE

In New Zealand we are lucky to have very clean wool and, as I usually prefer to spin in the grease, I only wash wool before spinning if I need to. However, I know of many spinners who have to buy wool that is simply too dirty to spin unwashed. Some drumcarders will soil if greasy wool is put through, so this is another instance when the wool can be washed first.

If the wool is very dirty, flick carding it before washing will open the staples and make it easier for the dirt to wash out. Wool in bulk is easier to handle (and does not block the drains) if an old net curtain is placed in the tub and the wool put into that.

Because wool shrinks during washing (up to 25 per cent in some wools), care should be taken to prevent over-shrinking and felting. If a fleece becomes even slightly felted in the washing process it may be impossible to spin. Do not rub the wool fibres together in water, and avoid rapid changes of water temperature when washing fleeces.

FELTING

Felting results from the tendency of wool to undergo an irreversible increase in bulk when subjected to heat, moisture and friction. The process of felting meshes the yarn or fabric together, strengthening and solidifying it. Felt is even waterproof enough to be used for making tents or boots.

Each sheep breed makes a different type of felt and some felt more quickly than others. The wool from Down breeds is too spongy to felt easily.

Several experiments have shown that it is easier to spin a finer, smoother worsted yarn if you spin wool in the grease. The finished yarn does not bulk up as much as yarn spun from a fleece from which the grease had been removed. So if I am spinning a worsted yarn I do not wash the fleece first, as long as it is very clean. If it is a dirty fleece, however, I use the cold-water washing method that leaves the grease in.

Leaving grease in the wool

Divide the fleece up into manageable portions based on the size of your tub. Choose a warm windy day and soak the portion in lukewarm water. The length of soaking time and the number of water changes will depend on how dirty the fleece is: a very dirty fleece may need to be soaked overnight. When the water is clear and the wool is clean put the portion in mesh bags or old pillowcases and put these through a spin cycle in the washing machine. When the excess water has been spun out, put the wool outside in a warm *shady* spot to dry, turning frequently. Remember that direct sunlight will yellow the wool.

This washing method removes the suint, which is water-soluble, but not the grease, as the water is not hot enough to dissolve it.

Removing grease and dirt

Very dirty fleeces

Divide the fleece into manageable portions. Pre-soak one portion in lukewarm water, then place it in a bath containing the following ingredients:

- 2.5g (half a teaspoon) of washing soda (sodium carbonate) per 1kg (2.2lb) of wool
- Nonionic detergent (e.g. Lissapol or Teepol)
- Water above 36°C (97°F)

The washing soda turns the grease into a water-soluble form, and as most greases dissolve at 36°C (about 97°F), nearly body heat, the water should be above this temperature.

Add the wool and leave it to soak for up to an hour. Do not agitate the wool (this causes felting) but turn it over once or twice. It is the immersion in the bath that removes the dirt, not movement. Rinse the wool several times in warm water, making sure *all* the soap is gone. Take care not to let the tap run directly onto the fleece.

Put the wool in mesh bags or old pillowcases and put these through a spin cycle in the washing machine. This removes much of the excess water and will hasten drying considerably.

Information in *Dyeing for Fibres and Fabrics*, edited by Janet De Boer (Kangaroo Press), states that nonionic detergents are good wetting agents. Household detergents, on the other hand, are anionic and will react with dyestuffs if not properly rinsed out. Most nonionic detergents are sold as concentrates and are about ten times stronger than household detergents, so a little goes a long way.

Not-so-dirty fleeces

Follow the instructions for dirty fleeces but use either nonionic detergent *or* a washing powder and washing soda. If using a soap powder remember to dissolve it well or the powder or flakes will give your fleece a dusting of what looks very like dandruff. The addition of washing soda improves the efficiency of soap powders, which are not as efficient as nonionic detergents.

Clean fleeces

Again, follow the instructions for washing dirty wool but use soap powder or household detergent.

Washing wool before dyeing

Before dyeing wool all the grease must be removed or the wool will take the dye unevenly. The washing method described for very dirty wool should do the trick.

Washing Merino fleeces

Many fine wools, such as Merino, have a high grease content. This grease collects dirt easily at the tips of the staples so it is easier to wash these fleeces before spinning. The wash also lessens the high shrinkage rate and the matting potential of these fine wools so the spinning is more controlled.

A small amount of fine wool will spin a very long thread, so wash small amounts at a time. Margaret Stove's book *Merino: Handspinning, Dyeing and Working with Merino and Superfine Wools* describes in detail how to prepare and spin fine wools. With her permission I will very briefly describe one of the processes here.

Wash each staple in very hot water, lathering it onto a cake of soap. Rinse in warm water, squeeze in a towel to remove excess moisture, and dry lying flat. The weathered tips can be pulled off before spinning.

Drying wool

Place the wool outside in a warm shady spot over netting or slatted tables to dry, turning it frequently and removing the cats at regular intervals. My cats love their warm wool beds and think I have made them especially. Never dry wool in a tumble-dryer. Make sure the wool is completely dry before storage.

STORING FLEECES

Every spinner has been told not to buy too many fleeces at once, and every spinner I know has ignored this very sound advice many

1.14 Drying wool

1.15 Good containers that will allow the wool to breathe. Many wool suppliers are now aware of correct storage requirements and these muslin and sacking bags are very suitable. Unbleached calico makes good wool-storage bags too.

times. I see lovely fleeces that I cannot resist, even when I have no immediate need for them, and then I have to store them.

Ideally, we should use fresh fleeces immediately after shearing, but even if you intend using the fleece immediately, keep it away from damp, out of direct sunlight and not in a plastic bag, as this causes condensation.

Wool does change in time. Unwashed, greasy wool becomes solid as the grease hardens, and the wool also loses its liveliness and bounce. But even if you do not intend to use the wool immediately, there are ways you can minimise the damage. If the fleece is very dirty, or if I intend to wash it anyway, I wash it before I store it. For my fleece rugs (as in Project 1), for example, I wash the wool immediately, on the first fine day after I buy it. This way it can be stored for a year or two without any damage.

Whether washed or unwashed, the fleece can be stored in sacking, muslin or calico bags. Another way is to lay the fleeces, staple by staple, in a cardboard box on layers of newspaper – it is a joy to spin from such a well-prepared fleece. If moths are a problem in your area there are mothproofing agents you can add to the final rinse, place in the wool containers, or spray on the wool. One spinner I know swears that placing cedar shavings in her wool keeps the moths away.

Lastly, label each box or bag of wool with all the information you have as to its weight, source, price, breed and date of purchase.

2 Analysis of Wool

For many years I chose spinning fleeces by breed. For example, I would ask for a Romney fleece if I wanted to spin a medium-weight yarn, and perhaps a Polwarth for finer yarns. As my spinning experience increased I noticed variations within the breeds and I began spinning to suit these variations. As my overseas teaching expanded, the differences within breeds became even more apparent to me. These days I still like to know the breed name but I advocate analysing individual fleeces and base my judgment on observations of that fleece.

The way spinners buy their fleeces is changing. Thirty years ago I would go to a woolstore or a sheep farmer to buy my fleeces. Because both those sources were very knowledgable about their wool I could ask for a Romney with a count of 48-50 (that was before the days of microns) and a staple length of 10-15cm (4-6in). The wool-classer or farmer would then produce exactly that type of fleece. Now we can buy fleeces from many other sources, such as craft shops, guilds and hobby farmers with a few specialised sheep. Some of these are very knowledgable but others may not be, so spinners need to know what they are looking for.

In the past, spinners have relied on the judgment and terminology of the people who handle wool the most. In New Zealand this has been the people who class wool for farmers and manufacturers. But spinners process the fleece differently from manufacturers. We buy individual fleeces, not large numbers to be graded and classed into different categories. We do not use strong chemical scouring agents and dyes to produce uniform yarns and colours; we treat our fleeces individually with tender loving care, doing little to change the character of the original fleece.

For these reasons, I feel that spinners should learn to analyse individual fleeces, so that we can choose one that is suitable for the end product we have in mind, and so we can spin it to make a unique yarn that enhances the character of the original wool.

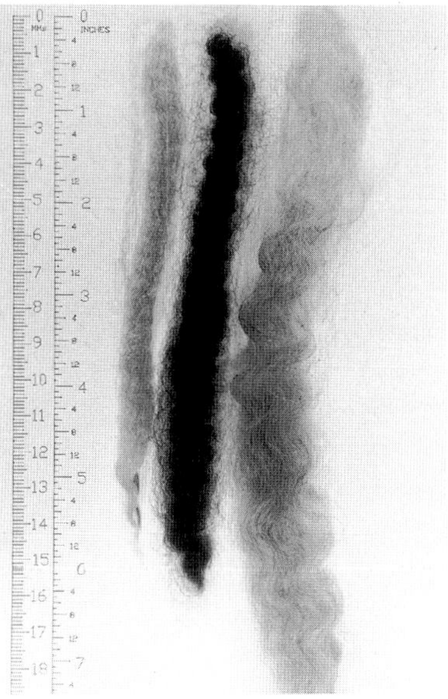

2.1 These three staples are all from Romney sheep but vary considerably in fibre diameter and crimp spacing and should be spun with differing amounts of twist into a range of yarn sizes.

HOW TO ANALYSE A FLEECE

Analysing a fleece is rather like following the clues in a detective novel. When we have enough clues we can decide not who the murderer is but what a fleece is suitable for. In one workshop I was handed a fleece to analyse and after some thought was forced to conclude that it was only suitable for stuffing cushions! How much better to make that decision now rather than struggle to spin a tender fleece.

> Fine wools usually felt more with washing than coarse wools, and this should be taken into account in considering the end use of the spun yarn. Fibres that felt easily also full well, which is very useful in the finishing of some articles. Fulling, or milling, is the process of meshing the fibres together while washing fabric to produce an integrated cloth.

The more we can find out about a fleece, the better we will be able to judge a suitable use for it, or to know whether it is suitable for the purpose we have in mind. For instance, there should be a direct relationship between the crimp number and fibre size of the wool to the twist number and thickness of the spun yarn. If coarse fibres are spun into very fine yarn with a lot of twist, the yarn will be stringy and harsh. These fibres should be spun with little twist into a thick yarn, which will be soft and bouncy. Conversely, if fine fibres are spun into a thick yarn with little twist, the yarn will break. They should be spun into a fine yarn with a lot of twist, which again will be soft.

A very helpful guideline, which will be discussed fully in Chapter Four, is that the number of twists per 2.5cm (1in) in the finished yarn (washed and plied) should equal the number of crimps per 2.5cm (1in) in the fleece. The number of twists per 2.5cm (1in) in relation to the thickness of the finished yarn will also be covered.

If you refer to Appendix B (Table of New Zealand wools) and Photo 2.8 on page 34 as you read the following pages, you will also be able to see how the 'clues' follow a pattern.

It is difficult for us to judge something as thin as a single wool fibre with the naked eye which is why it is easier to analyse a fleece if we break down our 'clues' into several categories. We will take into account not only crimp number and fibre size, but also the length, shape, colour and lustre of the staple. Do read through the background information under each heading and refer back to these explanations as you practise analysing fleeces for yourself.

Length and shape of staple

A staple is an individual lock of wool and its length determines the type of spinning for which that fleece is best suited: worsted or woollen or any of the varieties in between. (For a description of worsted and woollen spinning see page 88.) Long-staple wools are generally suited to worsted spinning, and short-staple to woollen spinning.

The length is also a pointer to the fibre size. Longer staples come from fleeces with a larger fibre diameter and consequently with coarser wool than shorter staples.

The shape of the staple tip, flat or pointed, gives us another clue. A pointed staple usually comes from a coarse wool; that is one with a larger fibre diameter. Lambswool is the exception to this, as fleeces are pointed or tippy before their first shearing.

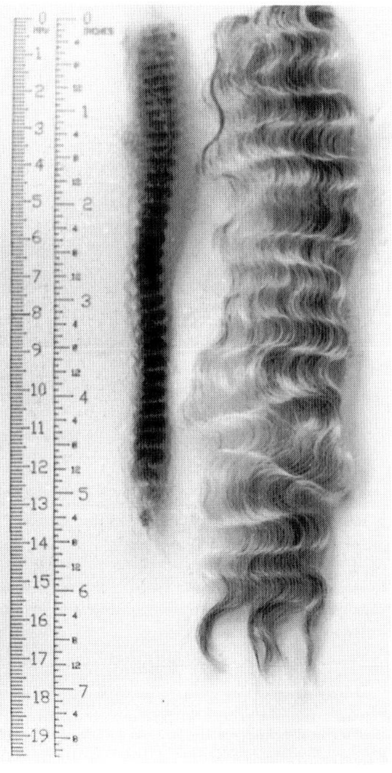

2.2. Two staples of wool, showing different degrees of crimp. The staple on the left has the most crimps and also contains the finest fibres.

Crimp patterns

The crimp pattern is probably the most helpful indicator for spinners. With few exceptions, the more crimps there are in 2.5cm (1in) of wool, the smaller the fibre diameter and the finer the wool.

The number of crimps will also indicate the elasticity of the fibre. As a general rule, the more crimps the more elastic the yarn. The other factor that affects elasticity is that each wool fibre contains chains of molecules arranged in folds. When you stretch the fibre the folds unfurl, so even a staple with no apparent crimps can have some elasticity. There can be stretch of 30% when dry and up to 70% in the wet.

When we look at crimp pattern in a staple we should not forget that a staple is made up of many fibres and each one crimps on a three-dimensional plane; that is, it will not lie flat on a surface. This ability will vary among the breeds; for example, Down breeds will have a pronounced 3-D crimp that adds to the elasticity of the staples. At the other extreme, a New Zealand Lincoln has a very flat staple.

Fibre size

The wool trade has developed a method of determining average fibre diameter after scouring by using the Airflow Apparatus, an instrument which measures the mean fibre diameter from the rate of air flow through a sample of wool.

Measurement in microns (one-millionth of a metre) is another method the wool trade uses, and this is replacing the old count or quality number system. If you buy wool already measured, the micron or count system can be helpful, but remember the two systems work opposite ways. The higher the count, the finer the wool; but the lower the micron number, the finer the wool (see Appendix B).

However, spinners mostly buy wool without knowing the fibre diameter, micron or count number and we should develop our own measuring system because knowing the diameter of the fibre is important to spinners.

For convenience I have divided wool into five categories: fine, fine/medium, medium, medium/bulky and bulky. The measuring system whereby we count the crimps per 2.5cm (1in) and then spin and ply that fleece to finish with the same number of twists actually gives us a much wider range than these five categories, but it is helpful in the beginning to be able to place wool in these general sections.

Fine:	13 crimps per 2.5cm (1in) or more
Fine/medium:	10-12 crimps per 2.5cm (1in) or more
Medium:	7-9 crimps per 2.5cm (1in) or more
Medium/bulky:	4-6 crimps per 2.5cm (1in) or more
Bulky:	3 crimps per 2.5cm (1in) and under

The crimp number is a reasonably accurate guide to fibre size, which will in turn let you judge the suitable twist and size of yarn to spin for a particular fleece. Your ability to judge crimp numbers and fibre size will improve with experience, and in later chapters I will show you how to spin to this correct fibre size.

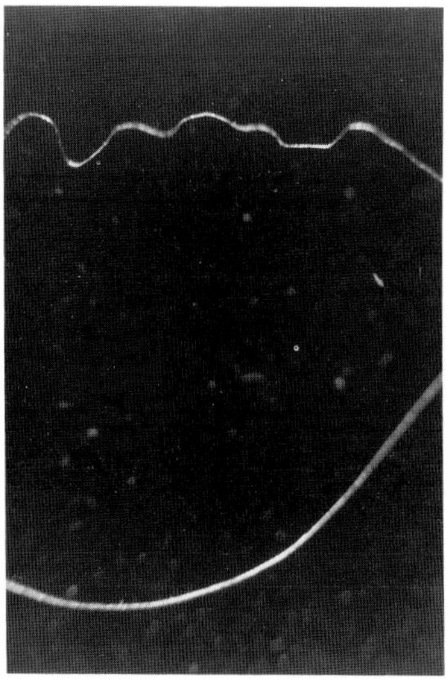

2.3 Magnification of fibres from a Merino (top) and an English Leicester (below) show comparative sizes.

2.4 This magnifying glass, which is marked out in inches, is a useful aid for determining the number of crimps per 2.5cm (1in) in finer wools. It is easier to use than a normal magnifying glass, which has to be held in one hand and has no measuring guide.

Colour

In a white fleece the colour can be an indication of the coarseness of the fibres: fine fleeces tend to be whiter than coarser fleeces. Of course this will not work with black and coloured fleeces. However, a dark brown fleece usually indicates a young sheep, as many of them,

2.5 New Zealand Romney sheep. *Courtesy NZ Wool Board.*

2.6 (L-R): Merino, Border Leicester, Romney rams.

like humans, go grey with advancing age. A younger sheep will usually have finer wool than an older sheep of the same breed.

Lustre

Lustre or shine is the ability of the wool to reflect light. It is also an indication of the fineness/coarseness of the wool, fine wools being generally less lustrous than coarse wools. Long-wool sheep, such as Lincoln and Leicester, have a relatively thin layer of scales on the outside of each fibre, although the scales themselves tend to be thicker. The degree of overlap is not great – only about one-sixth of each scale is covered – and it is thought this contributes to the lustre of this type of wool.

To test for lustre, move the wool staple around under either natural or artificial lighting and see if it reflects light. If you think it might be grease causing the lustre, wash the staple in hot soapy water and try again.

Bulk

This quality can be defined as the ability of the wool to spring back after it is compressed. Spinners need to know the bulk of a fleece before it is spun because the degree to which the wool springs back will affect the diameter of the finished yarn as well as the end use of that yarn.

When we spin we are compressing the wool. Some of this compression is released when the yarn is washed and the wool will try to return to its former state. A high-bulk wool can increase in diameter by up to twice its size with washing, yet a low-bulk wool will remain nearly the same size.

As spinners often spin to a desired thickness, it is helpful to learn how to estimate the bulk of a particular fleece.This can be done by taking a handful of fleece and squeezing it between two hands, pushing the air out. Open up your hands and see how much the wool springs back. High-bulk fleeces, such as a Cheviot, the Down breeds and Perendale, will spring back. A low-bulk fleece, such as a Border Leicester, will be more inert.

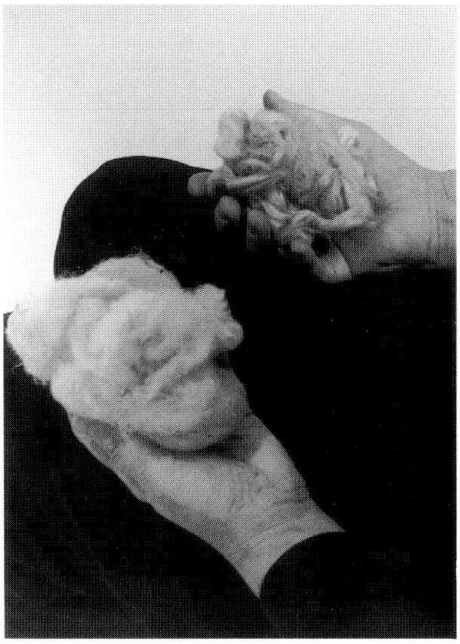
2.7 Measuring bulk

Wool's ability to spring back after compression accounts for some of the disappointment spinners feel when they try to spin a very fine yarn from a high-bulk fleece. The yarn looks just the right size when spun, but after washing it suddenly becomes a medium yarn. Yet it is this very factor that gives wool yarn and fabric one of its most desirable attributes: it does not crease easily and retains its original shape after washing.

Cleanliness

The cleanliness of a fleece affects the amount of preparation prior to spinning: making a judgment before you start spinning will let you plan better. Rank your fleece in one of these three categories.

1. Clean fleece: needs nothing further done to it.
2. Reasonably clean: may need further skirting (see page 24), a good shake, or just a lie in the sun to loosen up the grease.
3. Dirty: will need washing before any preparation.

Soundness

Always test and grade a fleece for soundness, as described on page 15. Again, there are usually three categories:

1. A good, sound fleece with no breaks.
2. Has a slight break, but spinnable.
3. Has a definite break or is tender. Wool with a break can be used for woollen or semi-worsted spinning as this wool is hand or drumcarded and the shorter fibres and noils are part and parcel of woollen yarn. A tender fleece should be discarded, used for felting, or washed and used for cushion stuffing.

To sum up all this information look at photograph below, which shows three different sheep breeds and illustrates the general pattern: as the wool becomes coarser the staple has fewer crimps and is longer and more pointed, with a high lustre. Because these staples are from coloured fleeces the other helpful clue, that fine wools are whiter than coarse wools, cannot be seen.

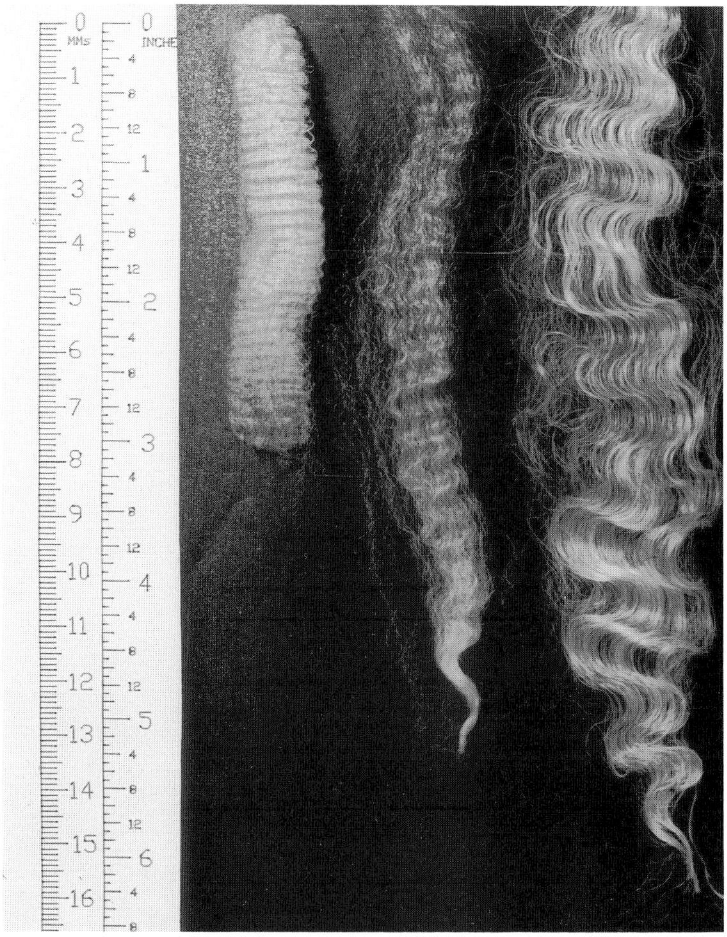

2.8 The Australian Merino staple on the left is finer, has more crimps, is shorter, has less lustre, and the shape of the staple tip is flatter than the other two staples.
The centre staple, New Zealand Romney, is coarser, has fewer crimps and is longer, with a more pointed tip and higher lustre.
The staple on the right, New Zealand English Leicester, is very coarse, with even fewer crimps and is very long with a very pointed tip and high lustre.

ANALYSING CARDED WOOL

Carded wool should be analysed slightly differently from raw fleece wool. The fibre length and crimp are harder to see, so take out a single fibre from the batt and pull it out between the finger and thumb of each hand until you are holding both ends. Do not stretch the fibre too tightly. This requires some patience, but do it with several fibres to calculate the average fibre length.

To determine the crimp, again remove one fibre from the batt and count the crimps on 2.5cm (1in). Do this for several fibres until you can estimate the average number of crimps. Do not stretch the fibres as you count but let them lie loosely. A magnifying glass such as the one in Photo 2.4 is very useful for this fine work.

THREE TYPES OF CARDED WOOL

Commercially carded wool

Wool commercially carded on large carding machines for the woollen industry is called tops, rovings or sliver. There is often confusion between these terms, so the definitions used in the wool industry will be given here. Wool prepared for both worsted and woollen spinning is carded, although on different types of machines, and comes off the machines in *sliver* form. Wool for worsted yarn is then gilled (thinned out), combed into a parallel formation and called *tops. Rovings* are a thinned-out form of the tops or sliver with a very slight twist or rolled effect to add strength.

The most important point for spinners to note when buying commercially carded wool is whether it is made of long, parallel fibres for worsted spinning, or randomly arranged short and long fibres ready for woollen spinning. Hold the wool up to the light to see if the fibres are parallel or not. Sample P on page 52 has been prepared for worsted spinning, and samples B and O for woollen spinning.

All types of commercially carded yarn will have been scoured and sometimes they will also have been dyed. Spinners can certainly spin with this wool, and it can be analysed using the same methods that I used with Samples B, O and P on pages 38, and 51-52. Commercially carded wool is usually smoother and has less character than the following two types.

Wool carded especially for handspinners

This wool retains the natural qualities of the original fleece because it has undergone less processing than the first type. The carding machines used for this process are similar to but smaller than those used in industry. This wool can be bought scoured or in the grease. In many cases it is possible to send your own fleece away to be carded.

Wool carded on hand or drumcarders by a spinner

This can also be analysed using the same method as Samples B and O, but as the spinner did the carding, the original fleece is usually available and it is easier to analyse this. When the wool is removed from the carder it is in the form of a batt – a flat pad of wool the width of the carder. This batt is often narrowed down into strips 5-30cm (2-12in) wide to make it more manageable for spinners.

If the crimp is too fine and too close to count, you may be looking at a Down breed. In one wool-classing manual I read, the crimp on these breeds was defined as 'not apparent', so if the wool classers cannot count the crimp, spinners certainly will not be able to. Just define these breeds as fine with high bulk, and spin accordingly.

We need another category for carded wool, as the processing has been taken several stages further. Has it been combed or carded for worsted or woollen spinning? To judge this, thin out a piece of the batt and hold it up to the light. If all the fibres are parallel and smooth, the batt has been prepared for worsted spinning. If the fibres are not parallel and the wool contains small noils, the wool is ready for woollen spinning.

> To help spinners assess carded wool, some sellers attach a lock of the original fleece to the outside of the bag of carded wool, with the fleece type named. This information is invaluable. If spinners insist that it is given to them at point of sale, all the carded-wool suppliers will eventually see the need and I, for one, would be happy to pay a fraction more for this service.

ANALYSING WOOL SAMPLES

On the following pages are photographs of samples of wool gathered from many sources in New Zealand and around the world. The photographs of each sample have been reproduced as close as possible to their actual size. Where I know the micron diameter and the breed name of the wool samples I have added this information.

To practise analysing wool, look at the samples and read the analysis I have made of each, comparing the photographs with the information. Try to see why I have made these observations and decide whether you agree. If you do not, ask yourself why. Your judgment should be based on factual analysis of that particular wool

> An asterisk placed beside the source of wool indicates that they sell wool to spinners, and you can order your own wool from them. I suggest you send a stamped addressed envelope and request samples first.

sample. Of course, I have had the added advantage of being able to handle the wool, but you have your own experience, and this is where differences in judgment will and should come in. For instance, you will no doubt be able to think of many more uses for yarn spun from the fleece in Sample A, but my suggested uses are based on my observations. Because the fleece is reasonably hard-wearing, I suggest it is not woven into soft garments to be worn next to the skin.

The first one or two samples will take a little longer, but with some practice it takes only about five minutes. What is five minutes when you consider how long it takes to spin the wool for just one project?

Begin with the samples of wool that you are familiar with. If you live in Australia, where the finer Merino wools are more common, look at this breed first. Some English spinners, on the other hand, may have never spun with Merino, so they should choose another breed. When you have read the analysis for some of these familiar breeds, choose another sample from the range of wools you like to spin, cover up my analysis, and write your own observations. Then uncover my analysis and see if we agree. Remember that we do not have to agree on all points.

When you have developed some confidence in analysing the samples in the book, try some of your own wool. It can be great fun to do this at a spinning day with a group of spinners, and then you have the added advantage of examining wool types you may not normally spin and taking advantage of the wide ranging experience of your group.

When I bought sample A, the only indication of its type was the word Crossbred on the label. In New Zealand this term means a sheep that is bred for both meat and wool, and they are of a long-wool type. In Australia and the USA, however, this term means a sheep breed that has been crossed with a Merino, such as Corriedale. You can see why the naming of wool by breeds can cause confusion to spinners when each country has its own terms and classification system.

KEEPING RECORDS

To make fleece analysis easy I have made up a record sheet with the necessary headings. (Appendix C). You may photocopy this for your own records. It is very helpful, for future reference, to keep these record sheets in some type of folder: the one in the photo has plastic sleeves and in New Zealand is called a flip file. Sheet protectors (another name for plastic sleeves) mounted in an A4 ring-binder are another excellent way to organise your wool samples and information. You can also add other information to your records, such as the source of the wool, the amount you bought and the price paid. Photos of any articles made from the fleece and/or swatches of cloth or knitted samples, together with a sample of the yarn, will make excellent resource material for other spinners or for you to refer back to.

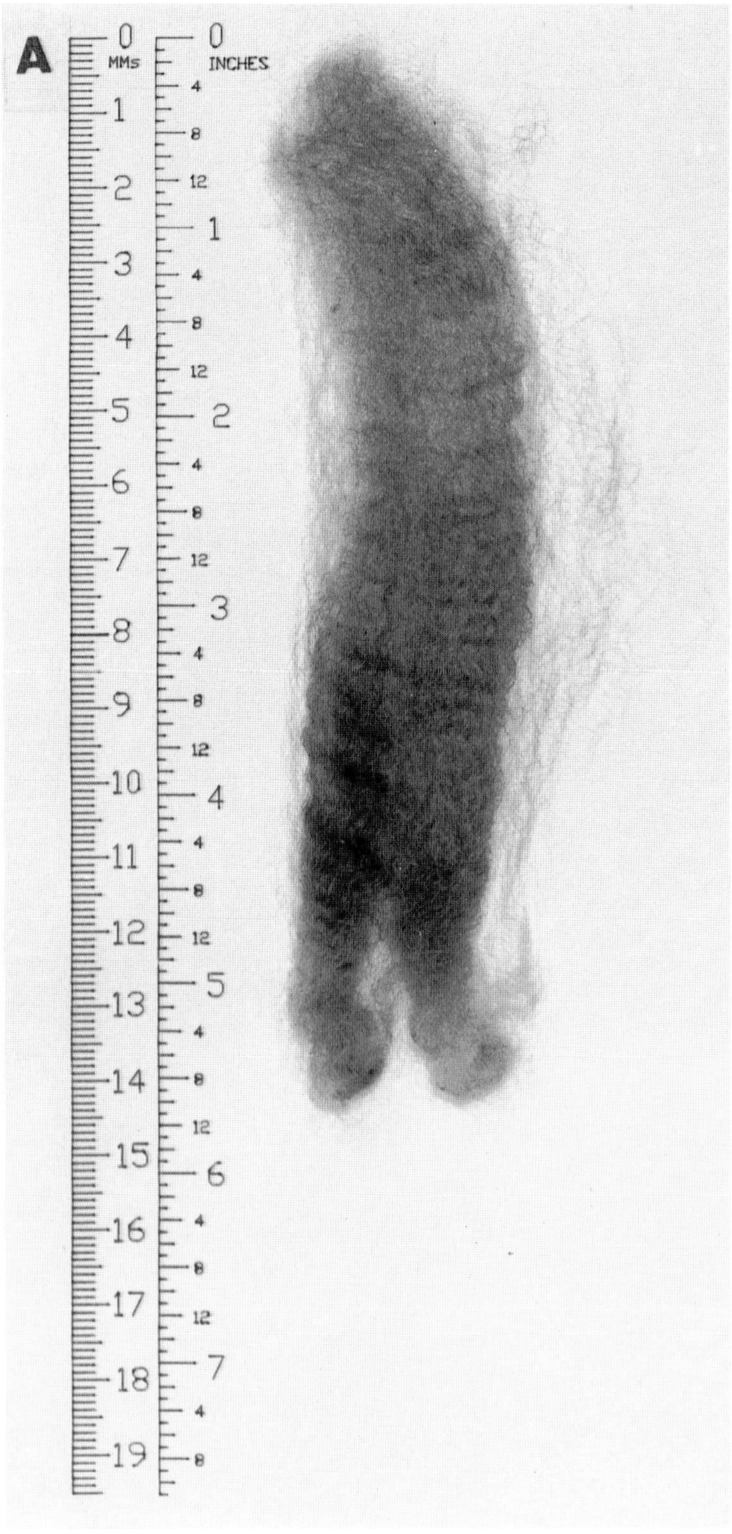

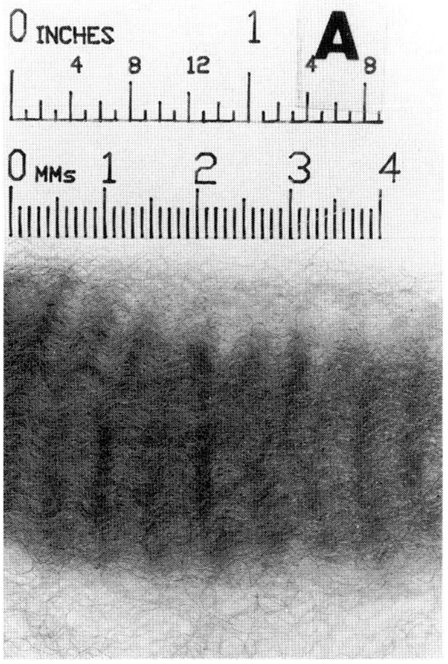

SAMPLE A

Staple length: 15cm (6in)
Staple shape: flat tip
Crimp pattern: 4 crimps per 2.5cm (1in)
Fibre size: medium/bulky
Colour: grey
Lustre: medium
Bulk: medium
Cleanliness: clean
Soundness: no break
Breed: New Zealand Crossbred.
Source of wool: Margaret Stewart, RD 12 Rakaia, New Zealand*

Suggestions for spinning

This wool should be spun into a medium/bulky yarn with 4 twists per 2.5cm (1in) in the finished yarn. Because the staple is long, this fleece would make a good worsted yarn, but it could also be spun semi-woollen. As it has a medium/bulky fibre size, the wool will be hard-wearing. Project 2, page 121 was spun from this fleece.

Suggested end uses

Knitting: A hard-wearing outer sweater or jersey, hats and mittens, afghans and throws. Weaving: Jackets and thick fabric, blankets and afghans. If spun finer, this yarn would make strong, hard-wearing upholstery fabric, cushion covers, and curtain fabric.

SAMPLE B (CARDED WOOL)

Staple length: 10-12cm (4-5in)
Staple shape: not known
Crimp pattern: 7 crimps per 2.5cm (1in)
Fibre size: medium
Colour: grey
Lustre: medium
Bulk: medium
Cleanliness: clean
Soundness: not known
Preparation of batt: carded for woollen spinning
Breed: not known
Source of wool: Hands, Ashford New Zealand Ltd, 5 Normans Road, Christchurch, New Zealand*

Suggestions for spinning

This wool should be spun into a medium yarn with 7 twists per 2.5cm (1in) in the finished yarn. It can be spun semi-worsted or woollen, but because it is already carded for woollen spinning it cannot be spun into a worsted or semi-woollen yarn.

Suggested end uses

Knitting: A medium-weight, reasonably hard-wearing outer garment, such as an outdoor sweater. It would also make socks (perhaps spun finer), hats, mittens and blankets.
Weaving: Use this yarn for clothing fabric. It is probably more suitable for coat, jacket and skirt fabric (spin finer for the latter) than for fine soft fabric. It would make good blankets and afghans.

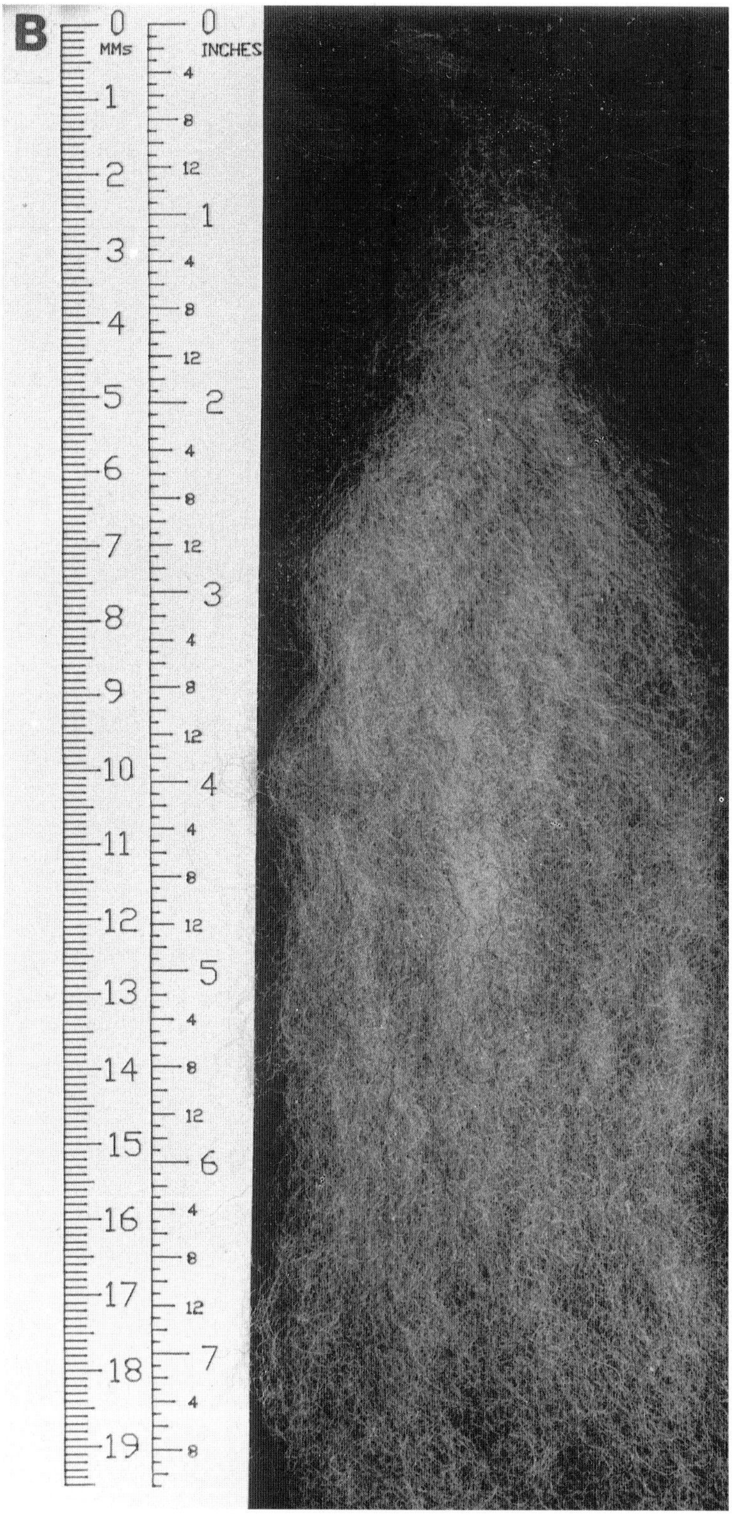

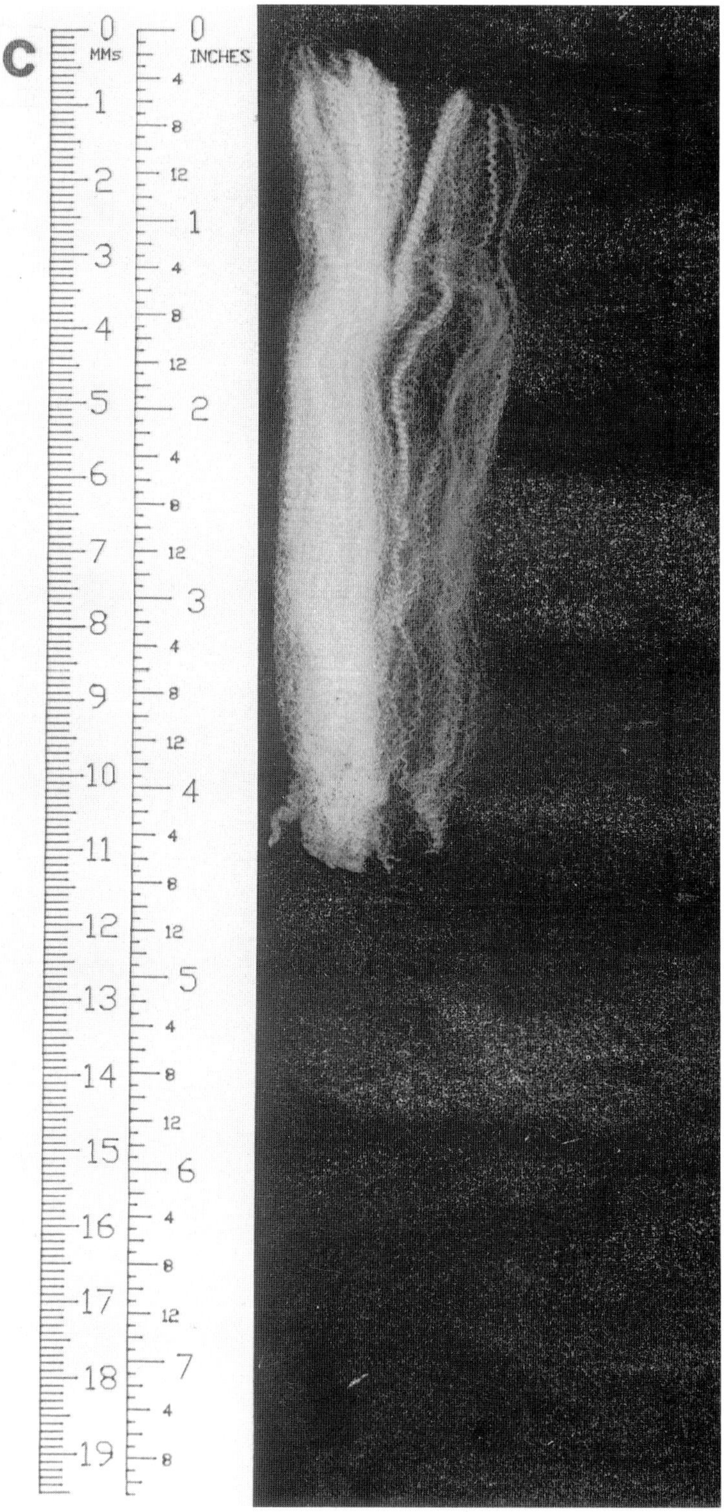

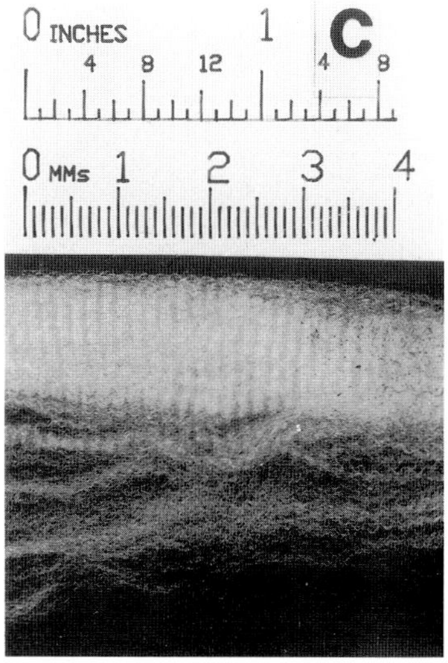

SAMPLE C

Staple length: 10cm (4in)
Staple shape: flat tip
Crimp pattern: 15 crimps per 2.5cm (1in)
Fibre size: fine
Colour: white
Lustre: low
Bulk: medium
Cleanliness: clean, apart from the tip, which contains much grease
Soundness: no break
Breed: Merino, 20 microns
Source of wool: Wrightson NMA, PO Box 106, Dunedin, New Zealand*

Suggestions for spinning

This wool should be spun into a fine yarn with 15 twists to 2.5cm (1in) in the finished yarn. Because of its length this wool would make a worsted yarn, but it could also be spun semi-worsted, semi-woollen or woollen. It is a fine wool and will be soft against the skin but guard against felting.

Suggested end uses

Knitting: Soft shawls, scarves, babywear, fine lacy jerseys and sweaters.
Weaving: Scarves, shawls and fine drapable fabric that will full well.

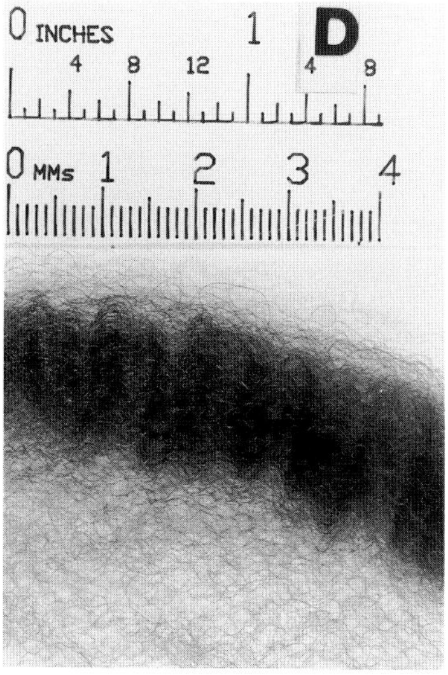

SAMPLE D

Staple length: 16cm (6.5in)
Staple shape: pointed tip
Crimp pattern: 6 crimps per 2.5cm (1in)
Fibre size: medium
Colour: light brown
Lustre: medium
Bulk: high
Cleanliness: clean
Soundness: no break
Breed: Perendale
Source of wool: Anne Paterson, Whiterock, Cannington, RD16 Cave, New Zealand*

Suggestions for spinning

This wool should be spun into a medium/bulky yarn with 6 twists per 2.5cm (1in). It could be spun worsted or semi-woollen but is probably too long in the staple for semi-worsted or woollen spinning. Because of the high bulk, spin this yarn finer than intended for the finished yarn as it will bulk up when washed.

Suggested end uses

Knitting: Scarves, shawls, medium-weight sweaters and jerseys, blankets, hats and mittens.
Weaving: Scarves, shawls, blankets and throws, medium-weight fabric for jackets, coats and other clothing fabric.

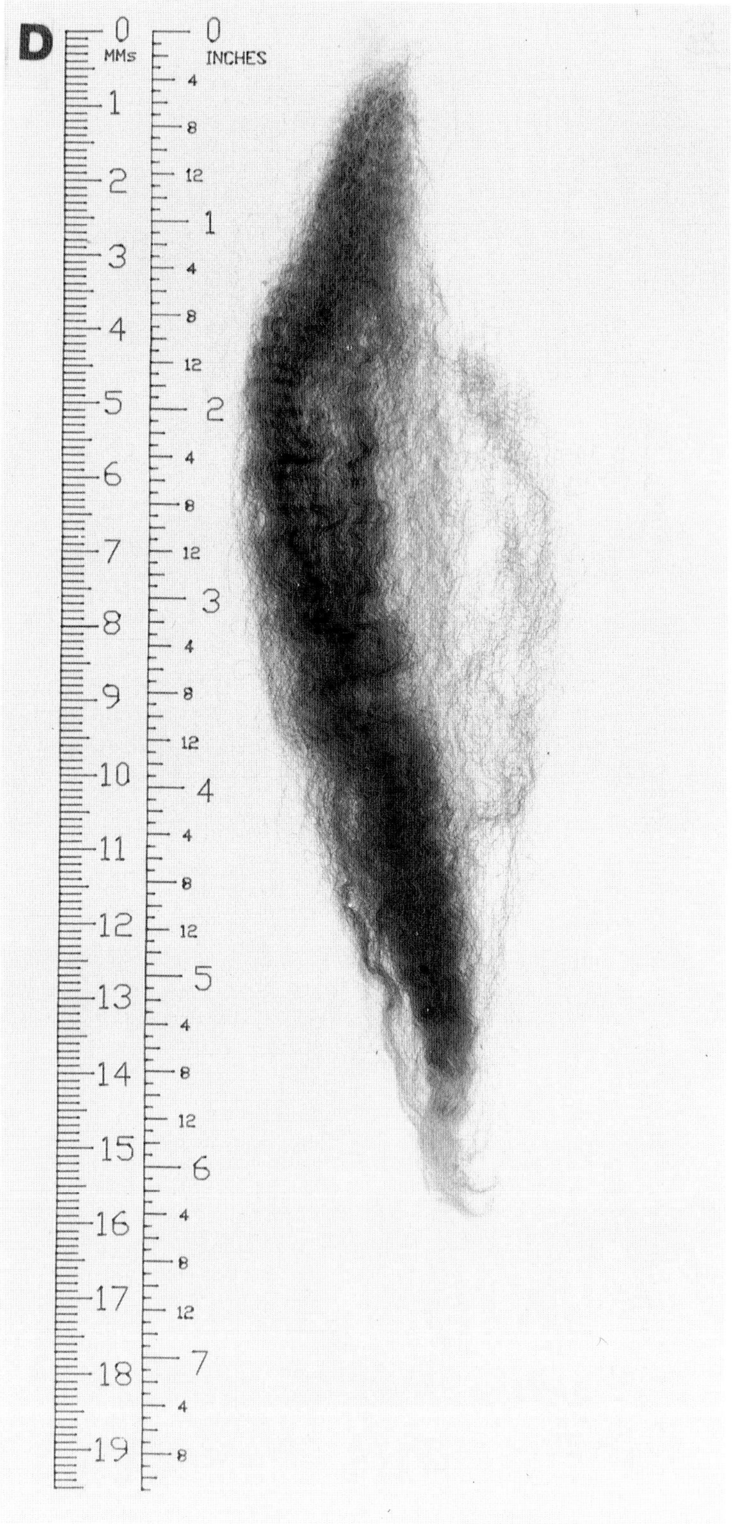

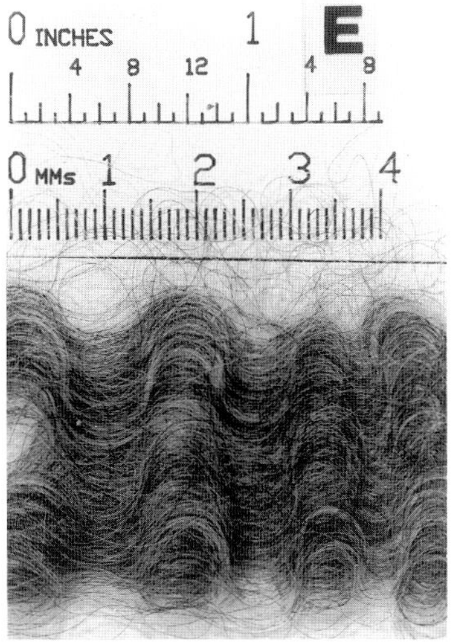

SAMPLE E

Staple length: 19cm (7.5in)
Staple shape: pointed tip
Crimp pattern: 2 crimps per 2.5cm (1in)
Fibre size: bulky
Colour: grey
Lustre: high lustre
Bulk: low
Cleanliness: clean
Soundness: no break
Breed: English Leicester
Source of wool: Elspeth Wilkinson, Mitcham, RD 2 Ashburton, New Zealand*

Suggestions for spinning

This wool should be spun into a very bulky yarn with 2 twists per 2.5cm (1in) in the finished yarn. It can be spun worsted or semi-woollen as it is too long in the staple for carding for woollen or semi-worsted spinning. This fleece would make a strong singles yarn for weaving or knitting.

Suggested end uses

Knitting: Bulky outdoor jackets, hats and mittens – but it is very limited in use.
Weaving: Excellent as the unspun weft for fleece rugs (see Project 1). It would also make a strong bulky rug yarn, either singles or plied. If this fleece was spun fine with plenty of twist it would make an excellent warp for floor rugs, giving a strong, shiny, smooth hard-wearing yarn.

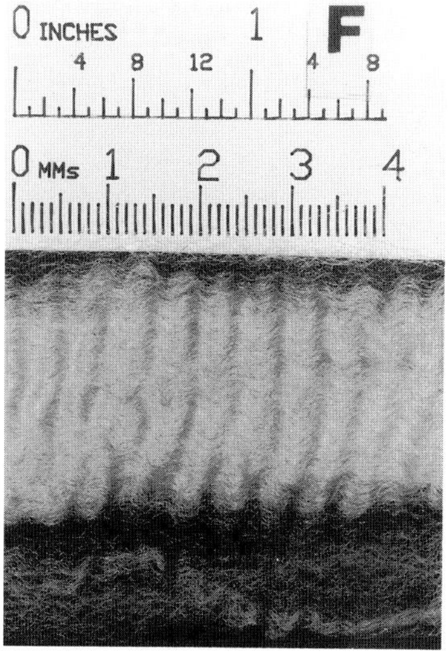

SAMPLE F

Staple length: 15cm (6in)
Staple shape: almost flat tip
Crimp pattern: 6 crimps per 2.5cm (1in)
Fibre size: medium
Colour: white
Lustre: low
Bulk: medium
Cleanliness: clean
Soundness: no break
Breed: Corriedale
Source of wool: Helen Heddle, Glenrachney, RD 3 Akaroa, New Zealand*

Suggestions for spinning

This fleece should be spun into a medium/bulky yarn with 6 twists per 2.5cm (1in) in the finished yarn. It could be spun semi-worsted or woollen but may be too long in the staple (unusually so for a Corriedale fleece) for worsted spinning. Take care when washing as this fleece will felt easily.

Suggested end uses

Knitting: A good yarn for a wide range of projects, including scarves, shawls, babywear, jerseys and sweaters, hats and mittens. It is not as hard-wearing as coarser fleeces. Weaving: Soft blankets, shawls, scarves, throws and afghans. It would make good clothing fabric as it will full well.

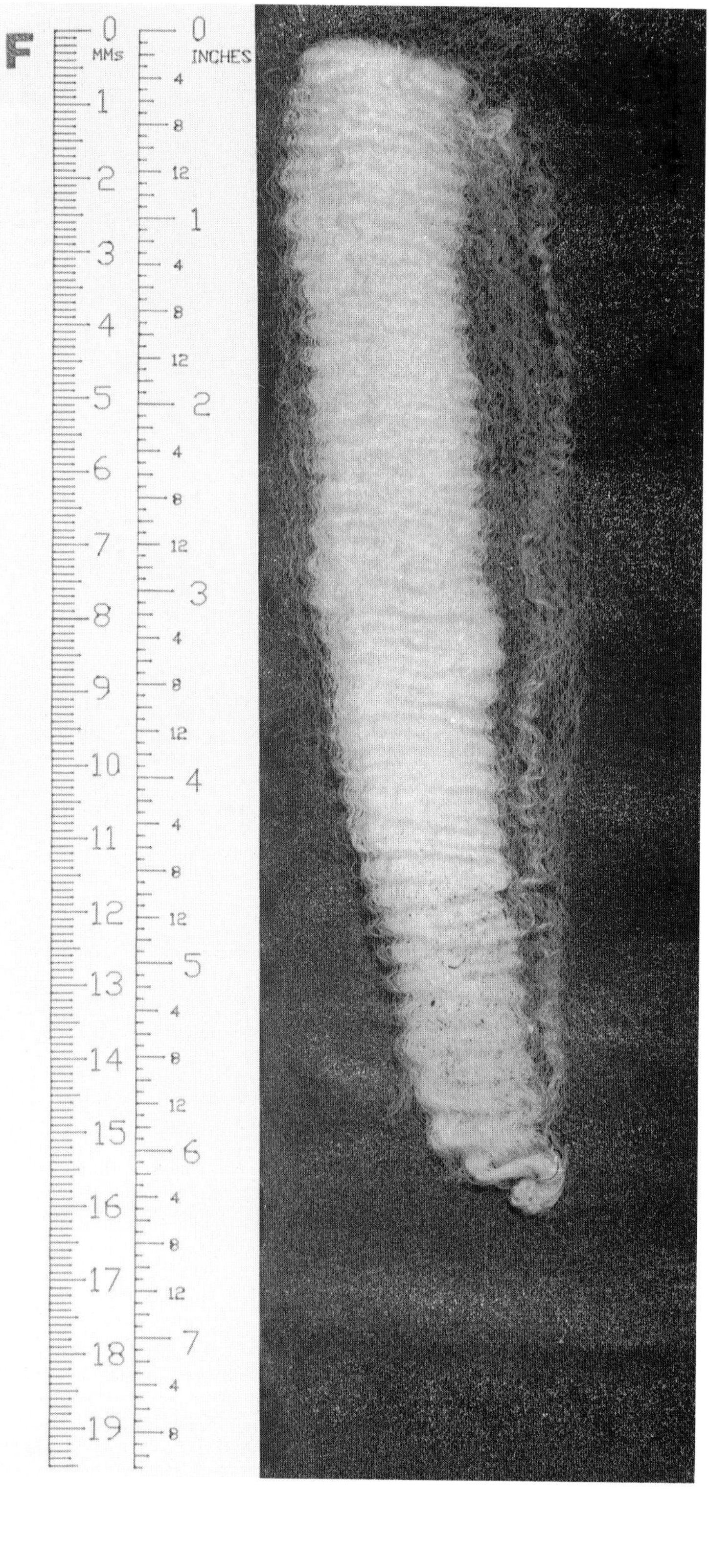

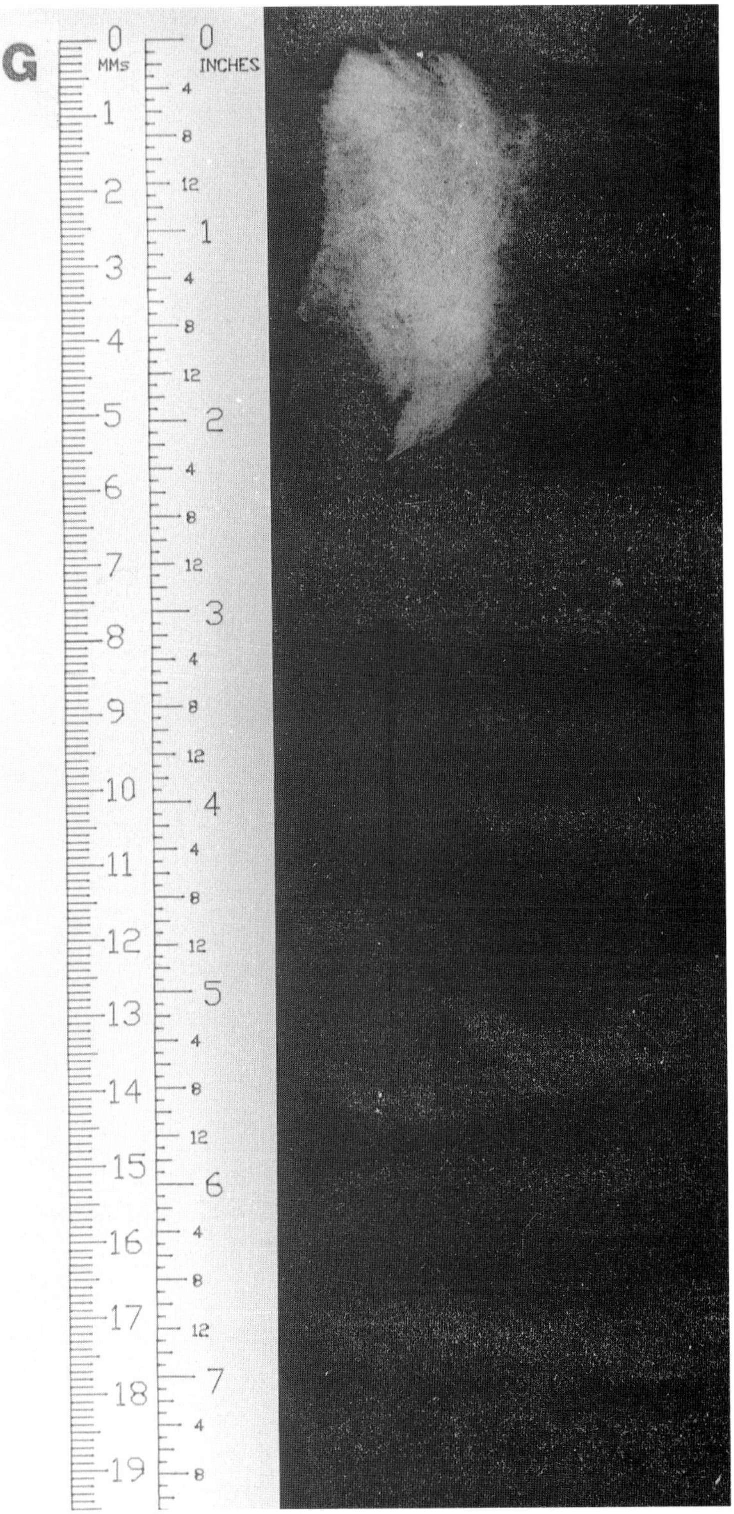

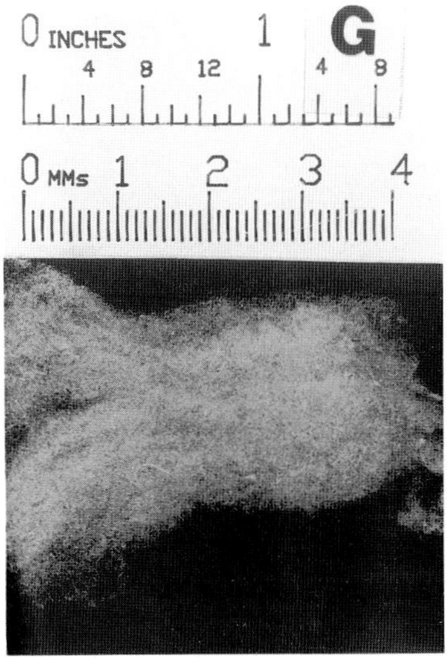

SAMPLE G

Staple length: 5cm (2in)
Staple shape: flat tip
Crimp pattern: lots! Impossible to count – more than 30
Fibre size: fine
Colour: creamy white
Lustre: very low
Bulk: very high bulk
Cleanliness: dirty at tips
Soundness: no break
Breed: Southdown
Source of wool: Pat Atwell, New Zealand

Suggestions for spinning

This wool should be spun very fine with a high twist. Because of its very high bulk it will more than double in size when washed. Because it has a very short staple it should be spun woollen or semi-worsted as the short fibres will be impossible to flick card or comb. The yarn will be uncrushable.

Suggested end uses

Knitting and weaving: Ideal for fine, soft babywear, shawls and scarves.

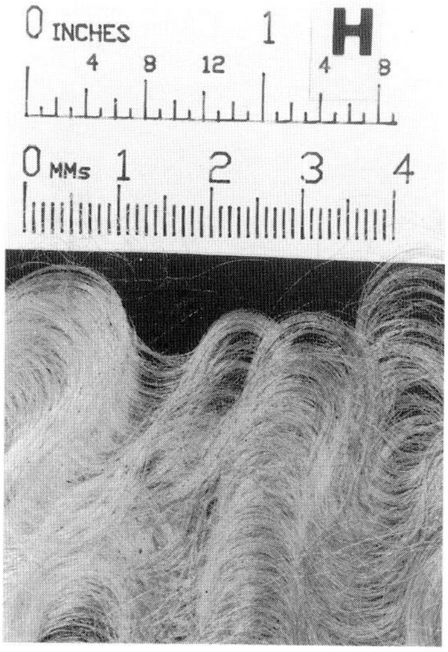

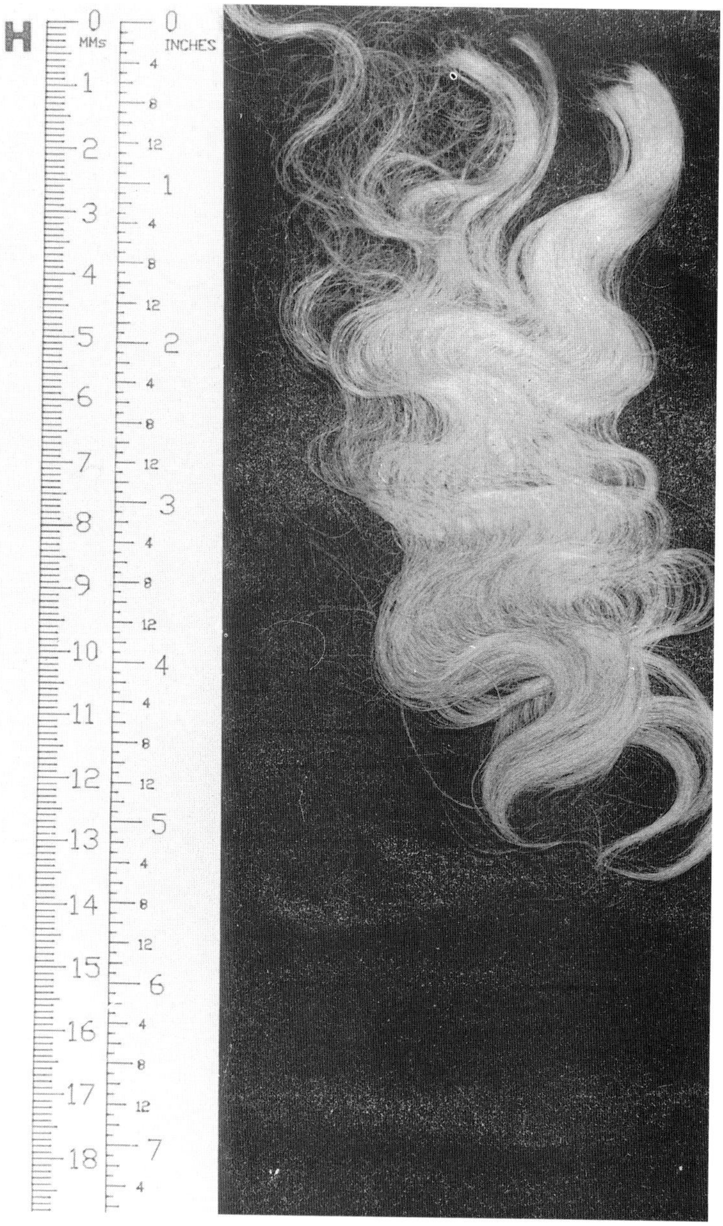

SAMPLE H

Staple length: 13cm (5in)
Staple shape: pointed tip
Crimp pattern: 1 per 2.5cm (1in)
Fibre size: bulky
Colour: creamy white
Lustre: high lustre
Bulk: none
Cleanliness: clean
Soundness: no break
Breed: Lincoln
Source of wool: Pat Atwell, New Zealand

Suggestions for spinning

Judging by the crimp pattern, this yarn should be spun with 1 twist per 2.5cm (in) in the finished yarn. This limits its use so much that this fleece is almost beyond the range of most spinners.

Suggested end uses

This yarn would be very hairy and coarse, not suitable for garments. It could be spun very loosely for a weft in woven tablemats, as a novelty yarn in decorative woven hangings, or as a spun weft in floor rugs. This particular Lincoln fleece is too short in the staple for use in weaving fleece rugs, as in Project 1, but a longer-staple Lincoln would make a good unspun weft for fleece rugs.

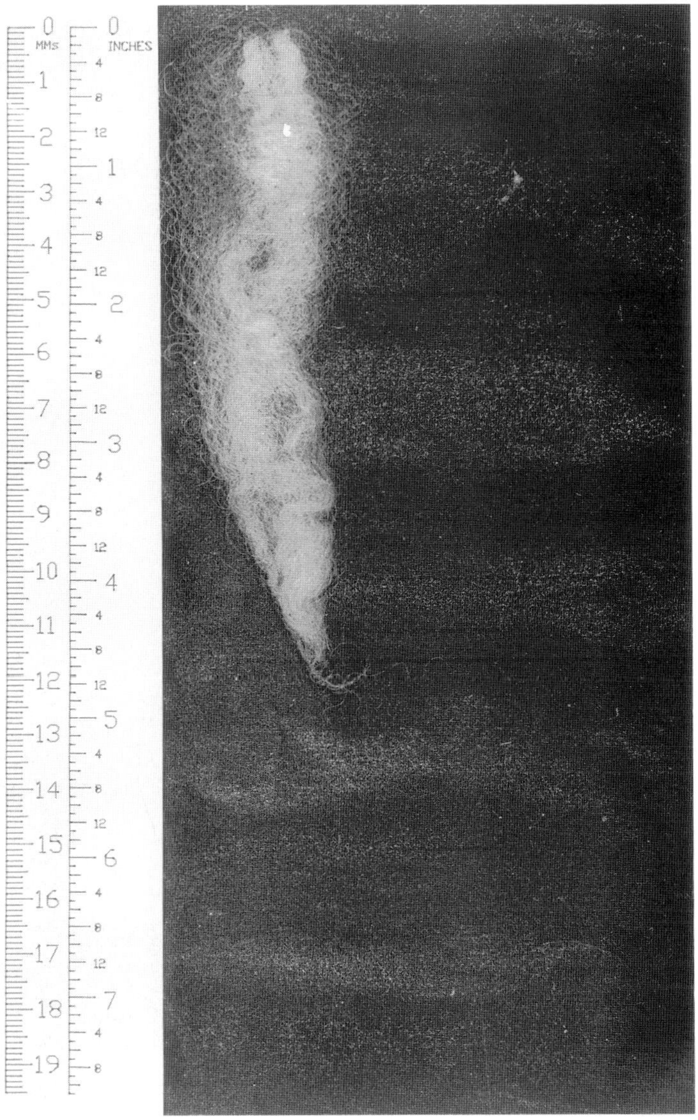

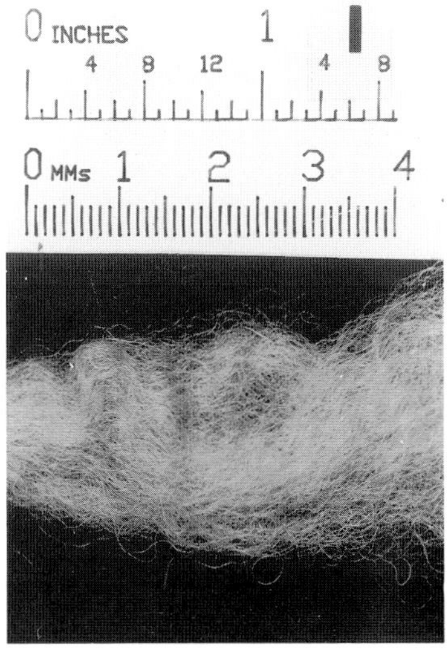

SAMPLE I

Staple length: 13cm (5in)
Staple shape: pointed tip
Crimp pattern: 4 crimps per 2.5cm (1in)
Fibre size: medium/bulky
Colour: creamy white
Lustre: very low
Bulk: high bulk
Cleanliness: clean
Soundness: no break
Breed: Cheviot
Source of wool: Pat Atwell, New Zealand

Suggestions for spinning

This wool should be spun with 4 twists per 2.5cm (1in) in the finished yarn, to make a medium/bulky yarn. Because of its high bulk the wool will double in size when spun. This will make it a very coarse yarn, particularly if spun woollen. To make the yarn more hard-wearing and less bulky, spin it worsted or semi-worsted.

Suggested end uses

Knitting: Bulky jackets and outer garments such as hats. It has good fulling properties, particularly if spun woollen.
Weaving: Blankets, knee-rugs or throws, or thick fabric and upholstery cloth.

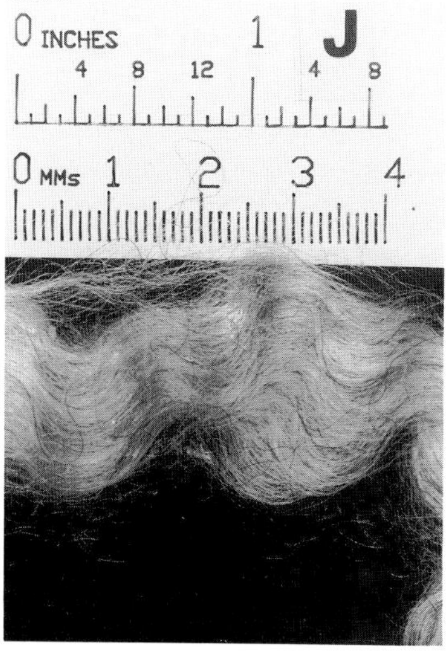

SAMPLE J

Staple length: 18cm (7in)
Staple shape: pointed tip
Crimp pattern: 2 per 2.5cm (1in)
Fibre size: bulky
Colour: light grey
Lustre: high
Bulk: low
Cleanliness: clean
Soundness: no break
Breed: Lincoln
Source of wool: Judith Lange, Cherry Ridge Ranch, 9845 Cherry Ridge Road, Sebastopol, CA 95472, USA*

Suggestions for spinning

This wool should be spun into a bulky yarn with 2 twists per 2.5cm (1in) in the finished yarn. It can be spun worsted or semi-woollen. The staple is too long for semi-worsted or woollen yarn, as it would be difficult to handcard or drumcard.

Suggested end uses

Knitting: Bulky outdoor garments, hats and mittens.
Weaving: Excellent for weaving fleece rugs (see Project 1). It would make a suitable bulky-spun rug yarn, either singles or plied. If this fleece was spun fine with plenty of twist it would be an excellent warp yarn for floor rugs, as this type of spinning would result in a strong, smooth shiny yarn with a hard feel.

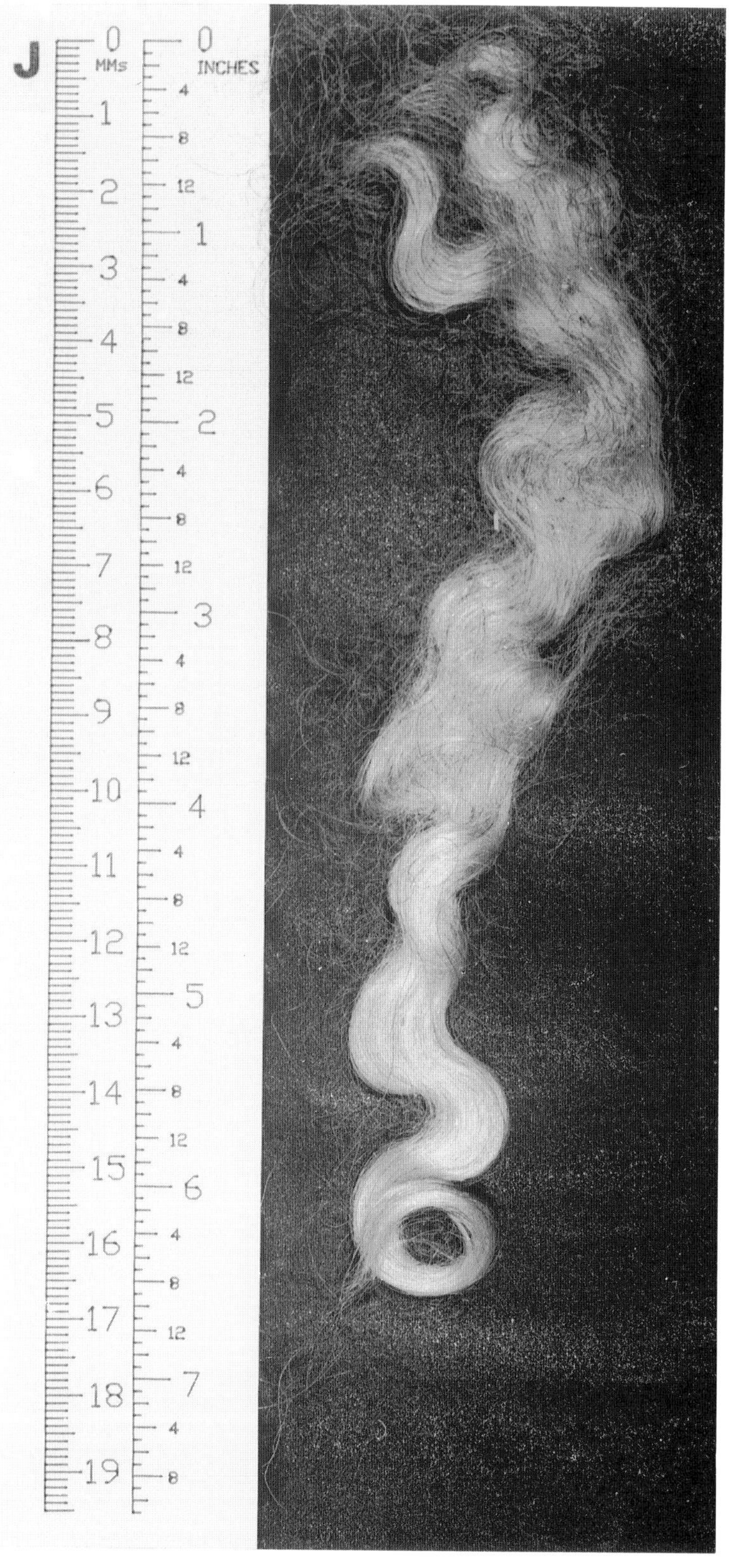

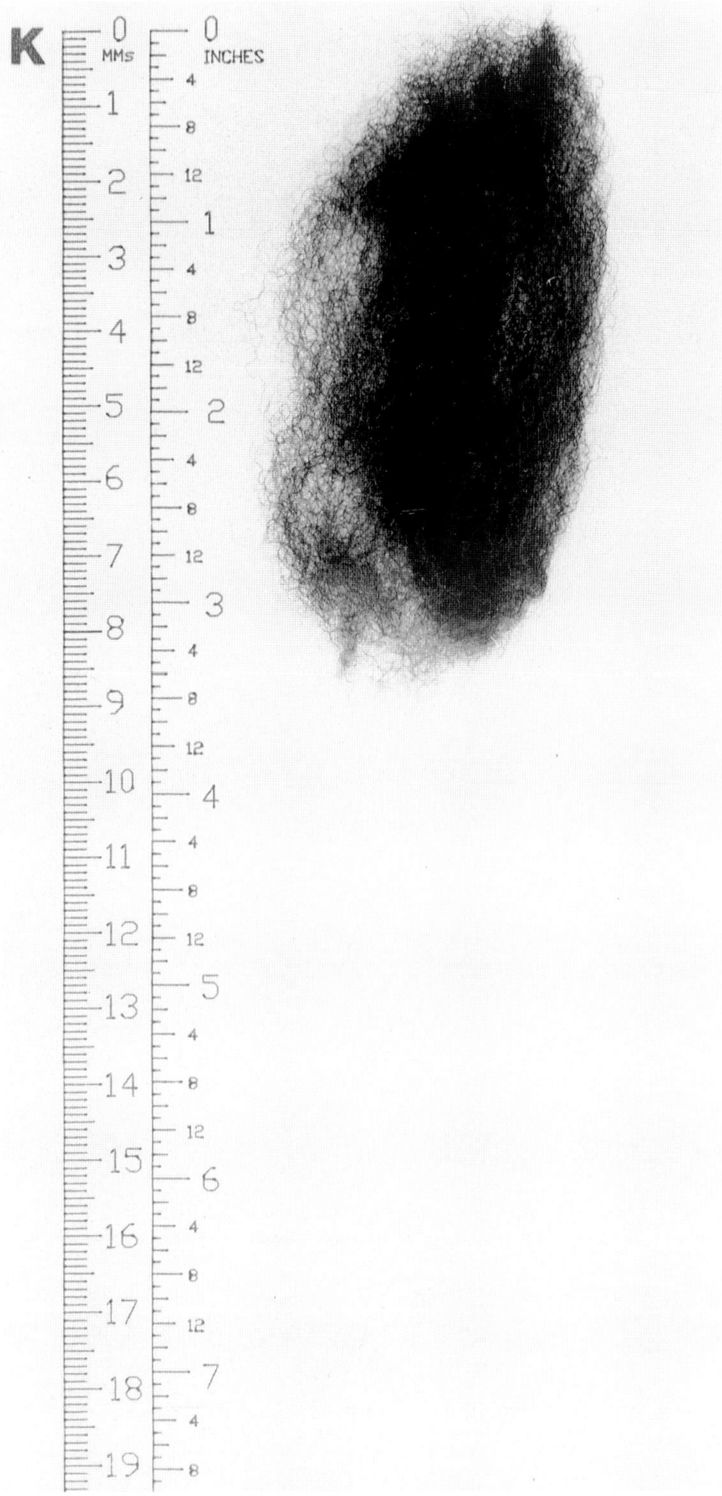

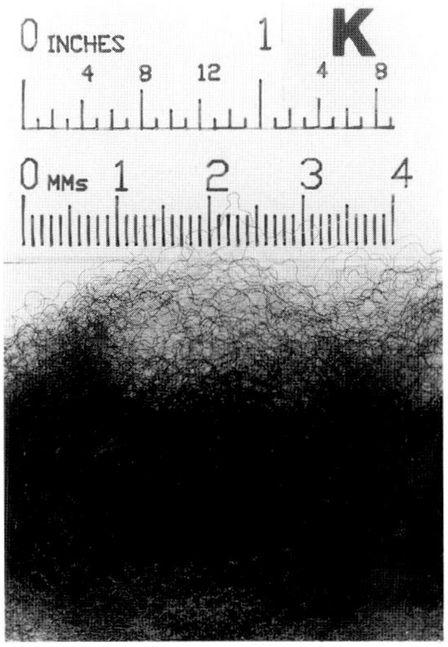

SAMPLE K

Staple length: 7.5cm (3in)
Staple shape: flat tip
Crimp pattern: 9 crimps per 2.5cm (1in)
Fibre size: medium
Colour: dark brown
Lustre: low
Bulk: high
Cleanliness: clean
Soundness: no break
Breed: Jacob and Suffolk cross
Source of wool: Ann Mulley, England

Suggestions for spinning

This yarn should be spun into a medium yarn with 9 twists per 2.5cm (1in) in the finished yarn. It has a high bulk so spin it fine and expect the yarn to almost double in size when washed if you have spun a woollen, semi-woollen or semi-worsted yarn. Spinning this yarn worsted would reduce the bulk in the finished yarn. Project 3, page 124, was spun from this fleece.

Suggested end uses

Knitting: Jerseys and sweaters, hats, mittens, shawls and socks.
Weaving: Jackets and vests (see Project 3), and any clothing fabric. Because of the high bulk it would also be suitable for blankets.

SAMPLE L

Staple length: 16cm (6in)
Staple shape: pointed tip
Crimp pattern: 3 crimps per 2.5cm (1in)
Fibre size: bulky
Colour: grey
Lustre: low
Bulk: medium
Cleanliness: clean
Soundness: no break
Breed: Border Leicester and Cheviot cross
Source of wool: Ann Mulley, England

Suggestions for spinning

This fleece should be spun into a bulky yarn with 3 twists per 2.5cm (1in) in the finished yarn. Because of the staple length it would be difficult to handcard or drumcard, so is most suitable for worsted or semi-woollen spinning. The Cheviot component of this fleece gives bulk to the otherwise low-bulk Border Leicester. Therefore this fleece will increase in size when washed, unlike sample E.

Suggested end uses

Knitting: Bulky outdoor garments, hats and mittens.
Weaving: Excellent yarn for weaving blankets because the yarn will increase in size (due to the Cheviot component) and retain its springiness. As a weft yarn in jackets this yarn would be strong but springy to touch.

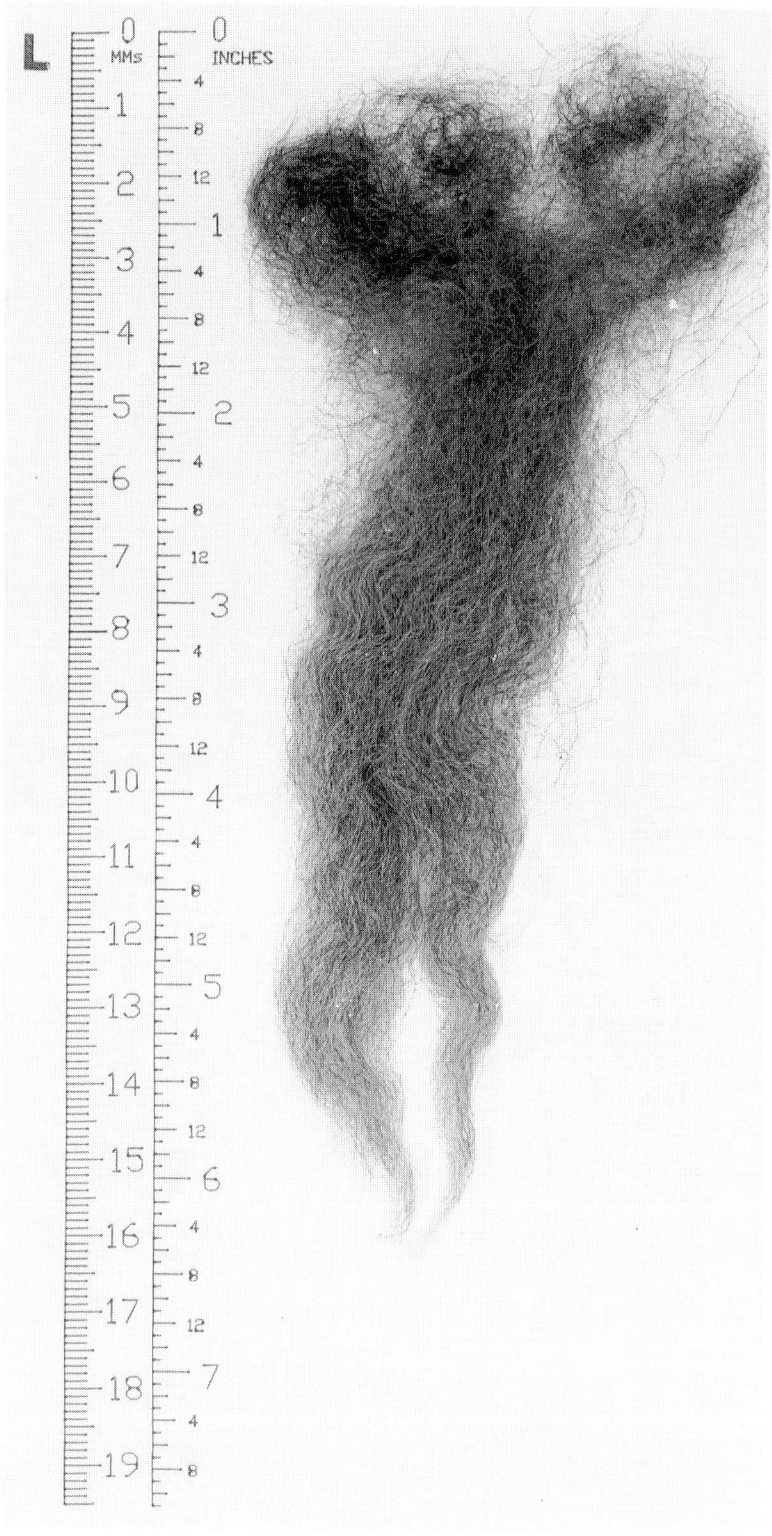

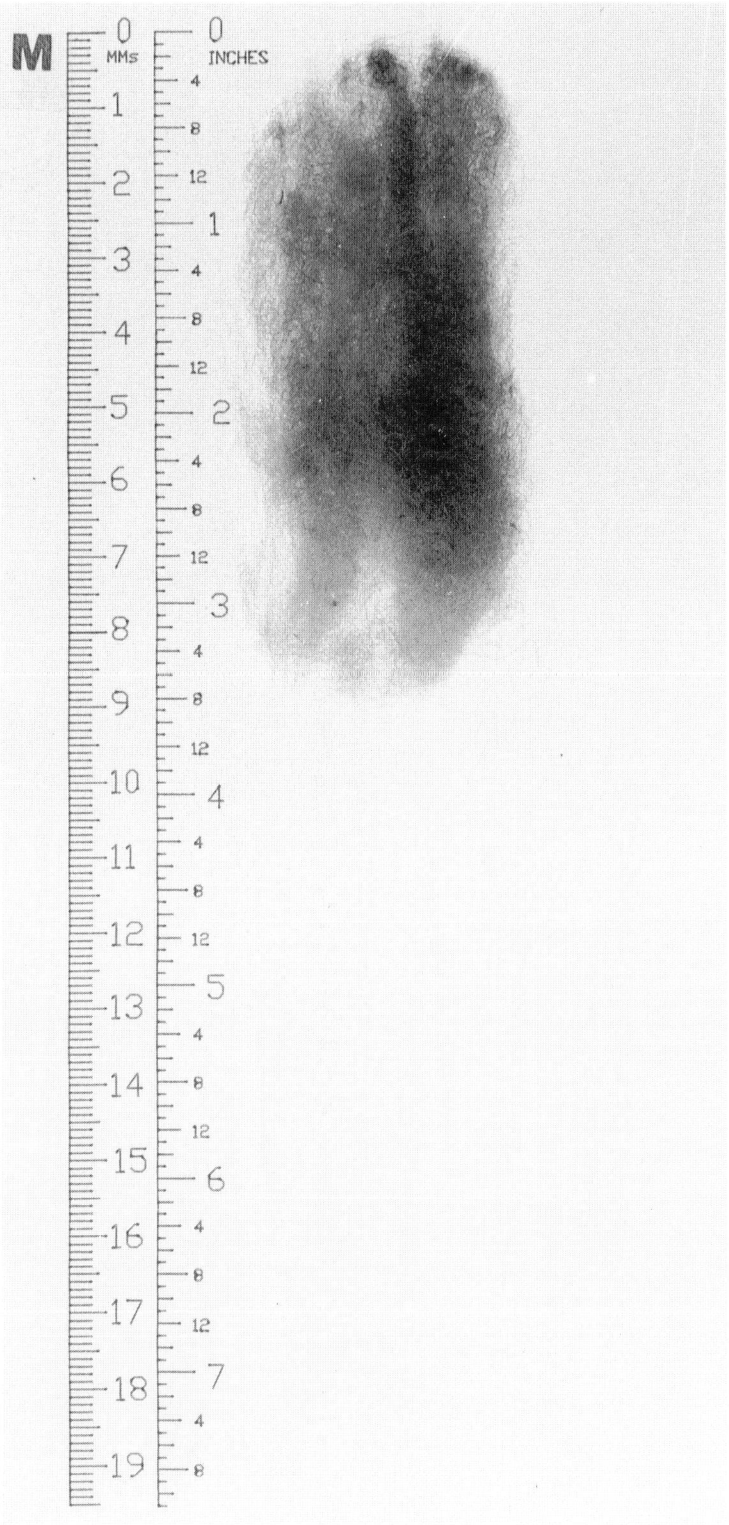

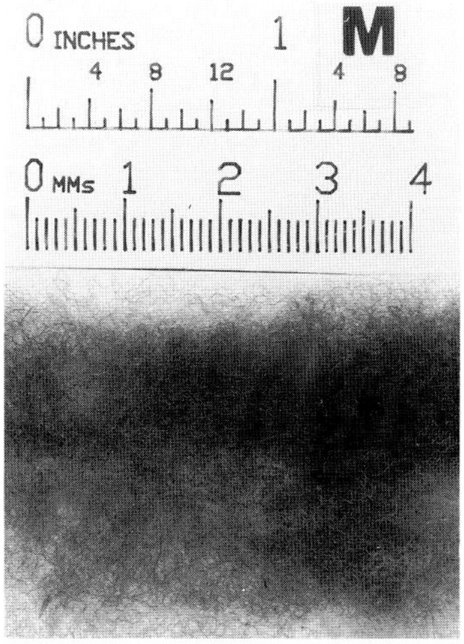

SAMPLE M

Staple length: 8cm (3in)
Staple shape: slightly pointed tip
Crimp pattern: approximately 12 crimps per 2.5cm (1in) – a very elastic fibre
Fibre size: fine/medium
Colour: light brown
Lustre: low
Bulk: high
Cleanliness: clean
Soundness: no break
Breed: Manx
Source of wool: Ann Mulley, England

Suggestions for spinning

This wool should be spun fine with 12 twists per 2.5cm (1in) in the finished yarn. The staple is probably too short for worsted spinning so woollen or semi-worsted would be best. Because of the high bulk, the yarn will increase in size when washed.

Suggested end uses

Knitting: Scarves, shawls, lightweight sweaters and jerseys.
Weaving: Scarves and shawls would be suitable, as the finished articles would be soft next to the skin.

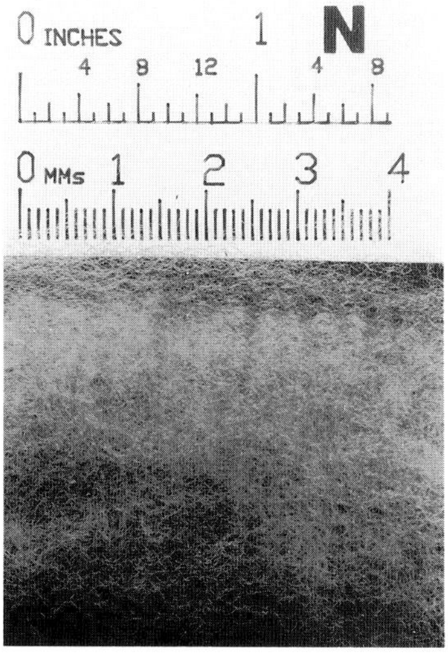

SAMPLE N

Staple length: 13cm (5in)
Staple shape: slightly pointed tip
Crimp pattern: 7 crimps per 2.5cm (1in)
Fibre size: medium
Colour: creamy
Lustre: medium
Bulk: medium
Cleanliness: clean
Soundness: no break
Breed: Lleyn
Source of wool: Ann Mulley, England

Suggestions for spinning

This wool should be spun into a medium yarn with 7 twists per 2.5cm (1in) in the finished yarn. It can be spun worsted, semi-worsted, semi-woollen or woollen.

Suggested end uses

Knitting: Scarves, shawls, medium-weight sweaters or jerseys, hats, socks, mittens, blankets, throws and afghans.
Weaving: Medium-weight fabric for jackets, coats and other clothing, including skirt fabric.

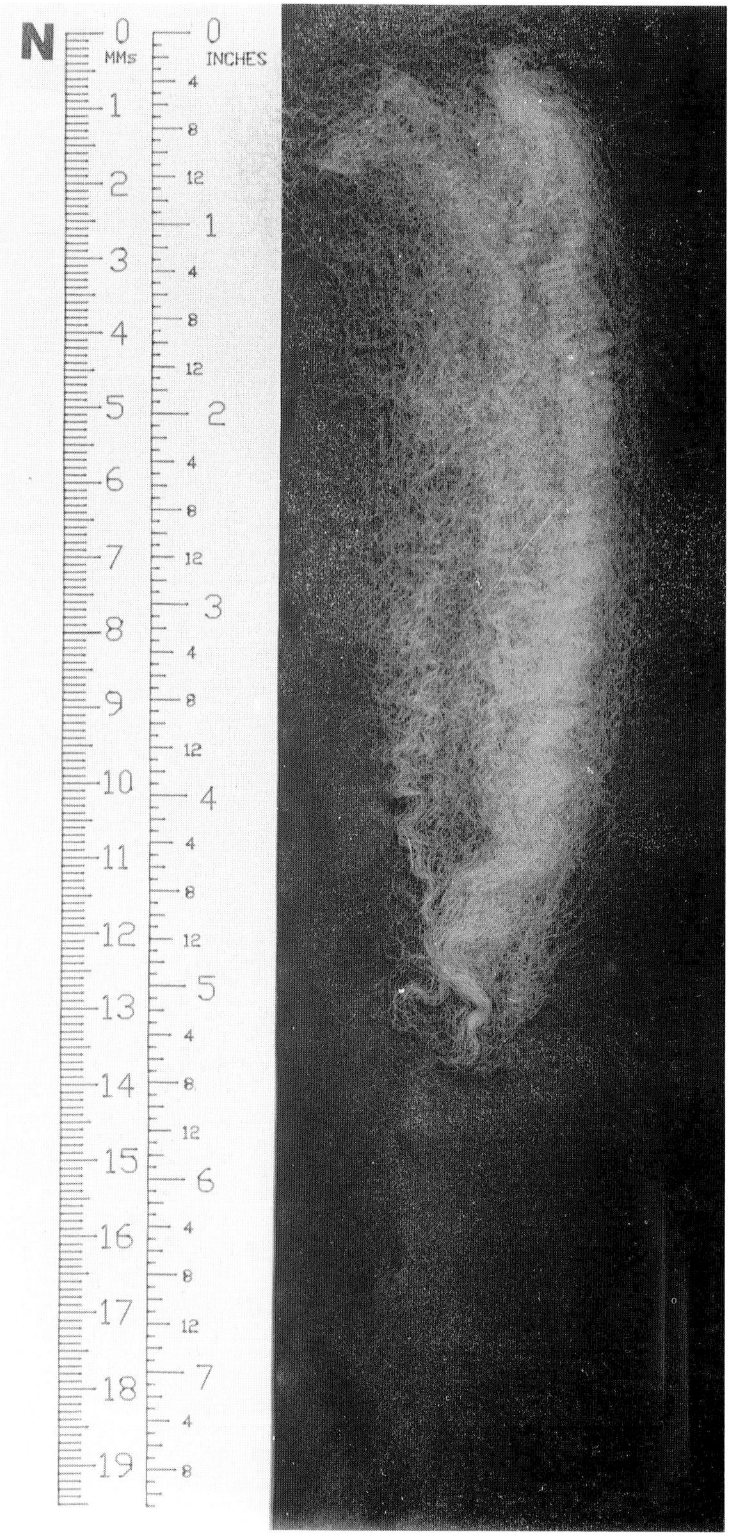

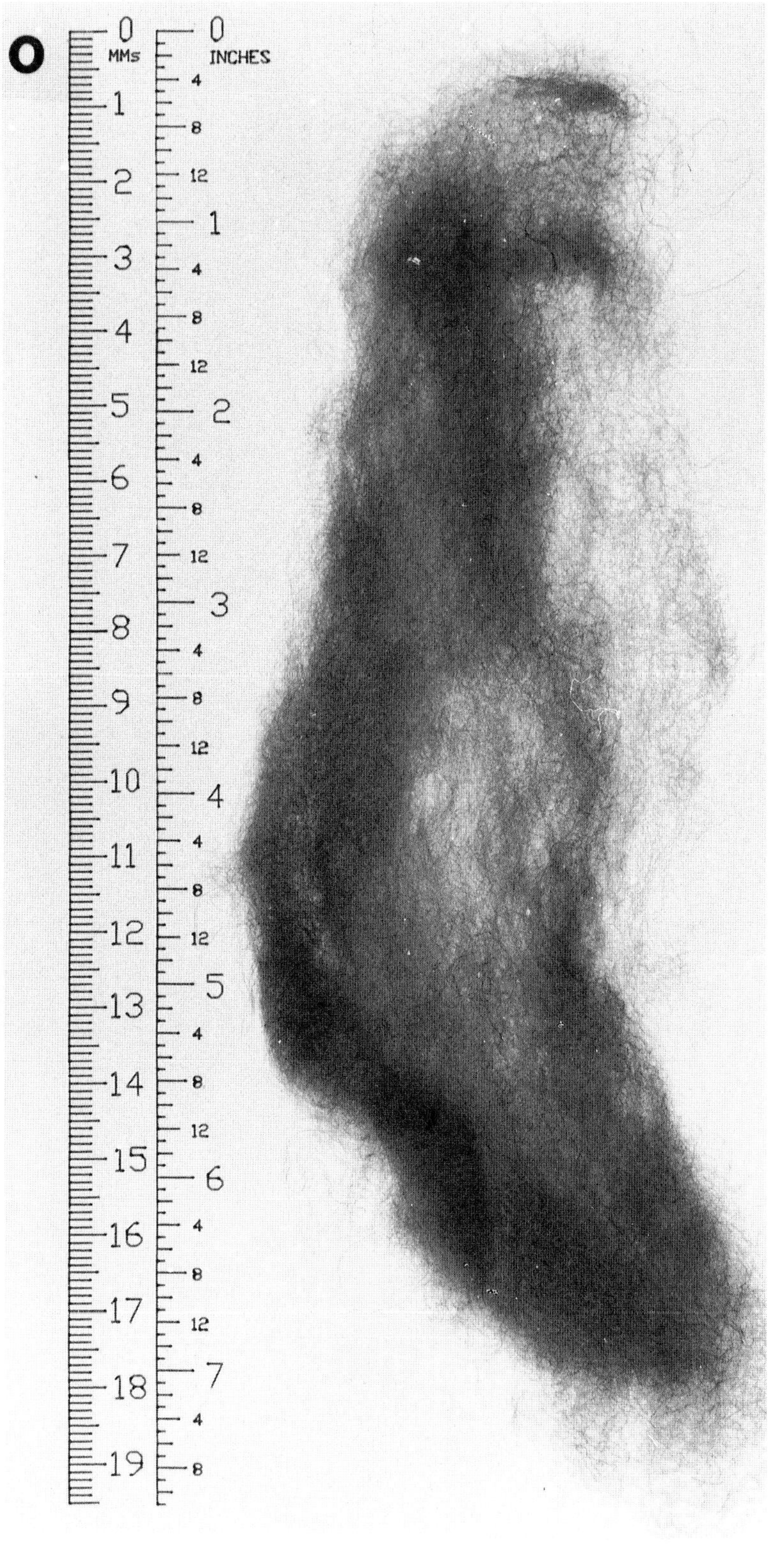

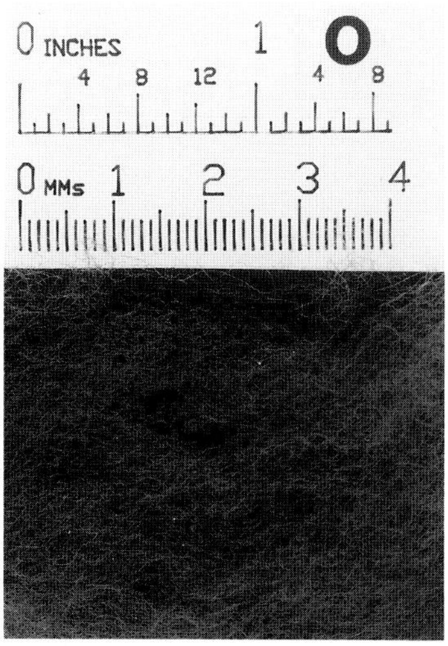

SAMPLE O (CARDED WOOL)

Staple length: 13cm (5in)
Staple shape: not known
Crimp pattern: 6-7 crimps per 2.5cm (1in)
Fibre size: medium
Colour: dyed blue/green
Lustre: medium
Bulk: medium-high
Cleanliness: clean
Soundness: not known
Preparation of batt: carded for woollen spinning
Breed: Romney/Dorset cross
Source of wool: Rotocard, RD 2 Nelson, New Zealand*

Suggestion for spinning

This wool should be spun with 6-7 twists per 2.5cm (1in) in the finished yarn. It can be spun semi-worsted or woollen but not worsted or semi-woollen, because it has already been carded. The wool spun for Project 6, page 132, and Project 8, page 138, came from this carded fleece. The yarn used in Project 5 is very similar to this sample and came from the same source.

Suggested end uses

Knitting: Medium-weight, reasonably hard-wearing outer garments such as sweaters or jerseys. It would also be suitable for socks, hats, mittens and blankets.
Weaving: Clothing fabric, blankets and afghans.

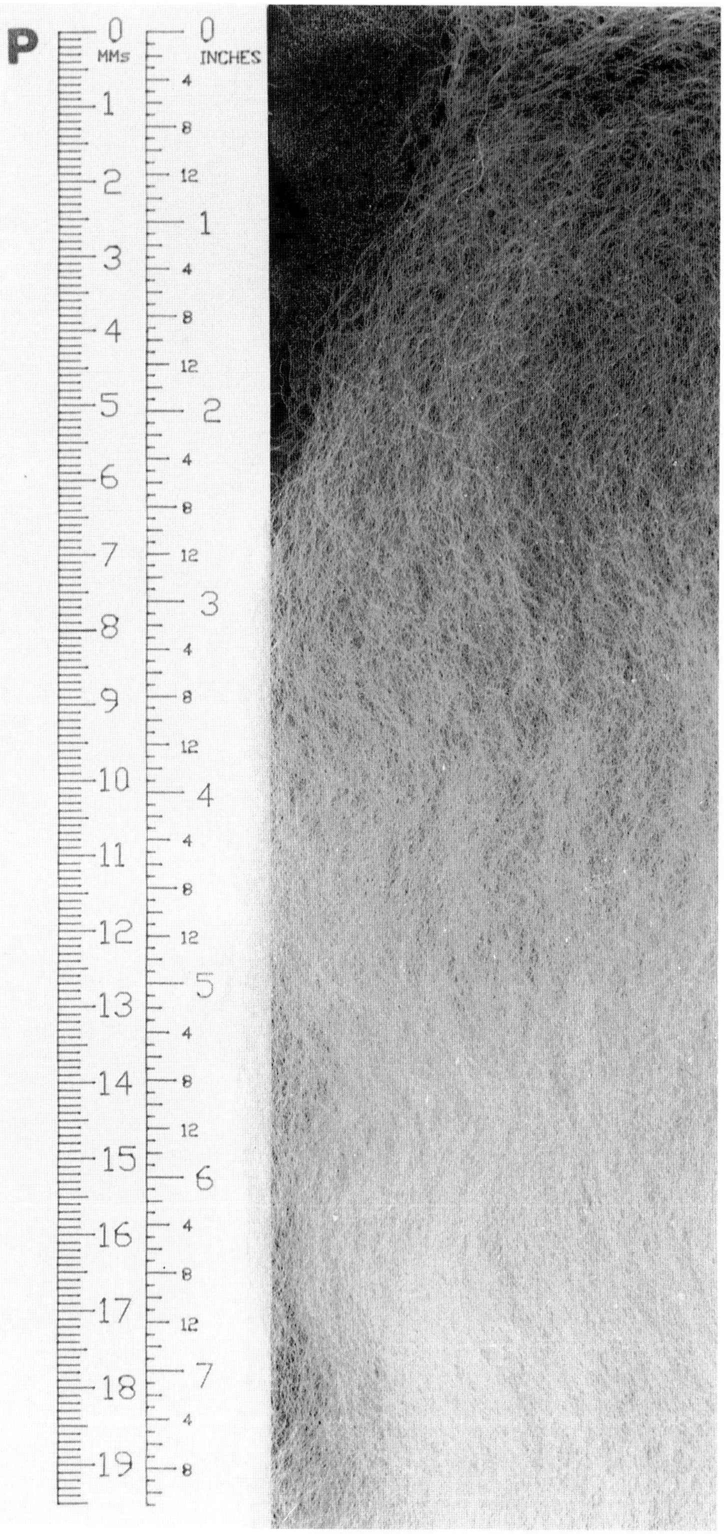

SAMPLE P (CARDED WOOL)

Staple length: 15cm (6in)
Staple shape: not known
Crimp pattern: 4 crimps per 2.5cm (1in)
Fibre size: medium/bulky
Colour: white
Lustre: medium
Bulk: medium
Cleanliness: clean
Soundness: not known
Preparation of batt: prepared for worsted spinning
Breed: not known
Source of wool: Not known. I acquired this sample somewhere in the USA from one of my teaching classes

Suggestions for spinning

This wool should be spun into a medium/bulky worsted or semi-woollen yarn with 4 twists per 2.5cm (1in) in the finished yarn. Because it has been prepared for worsted spinning it cannot be spun satisfactorily into a woollen or semi-worsted yarn. You can see how all the fibres are parallel.

Suggested end uses

Knitting: A good worsted yarn for bulky outer garments such as jackets and hats as it would be very hard-wearing.
Weaving: A weft yarn in floor rugs.

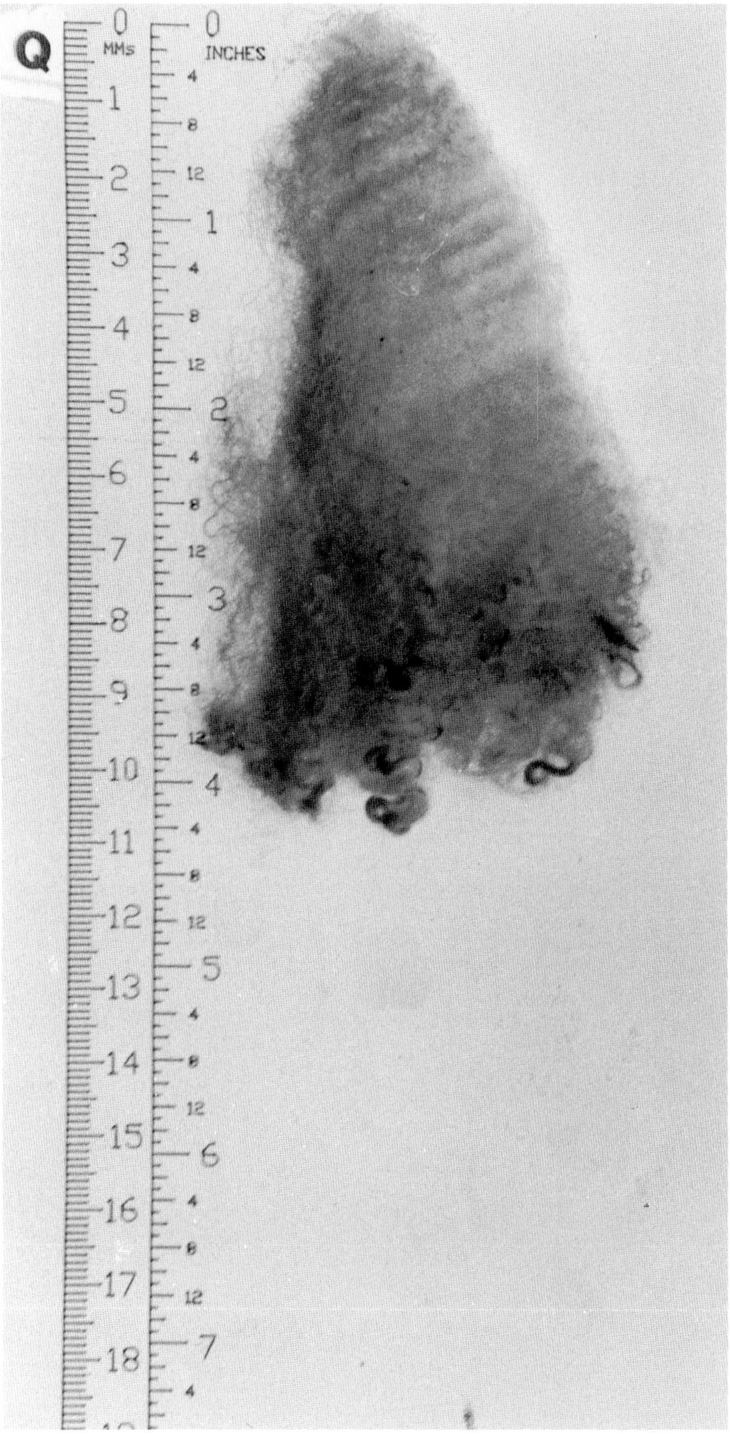

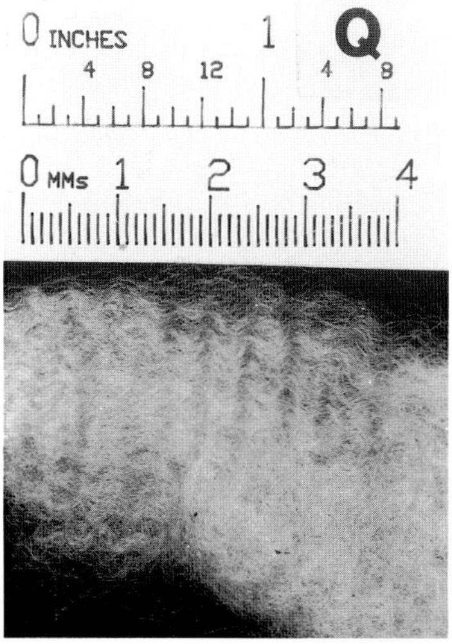

SAMPLE Q

Staple length: 12cm (4.5in)
Staple shape: slightly pointed tip
Crimp pattern: 7 crimps per 2.5cm (1in)
Fibre size: medium
Colour: creamy white
Lustre: low/medium
Bulk: medium
Cleanliness: clean
Soundness: no break
Breed: Corriedale
Source of wool: Joyce Chance, USA

Suggestions for spinning

This fleece should be spun into a medium yarn with 7 twists per 2.5cm (1in) in the finished yarn. It could be spun worsted, semi-worsted, semi-woollen or woollen. Guard against felting when washing.

Suggested end uses

Knitting: A wide range of articles, including scarves, shawls, jerseys and sweaters, hats and mittens.
Weaving: Ideal for blankets, afghans and throws, as well as clothing fabric, as it will full well.

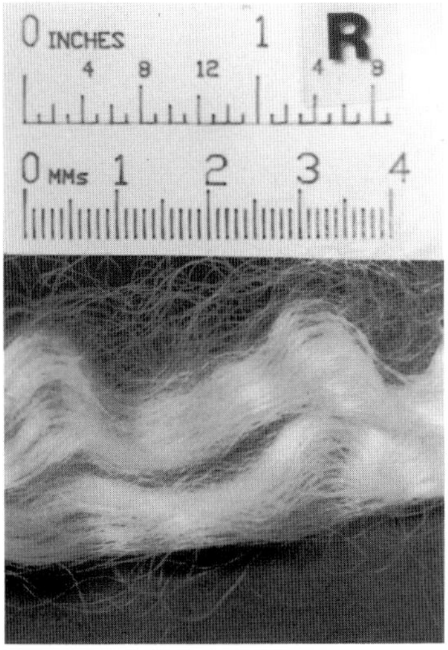

SAMPLE R

Staple length: 18cm (7in)
Staple shape: pointed tip
Crimp pattern: 2 crimps per 2.5cm (1in)
Fibre size: bulky
Colour: creamy white
Lustre: high
Bulk: low
Cleanliness: clean
Soundness: no break
Breed: English Leicester
Source of wool: Ethel Stephenson, The Homestead, RMB 2660, Goorambat, Victoria 3725, Australia*

Suggestions for spinning

This wool should be spun into a very bulky yarn, with 2 twists per 2.5cm (1in) in the finished yarn. It can be spun worsted or semi-woollen, as it is too long in the staple for carding for woollen or semi-worsted spinning. This fleece would make a strong singles yarn for weaving or knitting.

Suggested end uses

Knitting: Bulky outdoor jackets, hats and mittens. Very limited in use.
Weaving: Excellent as the unspun weft for fleece rugs (see Project 1). It would also make a strong bulky rug yarn, either singles or plied. If this fleece was spun fine with plenty of twist it would make an excellent warp for floor rugs, as this method of spinning would result in a strong, shiny, smooth hard-wearing yarn.

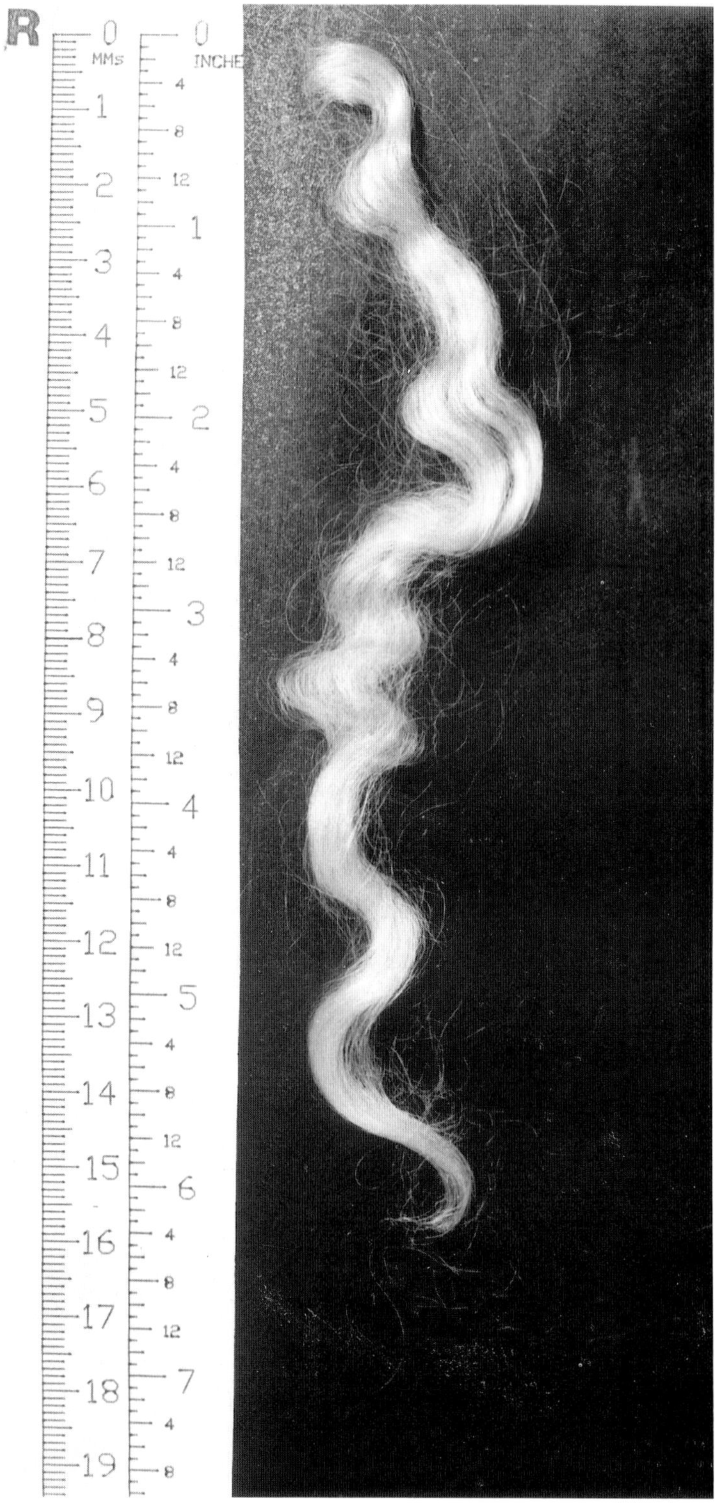

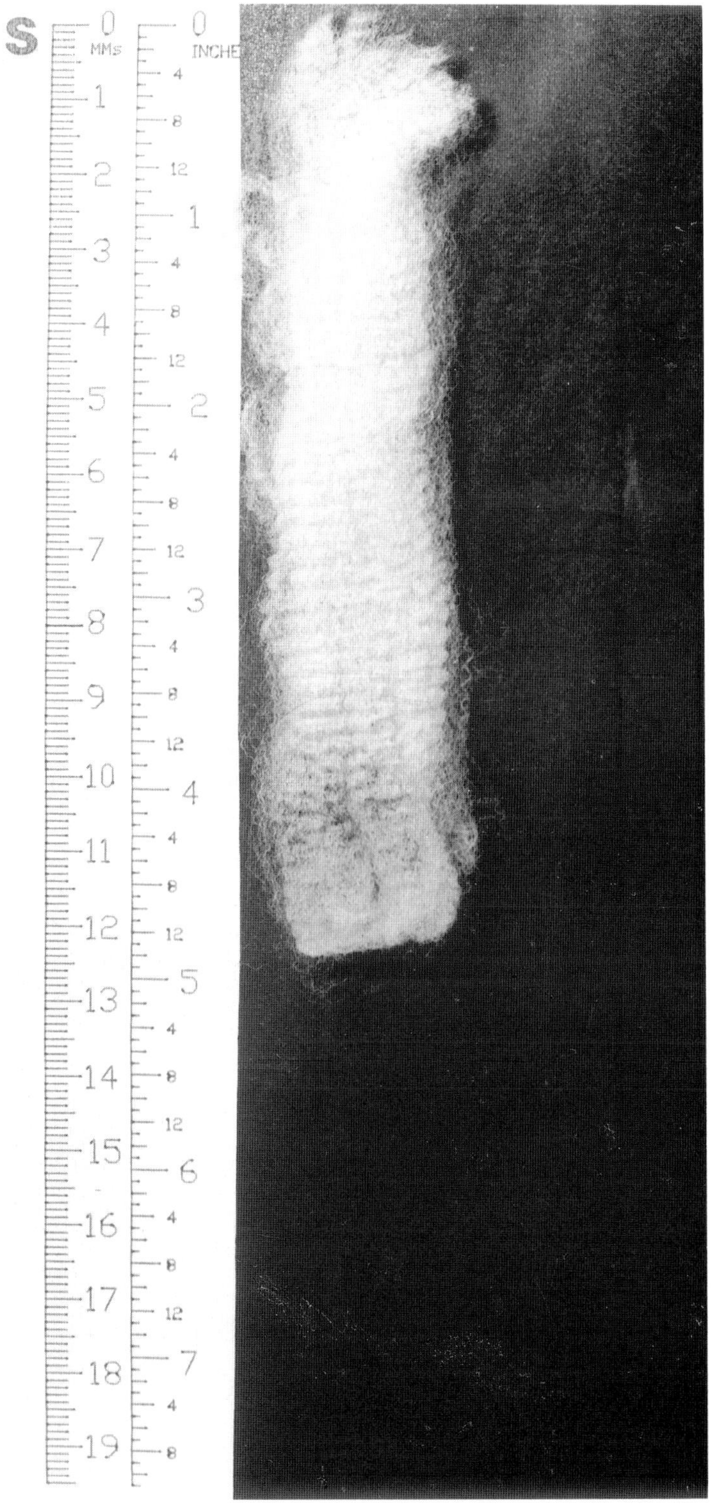

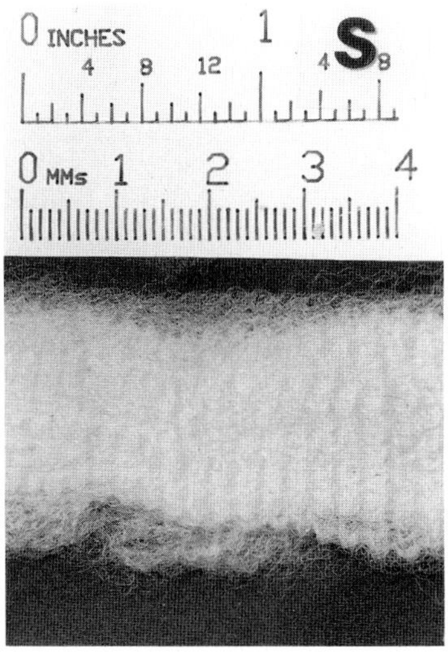

SAMPLE S

Staple length: 13cm (5in)
Staple shape: flat tip
Crimp pattern: 10 crimps per 2.5cm (1in)
Fibre size: fine/medium
Colour: white
Lustre: low
Bulk: medium
Cleanliness: clean
Soundness: no break
Breed: Merino
Source of wool: Shirley Caldwell, Mole Station, Tenterfield, NSW 2372, Australia*

Suggestions for spinning

This wool should be spun into a fine to medium yarn with 10 twists per 2.5cm (1in) in the finished yarn. It is very suitable for woollen or semi-worsted spinning but because of its length, which is long for a Merino, it could be spun worsted or semi-woollen to make a stronger yarn.

Suggested end uses

Knitting: Soft shawls, scarves, babywear, fine lacy jerseys and sweaters.
Weaving: Scarves, shawls and fine, drapable fabric that will full well.

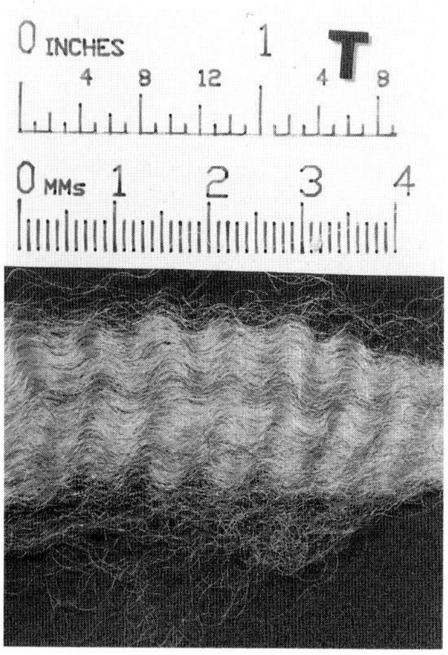

SAMPLE T

Staple length: 14cm (5.5in)
Staple shape: slightly pointed tip
Crimp pattern: 4 crimps per 2.5cm (1in)
Fibre size: medium/bulky
Colour: grey
Lustre: medium
Bulk: medium
Cleanliness: clean
Soundness: no break
Breed: Romney
Source of wool: Jenny Williams, Ashwood, RD 6 Ashburton, New Zealand*

Suggestions for spinning

This wool should be spun into a medium/bulky yarn with 4 twists per 2.5cm (1in) in the finished yarn. Because of the staple length this fleece would make a good worsted yarn, but it could also be spun semi-woollen. It is probably too long in the staple to be handcarded for woollen or semi-worsted yarn.

Suggested end uses

Knitting: A hard-wearing outer sweater or jersey, hats, mittens, afghans or throws.
Weaving: Jackets, upholstery fabric, cushions and, if spun finer, would be excellent for hard-wearing skirt fabric.

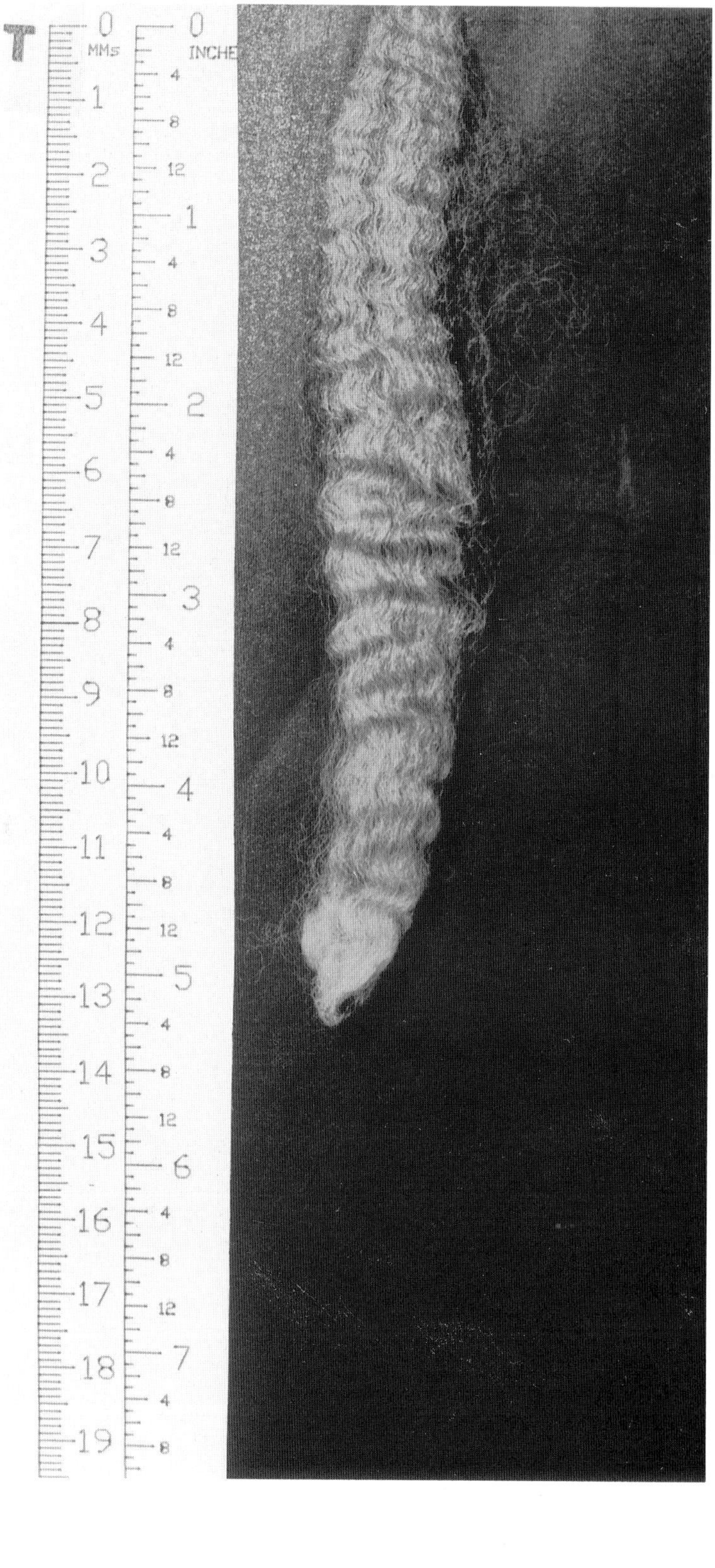

U

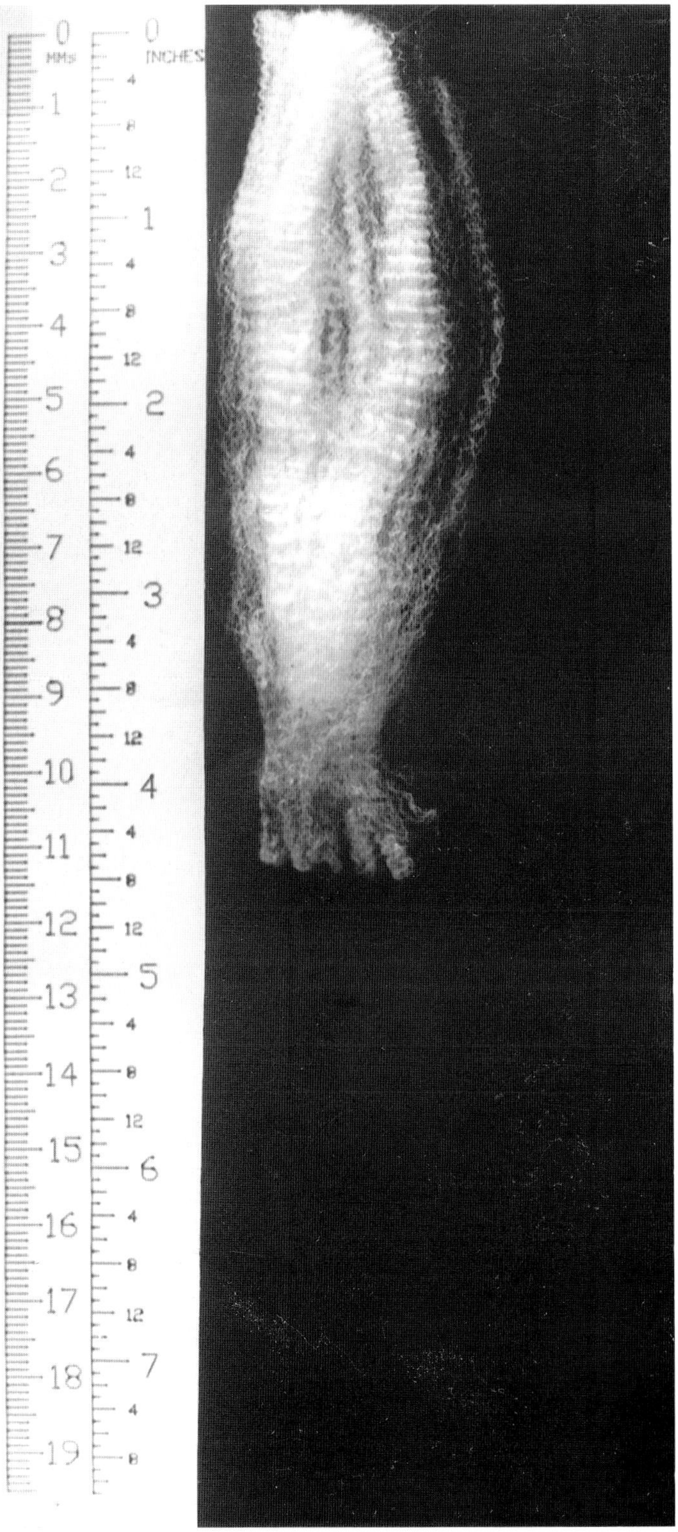

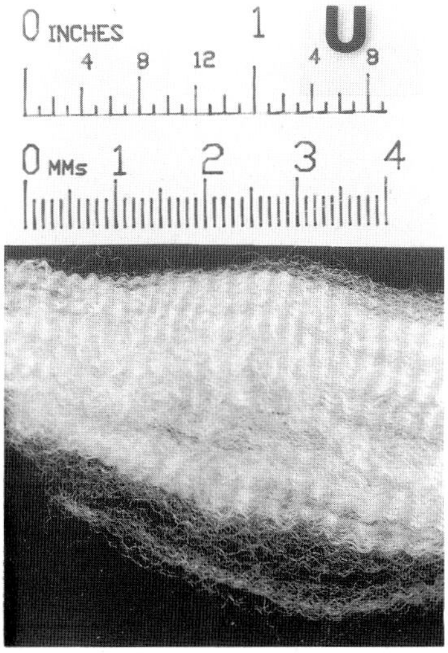

SAMPLE U

Staple length: 11.5cm (4.5in)
Staple shape: flat tip
Crimp pattern: 13 crimps per 2.5cm (1in)
Fibre size: fine
Colour: white
Lustre: low/medium
Bulk: medium
Cleanliness: clean
Soundness: no break
Breed: Polwarth
Source of wool: Helen Heddle, Glenrachney, RD 3 Akaroa, New Zealand*

Suggestions for spinning

It should be spun into a fine yarn with 13 twists to 2.5cm (1in) in the finished yarn. This wool could be spun woollen, semi-woollen, semi-worsted or worsted. The Polwarth breed is a cross between Merino and Lincoln, with the Merino predominant. It is a very useful breed for fine spinning as it does not have the high grease content of the Merino, so Polwarth fleeces are easier to prepare for spinning than Merino.

Suggested end uses

Knitting: Soft shawls, scarves, babywear and lightweight jerseys and sweaters. It will be a soft yarn but not very hard-wearing. Wash the garments carefully to prevent too much shrinking or felting.
Weaving: The same garments as mentioned above as well as fine, drapable fabric.

Remember that the analyses I have given are just suggestions, not absolute rules, to enable you to make informed decisions. For instance, I have taken a fleece with 5 crimps per 2.5cm (1in), which, strictly speaking, should have been spun into a medium/bulky yarn with 5 twists per 2.5cm (1in), and spun a finer yarn with 9 twists per 2.5cm because I wanted to weave a hard-wearing upholstery fabric. This outcome was the result of careful study and deliberate decision; the spinning and weaving were not just some happy accident. (I have made a few of those in my time, but the problem is that you do not know how you achieved the result so you cannot repeat it!)

CHANGING THE CHARACTERISTICS OF A FLEECE

I am very good at breaking the rules. If someone tells me there is only one way to do something I will immediately try to find others. My friends call this lateral thinking; others call it stubbornness! But with some experience in analysing wool it soon becomes apparent that you can use this knowledge to break the rules. This means I often spin yarn with different twists and sizes to those suggested by the wool and crimp pattern.

Project Two is handwoven fabric for a skirt length. I wanted this fabric to be hard-wearing and hang well without bagging or pilling. I took the fleece shown in Sample A, with 4 crimps to 2.5cm (1in), and spun a fine yarn with 10 twists to 2.5cm (1in) in the finished yarn. This was more than double the twist that should have been put into this yarn to retain its original characteristics. The resulting yarn, spun worsted to increase its strength, lustre and smoothness, was correct for that skirt length. Of course, I lost the springiness, softness and bounce of the original fleece, but this was not what I was aiming for in this particular project. If I had chosen a fleece with 10 crimps to 2.5cm (1in) the yarn would have been too soft for a hard-wearing skirt fabric.

Another project requiring hard-wearing yarn is woven upholstery fabric. Again, I would spin this type of yarn with more twists than the crimp number in the original fleece calls for. The main thing to remember is the more twists the stronger the wool, and this can be very useful when making hard-wearing garments. A knitted sweater or jersey that will be subjected to hard wear will also benefit from slightly more twist than the crimp number.

The opposite type of spinning is to put fewer twists than the crimp number when you want a softer bouncier yarn. A woven or knitted shawl that gets little wear and tear can be spun with less twist.

You can also combine these two factors. Using the same fleece, spin the wool for the sole of a pair of socks with more twist, and the wool for the rest of the sock with slightly less. A weaver can spin a warp yarn with more twist and a weft yarn with less twist, using just one fleece for the whole project.

When you can design yarns this way, based on a wide knowledge of wool, the variety is endless. Once you become familiar with wool analysis and get to know the characteristics of a fleece you can alter them by using a variety of spinning methods. Try this out for yourself and see what interesting yarns you come up with.

Part Two

SPINNING WHEELS

CORRIEDALE

3.1 Spinning wheel with named parts

3 Understanding Your Wheel

Most spinners will argue that their favourite wheel is the best. We become very attached to our wheels and experienced spinners are dextrous enough to overcome any basic faults they have. But if we ignore their peculiarities, the bad habits we use to overcome them can be very hard to unlearn if we change wheels, and often it is only some small adjustment that is needed to correct a fault.

Understanding the basic workings of spinning wheels will enable you to get the best out of yours.

There are many different types of spinning wheel, but the wheels discussed in this book will be the bobbin and flyer wheels. There are enough variations of this type to merit a book or two of their own. We will not cover great wheels or charkha wheels, both of which operate on the same principle as a spindle, with the wool winding onto a spindle rather than a bobbin.

BOBBIN AND FLYER WHEELS

All bobbin and flyer wheels have the following features in common:

- The **drive wheel** – the large wheel turned by the foot treadle – provides the momentum to rotate the flyer and/or the bobbin.
- The **flyer** is a U shaped piece of wood or metal with hooks to carry the yarn, and a central shaft on which **bobbins** and/or **whorls** are placed.
- The **shaft**, acting as a spindle, is enlarged and hollowed out at the end nearest the spinner, and this section has the **orifice** through which the yarn passes on its way to the bobbin.
- The **whorls** or **pulleys** are the circular grooved pieces holding the drive band.
- The **drive band** connects the drive wheel to the flyer and/or the bobbin.

There are three ways the drive band connects the drive wheel to the flyer or bobbin, and each of these defines a specific type of bobbin and flyer wheel.

Single-drive flyer-lead wheel (scotch tension)

A single drive band goes from the drive wheel to the whorl on the flyer. The flyer goes faster than the bobbin because a separate brake band slows the bobbin.

Single-drive bobbin-lead wheel

A single drive band goes from the drive wheel to the bobbin whorl. The bobbin therefore goes faster than the flyer, which is held back by a brake.

Double-drive wheel

A doubled drive band goes around the drive wheel, with one loop around the bobbin whorl and one around the flyer whorl. The flyer travels more slowly than the bobbin because the flyer whorl is larger.

To check what type of wheel you have, follow the drive band back to the flyer and bobbin and compare it with the following illustrations.

A treadle that has room for both feet is better for most spinners. Treadling with both feet makes you sit straight in front of a wheel and the work is shared by both feet.

Single-drive flyer-lead wheel (scotch tension)

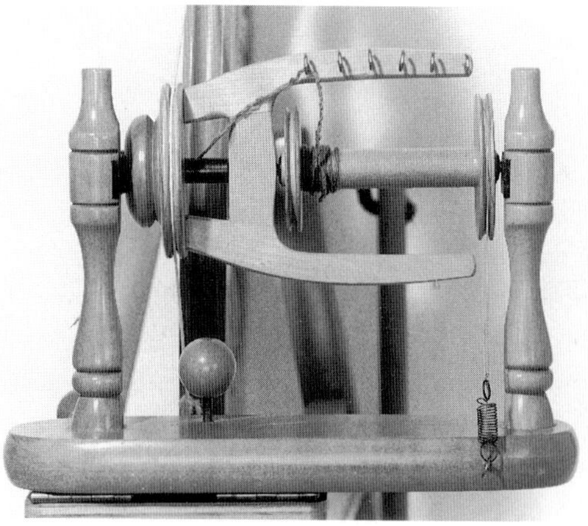

3.2 Ashford wheel, with closeup of flyer

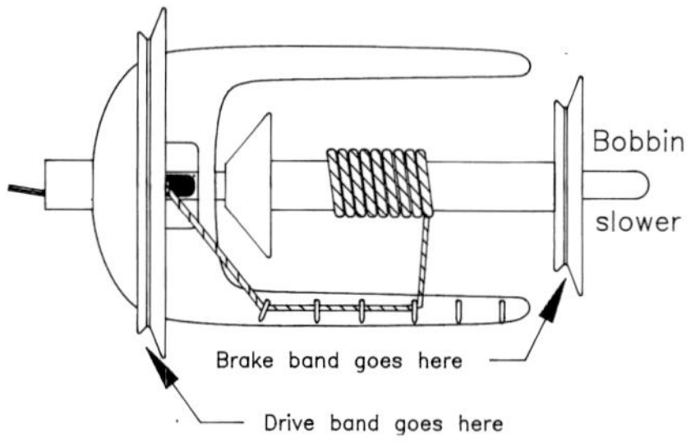

Fig. 3.A Single drive, flyer lead

Single-drive bobbin-lead wheel

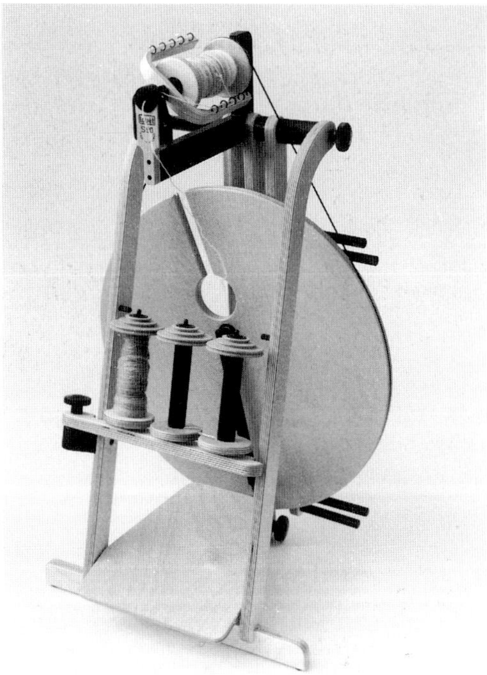

3:3 Louet wheel, with closeup of flyer

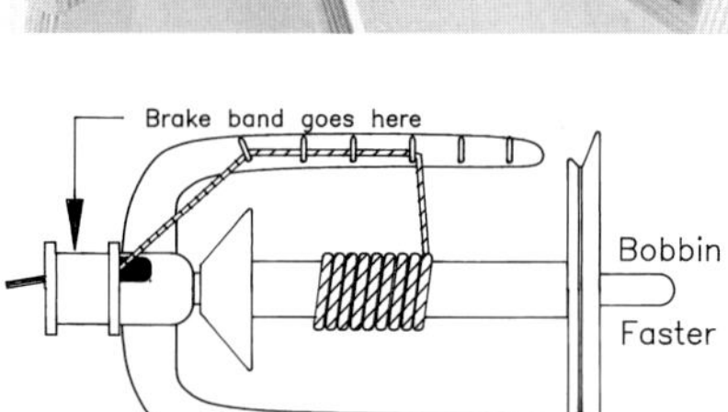

Fig. 3.B Single drive, bobbin lead

Double-drive wheel

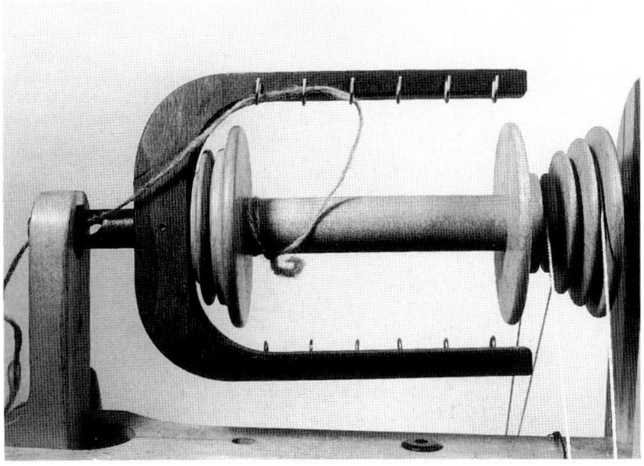

3.4 Schacht wheel, with closeup of flyer (top)

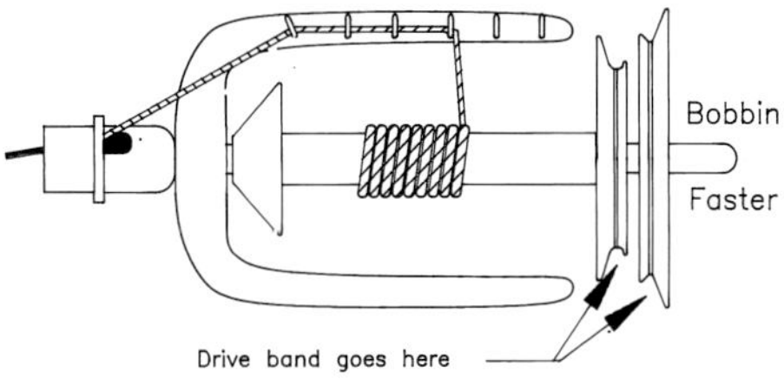

Fig. 3.C Double drive

Many wheels have the provision to operate either as double-drive or single-drive flyer-lead wheels. Changing over from double to single drive (scotch tension) is a simple matter of putting the doubled drive band in the flyer whorl, and putting the brake band over the bobbin whorl. Note in the Schacht wheel in Photo 3.4 the bobbin is also reversed so the larger end holds the brake band, but this may not be the case with other wheels.

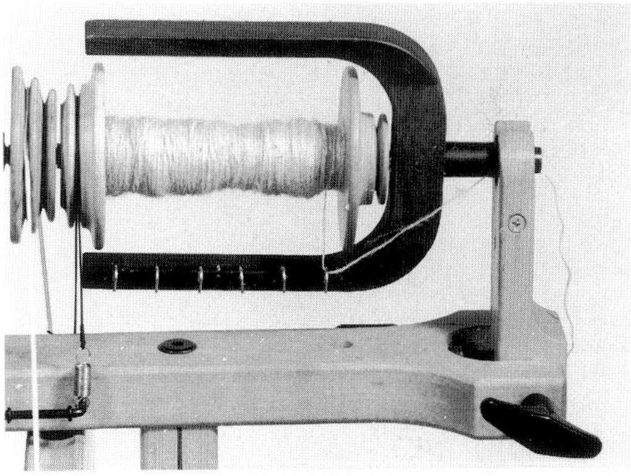

3.5 Schacht wheel changed to single drive, flyer lead

Flyer and bobbin speeds

You will notice that in all these variations the bobbin and the flyer travel at different speeds. It is this factor that pulls the spun wool onto the bobbin. If the bobbin and flyer revolved at the same speed the wool would not pull on.

Single-drive flyer-lead wheels, as in Fig. 3.A, have a brake band at one end of the bobbin, an adjustable cord that slows down the bobbin speed in relation to the flyer speed. This system gives the spinner slightly more time when drafting the wool into yarn and can make these wheels easier for beginners. The yarn is held back while

Spinners often argue about what makes a good drive band. I usually use a tightly plied cotton fishing line. The cord should have some elasticity to enable tension adjustments, but not too much. Whatever you use, do not join the cord with a large knot and leave the ends dangling. This knot will not revolve easily around the whorls, and it is distracting to have a knot whizzing past on every revolution. Splicing is an ideal way to join a cord. Check that the cord fits snugly into the grooves on the flyer and/or bobbin. If it is too large or too small, the necessary traction will be lost.

spinning to allow the twist to enter, and then released onto the bobbin. While the yarn is held back and twisted, the bobbin will slip on the brake band and the bobbin and flyer will revolve. When the yarn pressure is released the bobbin brake slows down or stops the bobbin and the yarn pulls on. When spinning long draw (see page 105) this is something to remember. A nylon brake band aids this slippage.

In Fig. 3.B the single-drive bobbin-lead wheel, the brake band is on the flyer, thus slowing the flyer down. When the yarn is held back and twisted, the flyer and bobbin both revolve. When the yarn pressure is released the flyer slows down or stops. This is exactly the same as the flyer-lead wheel but it is the flyer that changes speed, not the bobbin. With these wheels the brake band may be nylon, or it can be a leather strip adjusted by a turnbuckle.

In Fig. 3.C the double-drive wheel, the flyer whorl is larger in diameter than the bobbin whorl and revolves more slowly. As both bobbin and flyer are driven by the drive band, the bobbin and flyer constantly revolve whether the yarn is under tension or not, unlike single-drive systems. However, the flyer does slow down slightly as the yarn pressure is released. When spinning long draw this factor does make a difference.

Drive band

The drive band should be firm enough to give traction with no slippage. The large diameter of the drive wheel means that the cord touches a large area of the wheel, giving the necessary traction at that end. Because the flyer or bobbin whorl is much smaller, with much less area, some added traction is necessary. On some wheels, usually the single-drive bobbin-lead wheels, the drive band is a thick, rounded nylon cord that fits snugly into the bobbin or flyer groove. This has one disadvantage in that it cannot be shortened or lengthened, so it should not be used on a double-drive wheel, where the cord needs some adjustment as you spin.

On single-drive wheels the groove on the bobbin or flyer whorl is V-shaped, allowing the drive cord to fit firmly into the V, giving that much-needed traction on a small area. The drive-band tension on these wheels does not need adjusting often; usually only when the band has stretched. If you find the wheel is hard to treadle, check the drive-band tension. Many spinners have this far too tight and then have to use a lot of treadle pressure to turn the wheel. Heavy treadling can cause the wheel to move away from you as you spin and this sort of 'travelling' wheel can be a real nuisance. The drive-band tension should be just firm enough to turn the flyer or bobbin without slipping.

If your wheel has an adjustment for drive-band tension, and most do, have the drive wheel and the bobbin or flyer whorl at their closest position when putting on a new cord. This will give you room to adjust the tension later as the band stretches.

Double-drive wheel

To adjust the tension of the drive band on a double drive-wheel, the complete mother-of-all is moved away from (or towards) the drive

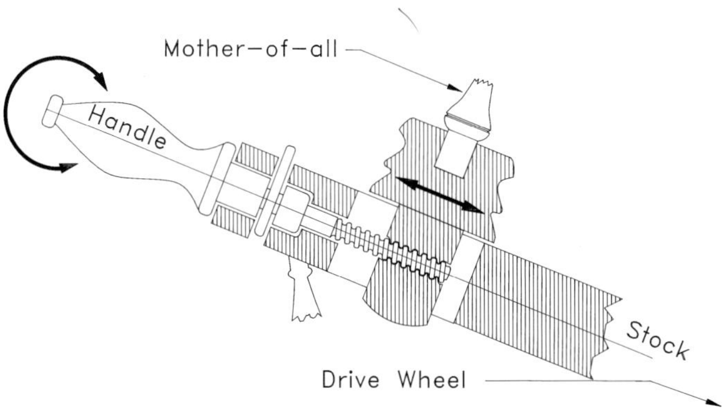

Fig. 3.D Cross-section of a tensioner for double drive wheels

wheel. Moving it away from the drive wheel causes the drive band to tighten and the yarn is pulled on faster. The mother-of-all fits into the stock, at the end of which is a handle, connected to a screw, which engages the mother-of-all. The amount of movement varies with different types of double-drive wheels but is usually up to 5cm (2in). Unlike on single-drive wheels, the drive-band tension is adjusted as you spin.

On double-drive wheels the flyer whorl is V-shaped to help traction, but the groove for the bobbin whorl is a rounded U shape, giving the necessary slippage. The brake and drive cords are one, and U- and V-shaped grooves give more slippage to one than the other.

It is interesting to note where the drive band crosses. When the wheel is moving in a clockwise direction for Z twist (see Fig. 4.B, page 76), which is usually when spinning singles, the band is crossed on the left on vertical upright wheels, and below the flyer on horisontal Saxony wheels. When the wheel is turning anti-clockwise (S twist, usually for plying), the cross moves to the opposite position.

There will be less friction on the drive band if the band that travels over the flyer whorl crosses *over* the band that goes over the bobbin whorl. The band going over the larger flyer whorl is pulled higher than the other portion of the band, over the lower, smaller bobbin whorl. If this higher band is on top, there will be less friction. The upper and lower position of the band also changes with the clockwise or anti-clockwise movement of the wheel. More time is spent spinning than plying, so it will reduce friction if the band is in the correct position for spinning.

3.6 U and V-shaped grooves on a double drive wheel

Brake band (scotch tension)

The placement of the spring or rubber-band makes a difference to the performance of the brake band. In Fig. 3.E you will see that the bobbin is turning from the fixed end to the sprung end. There has been much dissension among spinners and wheel manufacturers about this point. However, experimenting with positions of the spring has led me to believe that the diagram shows the correct direction. The bobbin runs smoothly and with less shake when it is turning away from the fixed end of the brake band. Most spinners spin with

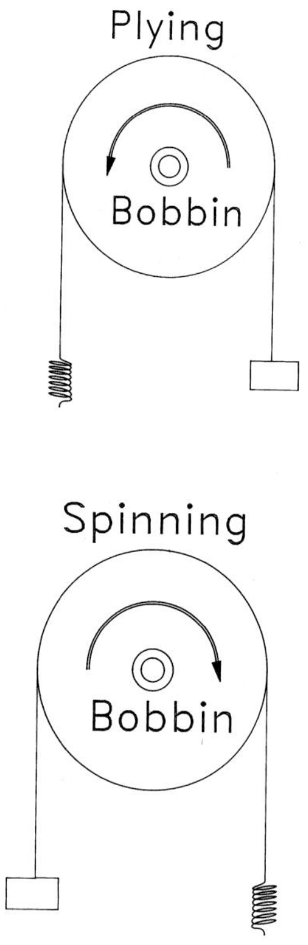

Fig. 3.E Brake band direction

the wheel turning clockwise and ply with the wheel turning anti-clockwise, so the spring or rubber-band on the brake band should be placed on the right side of the flyer for spinning, and the left for plying. Try this and see how smoothly the bobbin and the brake band run. On some wheels it may be possible to reverse the brake-band direction when spinning and plying.

Differences between single- and double-drive systems

1. There is usually a greater amount of brake-band adjustment possible with the single-drive flyer-lead wheel. Beginners, in particular, can change the speed of the bobbin to quite a degree, making it easier for them to spin uneven yarn.
2. The single-drive flyer-lead wheel is usually the most versatile because the brake band and drive band can be adjusted separately.
3. The single-drive bobbin-lead wheel has the brake band going around the flyer. The orifice end of the flyer, where the brake band is attached, sits in a U-shaped groove, and even with all the tension released from the brake band, the friction of the flyer in that groove means there is always some tension. For very fine spinning, where a very light tension is required, this can be a disadvantage. Because the strong drive band drives the bobbin, this type of wheel is suitable for bulky spinning, as a heavy bobbin will not slow down and can still be driven by the drive band.
4. Once the drive band is adjusted to its correct length, double-drive wheels provide a very consistent tension. For beginners there may not be enough adjustment to allow very uneven wool to pull on.
5. With the double-drive band wheel, the yarn will continue twisting as it is fed onto the bobbin. This is why some spinners overspin with their double-drive wheels but not with their single-drives. With the single-drive flyer-lead wheel (scotch tension) the yarn will receive little or no twist as it is propelled towards the orifice. So when spinning on a double-drive wheel you must begin to propel the yarn forward *before* it has the correct amount of twist. By the time it has reached the bobbin it will have gathered the rest. This does make the long-draw and medium-draft methods of spinning slightly different on these two types of wheel.
6. Because the action on the double-drive system is all positive – there is no brake band to retard the flyer or bobbin – there seems to be less friction and the action feels smoother.

More spinning wheel manufacturers are producing wheels with both double-drive and scotch-tension options on one wheel, and many beginners use the scotch-tension option first and change to the double-drive band when they have more experience.

Differences in tension for full and empty bobbins

As the bobbin fills with wool two things happen: it becomes heavier and the circumference increases. More yarn is then necessary to complete one circle of the bobbin and it takes longer for each length to wind on. To spin a consistent yarn with an even number of twists to the cm (in) it is necessary with some types of wheels to change the tension as the bobbin fills. The reason is that with the double-drive system the bobbin goes faster than the flyer, and the reverse happens with the single-drive systems.

With the single-drive flyer-lead wheel, as the bobbin fills and becomes heavier it slows down. At the same time, the increasing circumference of the bobbin causes each revolution of the flyer to lay longer lengths of yarn onto the bobbin, and the yarn will feel as if it is being pulled on more firmly. The slowing of the bobbin *increases* the difference between the relative speeds of the bobbin and flyer, giving the added pull necessary for the increased circumference. The brake-band tension does not usually need any adjustment.

With the double-drive wheel, as the bobbin fills and becomes heavier it also slows down. This *reduces* the difference between the relative speeds of the flyer and bobbin necessary for winding on and the yarn becomes overtwisted. The slowing bobbin overrides the increased pull due to the larger circumference. To make the bobbin faster again, tighten the drive-band tension as the bobbin fills.

With a single-drive bobbin-lead wheel the bobbin will not slow much as it becomes heavier because as it is driven by the strong traction of the drive wheel. The other factor, the increased circumference of the bobbin, which causes the increased pull, will make the yarn undertwisted unless the brake-band tension is loosened slightly.

As these adjustments are made it may be necessary to check that the twist per 2.5cm (1in) remains the same by measuring and counting, as shown on page 74.

WHEEL MAINTENANCE

Keep the orifice clean from grease and dirt by scraping out the grease with a matchstick and then a cotton bud (or cotton wool wrapped around a matchstick) soaked in methylated spirits. Make sure the bobbins run smoothly on the spindle shaft and keep the shaft lubricated. Some spinners use Vaseline as it does not spray everywhere the way oil does. If your spinning wheel has leather washers, either on the footman or the flyer, Vaseline is also useful for keeping them supple. For other moving parts use mineral oil. A good piece of advice is: if it moves, oil it, *but* the one moving part that should *never* be oiled is the drive band, as this will cause it to slip. If it is slipping, try applying some resin or beeswax.

WHEEL TYPES

Horizontal wheels

These wheels have the flyer on the same horizontal plane as the wheel and are often called Saxony wheels. Because the flyer is beside the wheel, not above or below it, the wheel can be large without affecting the height of the flyer. The flyer height should be such that the orifice is within easy reach of the spinner's hands. A large-diameter wheel is usually more efficient for faster yarn production.

The wheel size may make these horizontal wheels harder to store and carry than vertical wheels. The drive-band tension is controlled by moving the mother-of-all away from or closer to the drive wheel, usually by moving it along or above the stock or frame. The flyer remains horizontal during these manoeuvres, as it is the complete mother-of-all that moves.

Vertical wheels

Also called upright wheels, these wheels are easier to transport than horizontal wheels because they take up less space. The flyer is

3.7 Leicester wheel, a horizontal wheel (Timbertops Spinning Wheels)

3.8 Traveller wheel. (Ashfords)

3.9 Irish Castle wheel. (Timbertops Spinning Wheels)

positioned above the drive wheel and as the flyer height must be within easy reach of the spinner's hands, the drive wheel is usually smaller than those on the horizontal wheels. The main upright that holds the drive wheel also supports the flyer mechanism. To control the drive-band tension, the mother-of-all is moved up or down the upright. Usually only the end of the flyer nearest the upright moves up or down, with the orifice end remaining stationary. This can angle the flyer and cause friction if the angle becomes too steep. Self-aligning bearings on both ends can overcome this problem. Photo 3.4 is another example of this type of wheel, with self-aligning bearings.

Castle wheels (as in Photo 3.9) are a type of vertical wheel with the flyer below the drive wheel.

With all these types of wheels, the orifice must be kept within easy reach of the spinner. This dictates the size of the drive wheel as well as its position. Yet many spinners like a large drive wheel because it gives more traction and momentum.

Two-wheel spinning wheels

To solve the dilemma of having a large drive wheel with the orifice still within reach, an accelerating wheel can be added to the main drive wheel. The diameter of both wheels can be quite small, yet these wheels are very fast, with economical foot movements and a wide range of drive ratios.

3.10 Chair wheel with accelerating wheel (Timbertops Spinning Wheels)

Drive ratio is discussed in the next chapter, but it is worth noting here that there is no set drive ratio on motorised spinning wheels. In the Ashford Spinner, as the rpm increases so does the speed of the flyer. The brake band is on the bobbin, as in any flyer-lead wheel, and it slows down the bobbin. As the flyer speed is variable, so is the drive ratio.

3.11 Motorised wheel (Ashford Electronic wheel)

Electric spinning wheels

There are many makes of motorised spinning wheels. They are small and therefore very portable, and can be excellent for spinners who find the treadling action of other spinning wheels tiring or painful. Some spinners find the noise of the motor irritating but you can always mask it by playing music while you spin.

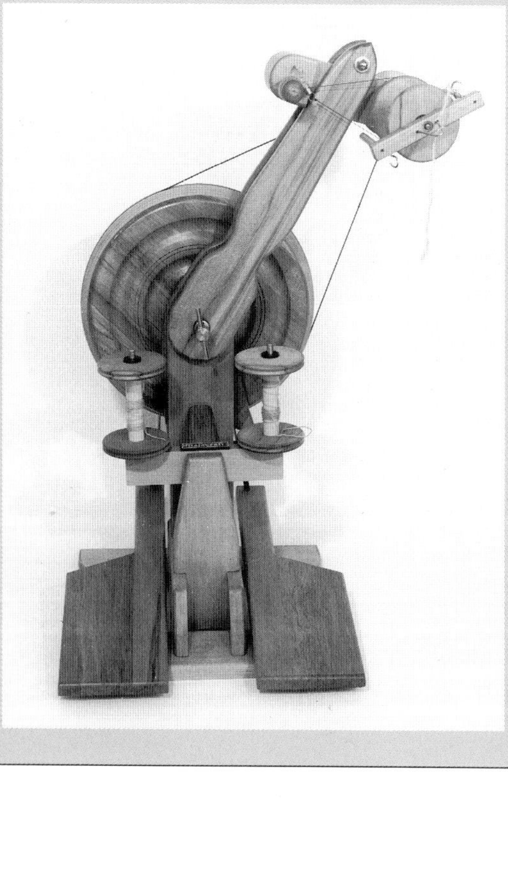

DIFFERENT TYPES OF ORIFICE

Most wheels have the spindle shaft hollowed out and you use a threading hook to pull the yarn through. A wire thread-holder, such as the one shown in Photo 3.12, is much easier to thread, as it does not require a threading hook.

To use this holder, called a delta orifice, the yarn must come from the peak or tip of the wire. If the yarn slips down the side a 'speed wobble' sets in and the yarn shakes about. When a spinner is sitting directly in front of the wheel the yarn has to be drawn in a straight line from the wire holder towards the body. This can make spinning with the long-draw method difficult, as the spinner's arm moves to its full extent to the right or left. With this particular wheel the upright can be tilted to the left or right, allowing the spinner to do the long draw and still keep the yarn coming from the tip of the thread-holder.

3.12 Majacraft wheel

Kitset wheels

Kitset wheels are usually cheaper than assembled wheels and you have a choice of stains or other finishes. In the assembly you will also learn how the wheel functions, which is very useful.

Second-hand wheels

If you are buying a second-hand wheel check for wear. I have seen a wheel that the seller insisted had never been spun on, yet there was a definite groove on the flyer where the yarn friction had worn the wood. It was still an excellent wheel, but we were able to bargain the price down when this was pointed out. Another tell-tale point of wear is the metal hooks on the flyer. On the wheel I used constantly for about 20 years I actually wore right through one set of hooks.

It is also important to check the drive wheel. A warped wheel is impossible to straighten and will throw the band. It is difficult to tell if a wheel is warped when you are sitting at the front spinning, so get someone else to treadle while you stand and look side on.

I advise my students not to buy a double-drive band wheel from an unknown maker, especially if it is someone who has made only one wheel and knows little about how they work. The relationship between the bobbin and flyer whorls, with their U- and V-shaped grooves, is critical and is difficult to correct.

BUYING A NEW WHEEL

In this chapter I have given only a few examples of different types of wheels; there is such a wide range available that it is impossible to illustrate them all. If you are buying a new wheel, do try spinning on it first. If a shop will not allow this, I would suggest trying another shop!

A wheel with at least two different drive ratios can spin a wider range of yarn than a wheel with only one drive ratio, as explained in the next chapter. And try to buy from an outlet that offers a back-up service for repairs, extra bobbins and so on. Getting bobbins made for antique wheels may be difficult.

If the flyer has the hooks on one arm only, the other arm should be slightly heavier for balance. These flyers will have only one opening on the spindle shaft for threading the yarn or leader through to the orifice. Some flyers have hooks on both arms but still only one opening. This gives the necessary balance on both arms, but remember to use only the set of hooks directly in line with the opening.

4 Drive Ratio, Twists and Yarn Sizes

DRIVE RATIO

Spinners need to know the drive ratio of their wheels because this will not only determine how many twists are inserted for each 2.5cm (1in) of yarn, but how thick or thin that yarn can be. In Chapter Two, on wool analysis, I explained that yarn should be spun with the same number of twists to the cm (in) as there are crimps to the cm (in). For example, if a fleece has 7 crimps to 2.5cm (1in), the finished washed yarn should have 7 twists to 2.5cm (1in). This finished yarn is usually two-ply, but can be a single.

Matching the crimps and twist retains the characteristics of the fleece and produces a soft-handling bouncy yarn. If you want to change the character of the yarn (e.g. to make it harder or softer) then the twist-to-crimp ratio changes.

There seems to be a feeling among spinners that drive ratio is a mysterious thing that is too complicated or mathematical for them to follow. I will show you, with practical exercises, that drive ratio is not the bogey it has been made out to be, but a straightforward and simple feature of your wheel.

The drive ratio is the difference in size between the circumference of the drive wheel and the circumference of the flyer or bobbin whorl. This determines the amount of twist in a fixed amount of yarn.

4.1 Drive ratio

With each treadle push, the drive wheel revolves once. The flyer will revolve a different number of times, depending on the difference in circumference. If the flyer revolves 6 times to one drive wheel revolution, (i.e. 6:1) then 6 twists are put into a given amount of yarn for that one treadle push.

In all the methods of spinning described in Chapters Five and Six, there is a time when the wool is stationary, that is, held back by the spinner, while the twist is inserted. For many years I was confused by the difference between drive ratio and the pull-on rate of wool. It helps if you can separate these two factors in your mind. The pull-on rate, discussed fully on pages 63-64, is caused by the relative speeds of the bobbin and flyer. Drive ratio, determining the twist, is the difference between the circumferences of the drive wheel and the bobbin or flyer whorl.

Determining the drive ratio

To find out the drive ratio of your wheel, do the following exercise.

Step 1

If you have a wheel the same as in Figs 3.A and C, tie a thread to one flyer arm. Revolve the flyer until the thread is lined up with the back maiden. Align the drive wheel so that the crank is at the very top of its stroke. Do not have any wool coming through the orifice but leave it all on the bobbin to avoid any tension on the flyer or bobbin.

Turn the drive wheel slowly by hand until it has completed a full circle and count the number of turns the flyer makes. Every time the thread on the flyer arm passes the maiden is one revolution. Do this two or three times to check the accuracy, then jot down this number on a piece of paper. The most common number will be between 5 and 9. If your flyer did 7 revolutions to one turn of the drive wheel, this ratio is written as 7:1.

You may have seen this figure written in the information that came with your wheel, but do your own verification anyway. Sometimes the number will be taken to one decimal point, e.g. 6.6:1, but for the following exercises it is easier to round it off.

If you have a single-drive bobbin-lead wheel, such as in Fig. 3.B, place a mark on your bobbin. A piece of tape will do, and is easily removed. Turn the drive wheel as described above, but this time count the number of bobbin revolutions to one turn of the drive wheel.

Many wheels have more than one size of whorl, with a different drive ratio for each one. At the moment, just use the whorl you use in your normal spinning. We will discuss the others later.

Step 2

Now we will try to spin, putting the number of twists you jotted down, into a given amount of yarn. It is easier than it sounds.

Use whichever spinning method you are most at ease with. I find the short forward or backward drafts (pages 94-95) are the easiest

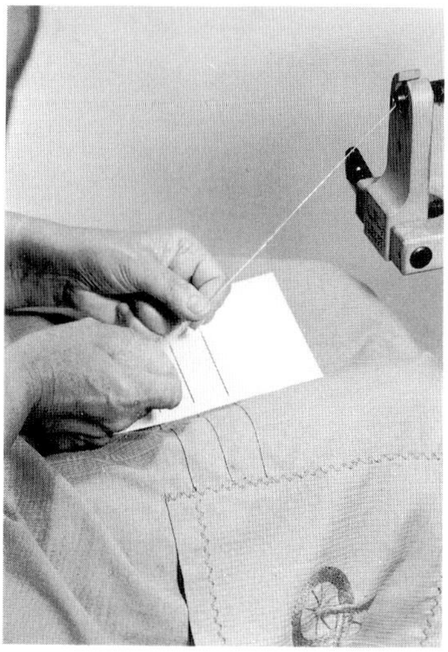

4.2 Measuring the draft

4.3. Counting the twist

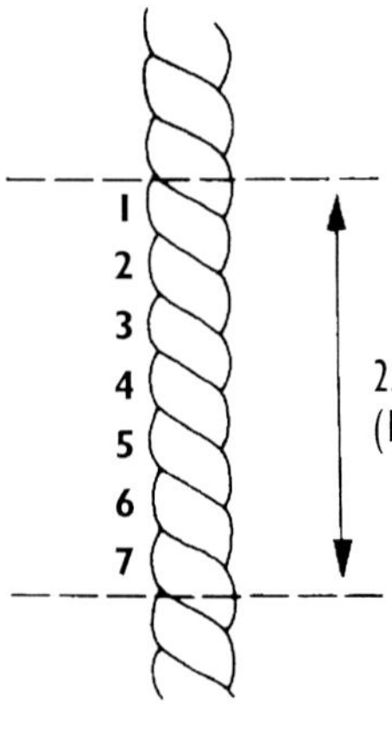

Fig. 4.A Counting the twists per 2.5cm (1in)

when visually measuring the amount of drafted fibres, but other methods may suit you better. The object of this exercise is to feed in 2.5cm (1in) of yarn for each revolution of the drive wheel. In other words, 2.5cm (1in) for each treadle push.

First, make an image of how much 2.5cm (1in) is. I find the distance between the tip of my thumbnail and the first joint of my thumb is just the right length. Some spinners have stripes on their spinning aprons, or you can mark out some measurements on a piece of card and lay this on your lap as a guide. It is surprising how accurate you will become at judging 2.5cm (1in) with some practice.

Begin spinning as you normally would, but count each treadle push. When you have the rhythm, saying 'one', 'one' every time your foot is at the top of the treadle push, and you are spinning smoothly, begin to monitor the amount of wool going onto the bobbin. It will help the rhythm if the wool is fed forward as your foot pushes down the treadle at the top of its stroke.

With the short forward and backward drafts, the distance between your two hands should be 2.5cm (1in) when they are farthest apart. This is not far, and your movements will be very jerky. With other spinning methods, experiment until you can feed on 2.5cm (1in) to each treadle push. If you are a long-draw spinner you will need perhaps 51cm (20in) to 20 treadles. It does help if the wool is carefully prepared and running smoothly, and the wheel is also running smoothly. If you have problems, refer to size of yarn, top of p. 75.

When you think you have it right, measure the amount of twist in the yarn. This can be done by pulling a length of yarn from the bobbin. Let it twist back on itself and count the twists in 2.5cm (1in). This is not a strictly accurate method of counting the twist, as the twist in the single yarn will unwind slightly as the yarn is allowed to double back on itself. I have found this loss of twist to be about one in six, that is; if I spun a single with 6 twists to 2.5cm (1in), the doubled yarn had 5 twists per 2.5cm (1in). Therefore, if your drive ratio is 6:1, the twist in your doubled yarn should be 5 per 2.5cm (1in). For the purposes of these exercises it will be enough if the doubled twist is just one or two twists less than the drive ratio of your wheel.

If you can do this at the first try, you are to be congratulated. Most spinners have to practise a little first. If there are too many twists in that given length, you are feeding on less than 2.5cm (1in), and if there are fewer twists you are feeding on too much. When counting the twists, count the bumps on one side of the yarn only.

Step 3

You will find feeding on 2.5cm (1in) to each revolution of the drive wheel is too jerky and slow. Exactly the same number of twists will be inserted if you spin with 5cm (2in) of yarn for 2 revolutions. Try this and see the difference in the treadle and hand rhythm. If this is difficult try 7.5cm (3in) for 3 revolutions.

The size of yarn in relation to the number of twists will be covered in detail later in this chapter (page 80), but for now these simple guidelines will suffice. If you are concentrating on putting the correct amount of twist into a set length of yarn for the first time, you will have enough to think about without going into the yarn size in detail. I always find it better for my students to master one step at a time.

It is more difficult to put a lot of twist into a thick yarn, as there is a definite correlation between the yarn thickness and the amount of twist. If you are having difficulty putting more twist into your yarn it may be that it is too thick. Experienced spinners seem to adjust for this automatically; for beginners it may be harder.

A practical guide is that if your yarn continually breaks there is not enough twist for the diameter of the yarn. In this case you can do either of two things: draft more wool into the given length of yarn, or add more twist to the yarn. In this exercise we are working with a fixed amount of twist so the first option is the practical answer here.

If the yarn kinks and curls there is too much twist for the diameter of the yarn. Either reduce the amount of yarn in the drafting area, or reduce the twist. For this exercise the first option is the way to go.

Step 4

If you have other whorls on your wheel, try the above steps with each whorl until you can match the twists in the yarn with the drive ratio of each whorl.

The number of twists per 2.5cm (1in) you have been putting into the yarn during these exercises is the correct number for the whorls on your wheel. Perhaps these exercises have also explained the difficulties experienced when you change to a new wheel, or try a friend's wheel with a different drive ratio.

If you have only one drive ratio on your wheel this will govern the amount of twist and also the yarn size that you can easily spin on that particular wheel. In other words, if the whorl on your wheel has a drive ratio of 7:1, then the wheel will easily and naturally spin with 7 twists to 2.5cm (1in). You can adjust this figure up or down one or two without difficulty, but beyond this you are beginning to take the wheel past its limits. I will show you what I mean.

Step 5

Halve the ratio of your wheel. In the above example, this would bring the figure to 3.5. Now try to spin with just 3.5 twists in your yarn. This means you will have to feed in 5cm (2in) to one treadle push. With a great deal of concentration it can be done but it is hard work. Your hands and feet are beginning to work against each other because to feed in that amount of yarn your hands need to move much faster than your feet and you lose the natural rhythm. The yarn also has to become thicker to give it the strength to prevent it breaking.

Step 6

Now double the drive ratio of your wheel. In our example this would be 14. To put 14 twists into 2.5cm (1in) we have to feed in 1.25cm

(0.5in) to each treadle push and the yarn must become thinner. This also requires concentration and the treadling becomes rather tiring as your feet are moving much faster than your hands.

An easy way to work out the number of cm (in) that should be fed onto the bobbin for each treadle push is to divide the drive ratio by the required twists per cm (in).

$$\frac{\text{Drive ratio}}{\text{Twists per cm (in)}} \quad = \quad \text{No. of cm (in) per treadle}$$

In Appendix D is a table giving the required length of the draft for every drive ratio (up to 18:1) for a given twist count (up to 15). This will save you doing your own calculations. The table also shows the impossibility of spinning a yarn with 15 twists per 2.5cm (1in) on a wheel with a drive ratio of 2:1. A spinner would need to draft one tenth of an inch (about 2mm) for each treadle! However, if you use the calculations when the drive ratio is near the twist count, the table will be useful. For example, if your drive ratio is 9, and you would like to spin with 7 twists per 2.5cm (1in), the draft length per treadle is 3.5cm (1.25in).

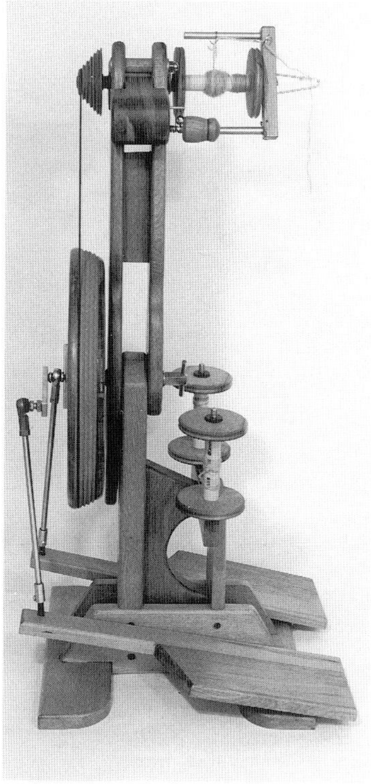

4.4 This Majacraft wheel has not only six whorls on the flyer but also five grooves on the drive wheel. A strong but stretchy co-polymer drive band enables the spinner to move the band from whorl to groove to achieve drive ratios from 4:1 to 14:1.

I hope these exercises will determine the range of yarn your own wheel produces best. You can see why spinning wheel manufacturers are giving spinners as wide a range as possible, with many interchangeable whorls.

I find it easier to change whorls or even spinning wheels, when I want to change the twists per 2.5cm (1in) and the size of my yarn. For example, when spinning fine yarn with 14 twists per 2.5cm (1in) I use a spinning wheel with 13:1 drive ratio. Then I do not have to change my treadling speed or hand movements as the wheel does it all for me. All I have to do is judge the correct amount of yarn, in both length and thickness, that I draft.

TWIST COUNT IN PLIED YARN

Knowing the drive ratio of the your wheel, you can now spin a singles yarn to a required twist. If you use single yarn, this is all you need to know to spin with a pre-determined number of twists per 2.5cm (1in). But most projects call for plied yarn as it is stronger and more stable. So the next step is to ply those singles together with the right amount of twist to ensure that the plied yarn has the twist count you want. In this section only two-ply yarns will be covered. We will look at three-ply yarns on page 79.

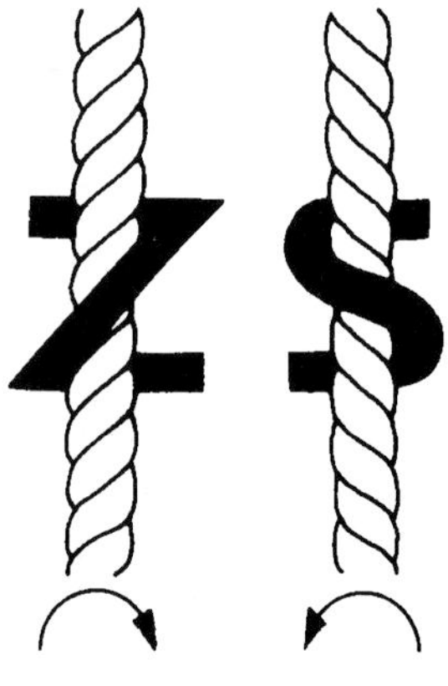

Fig. 4.B Z and S twist

Several things happen to single yarn when it is plied. To start with, the singles untwist slightly as the wheel is turning in the opposite direction, effectively softening the single yarn. Then we complicate matters by adding twist in the opposite direction.

Plied yarn should be balanced, that is, with no final twist in either

4.C COMPARATIVE SPINNING AND PLYING TWIST AND SIZE				
A Crimps per 2.5cm (in) in fleece wool	**B Twists per 2.5cm (in) in singles**	**C Wraps per 2.5cm (in) in singles**	**D Twists per 2.5cm (in) in two-ply yarn**	**E Wraps per 2.5cm (in) in two-ply yarn**
2	3	6	2	4
3	4.5	9	3	6
4	6	12	4	8
5	7.5	15	5	10
6	9	18	6	12
7	10.5	21	7	14
8	12	24	8	16
9	13.5	27	9	18
10	15	30	10	20
11	16.5	33	11	22
12	18	36	12	24
13	19.5	39	13	26
14	21	42	14	28
15	22.5	45	15	30
16	24	48	16	32
17	25.5	51	17	34
18	27	54	18	36
19	28.5	57	19	38
20	30	60	20	40

direction. To achieve a balanced yarn when plying two strands together, the plying twist should be two-thirds of the spinning twist. Therefore, if a singles is spun Z with nine twists per 2.5cm (1in), these two singles should be plied together with six S twists per 2.5cm (1in).

If six twists are required per 2.5cm (1in) in the two-ply yarn (column D in Fig. 4.C), then the singles should be spun with nine twists (column B). The plied yarn then has the necessary two-thirds twist of the singles. If you are matching the crimp in the fleece with the twist in the yarn, this means that this fleece should have six crimps per 2.5cm (1in) (column A).

4.5 Balanced plied yarn

Balanced plied yarn

To check that your plied twist is balanced, pull a loop of the plied yarn from between the hooks on the flyer as you are plying. This loop should hang almost straight with few kinks and curls. Another test is that the finished skein will hang straight after it is taken from the niddy noddy, as explained on page 96, Photo 5.31.

Measuring the twist in plied yarn

It is easy to put a measured twist into plied yarn. Sit comfortably at your spinning wheel. Place the lazy kate (with the bobbins holding the singles) to one side and slightly behind your chair. I put the lazy

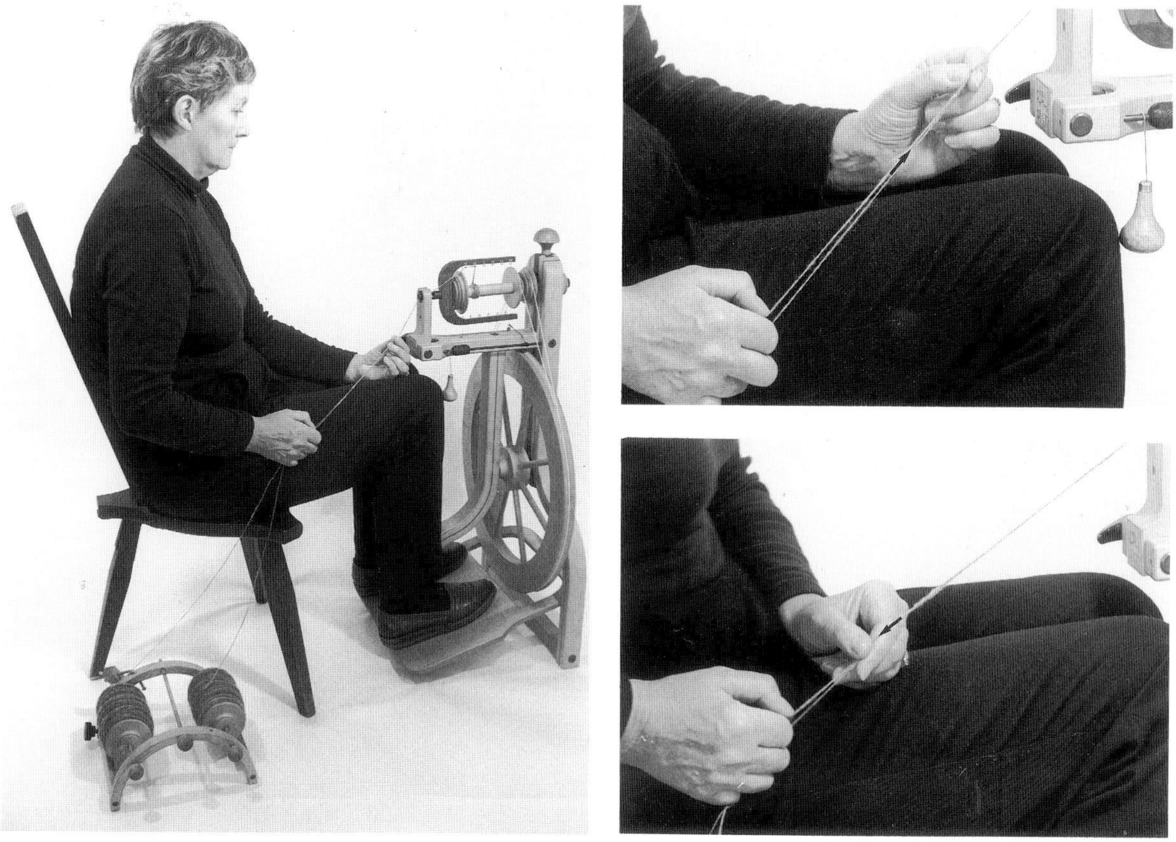

4.6-4.8 Position of hands and body for plying

kate on my right side, probably because I am right-handed (**4.6**).

Take the two ends in the thumb and forefinger of your front hand, overlapping the leader from the empty bobbin on your wheel. Begin treadling anti-clockwise and pinch the leader and the two ends until they twist together. Your back hand rests on the nearest hip, remaining stationary for the entire process. The two strands run through the fingers of this hand, which separate and keep them under a light tension (**4.6**).

When the singles and the leader are twisted together, propel the two strands towards the orifice (**4.7**).

Release the pinch of your front hand slightly and let the twist run back, supporting and accompanying the twist with this hand until both hands nearly meet (**4.8**). Repeat these last two steps.

There are slight differences for woollen and worsted yarn, which will be described in later chapters, but the general principle is the same for both. Plying this way allows a fixed amount of yarn to feed on. Count the treadles it takes to propel the yarn onto the bobbin. For example, it could be six treadles – five while the yarn is feeding on and one when your hand is sliding backwards. After a metre (yard) or two, test the twist. Pull some yarn off the bobbin and see if it looks a well-rounded, balanced yarn. Let it hang down as in Photo 4.5 and see if it hangs almost straight. Then count the twists in the plied yarn: it should be two-thirds of the singles twist. If there are too many twists, reduce the number of treadles to each draft of plied yarn. If there are too few, increase the treadles.

There is another, more accurate method of plying with two-thirds of the singles twist. Measure the distance between the stationary back hand and just in front of the orifice. I find 46cm (18in) a comfortable distance. If the drive ratio on the wheel is 9:1, and the singles are spun with 9 twists per 2.5cm (1in), I know that when 46cm (18in) is propelled forward for 18 treadles there will be 9 twists per 2.5cm (1in), as in Step 3. This is equal the number of twists in the singles. To ply with the correct *two-thirds* plying twist, in this case 6, I need 12 treadles for my 46cm (18in).

If the drive ratio and twists per 2.5cm (1in) in the singles are the same, as in the above example, the calculations are simple enough, as the number of treadles when plying will always be 12, (two-thirds of 18). When the drive ratio and twists per 2.5cm (1in) are different, for example if the drive ratio is 9:1 and the singles are spun with 7 twists per 2.5 cm (1in), the calculations are more complex. In *The Essentials of Yarn Design for Handspinners*, Mabel Ross has these calculations in table form for easy reference.

When you have the correct amount of twist, ply all the singles with the same treadle count. Of course there will be variations as even the best of spinners cannot keep the yarn even all the way through, and the thin areas will have more twist than the thick places. I am an optimist and always hope that a thin bit on one single will meet up with a thick bit on the other single when plying! Sometimes I get two thin bits meeting, or two thick bits, but it is amazing how the plied yarn does even up.

There are some projects for which a balanced plied yarn is not required, for instance a warp yarn for weaving, which needs more twist. In this case you could ply with an equal amount of twist as in the singles. The skein will not hang straight but the twist will set with washing and the yarn will be manageable, perhaps with a few kinks.

If the project calls for knitting yarn it is best to aim at an almost balanced yarn as a very unbalanced yarn can cause the knitting to skew to one side. However, for a very hard-wearing jersey or sweater I often ply with slightly more twist than the usual two-thirds. For a soft shawl I may ply with fewer twists. Unbalanced yarns are not as crucial for weaving yarns, particularly if the overtwisted plied yarn is used for the warp and the balanced yarn for weft, as the warp is held under tension on the loom.

THREE-PLY YARN

When three singles are plied together, the plying twist should be three-quarters of the spinning twist. The final yarn is approximately twice the size of each of the singles. In Photo 4.12 the singles (A) has 23 wraps per 2.5cm (1in). When this single was three-plied it measured 12 wraps (see below). Wraps per 2.5cm (1in) are described on page 80.

A three-ply yarn is more even than a two-ply yarn.

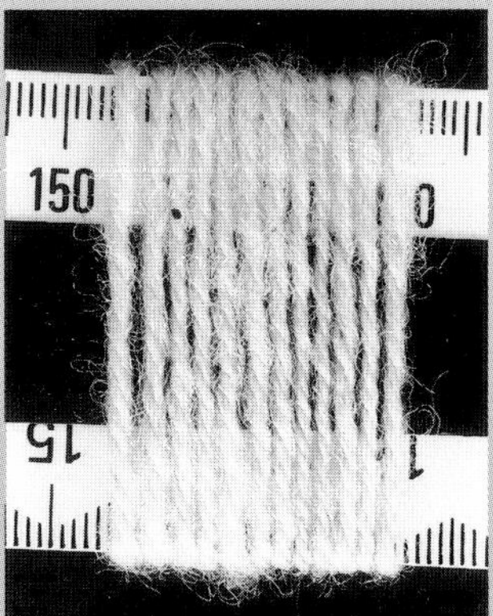

4.9 Three-ply yarn

WASHING PLIED YARN AND SETTING THE TWIST

The next step after spinning and plying is to wash the yarn. This does not change the twist but it is essential for setting it. Even if the fleece has been washed before spinning, the plied yarn should be washed again. The recipes for washing fleece wool, on page 26, can

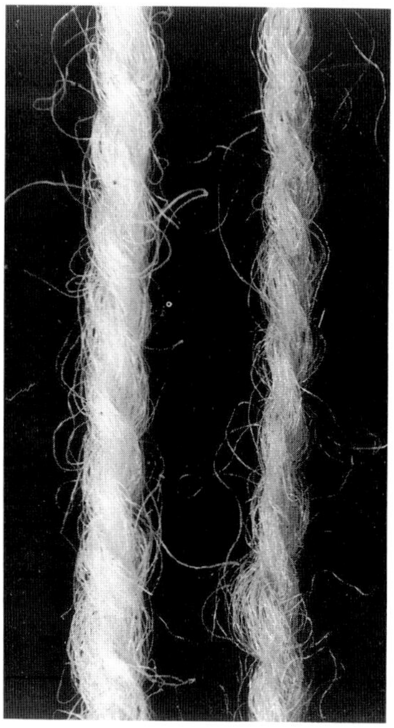

4.10 Plied and washed yarn – comparative sizes between washed (left) and unwashed yarn (right)

be used for the yarn also. After washing and drying the yarn will puff up and increase in size, and the degree of this increase will depend on many factors: the type of fleece, the method of preparation and spinning, the amount of twist, and whether the fleece was washed before spinning.

I do not weight my skeins as they are drying. I have tried it but I feel they lose elasticity. I have washed woollen jerseys or sweaters and hung them out dripping wet only to find the garment has stretched irreversibly with the weight of the water and I feel the same thing will happen if I weight wet skeins.

Some spinners claim that putting a weight onto the wet skeins straightens out the kinks and curls in overtwisted yarn, but I find even when I wash singles that are full of kinks, the wet yarn seems to straighten out of its own accord. After washing and before hanging the yarn up to dry I usually put the skein over both hands and give it a good sharp tug by pulling my hands quickly apart. Then I move the skein around and repeat the process. This seems to straighten out most kinks

MEASURING YARN SIZE

Most spinners aim at a producing a rounded, soft-handling yarn that will not break easily. Variations will be discussed in Chapters Five and Six, but in general terms this type of yarn is our goal. To achieve it spinners need to know how much twist to put into various yarn sizes, so we need a way of measuring yarn.

The 'wraps per 2.5cm (1in)' method has become the main method of measuring yarn for handspinners. To measure the size of plied, washed yarn wind it round a ruler or gauge for 2.5cm (1in) without stretching the yarn and with each thread touching the adjacent thread. Count the number of times the yarn goes round the gauge or ruler for 2.5cm (1in) and that gives you the wraps per 2.5cm (1in).

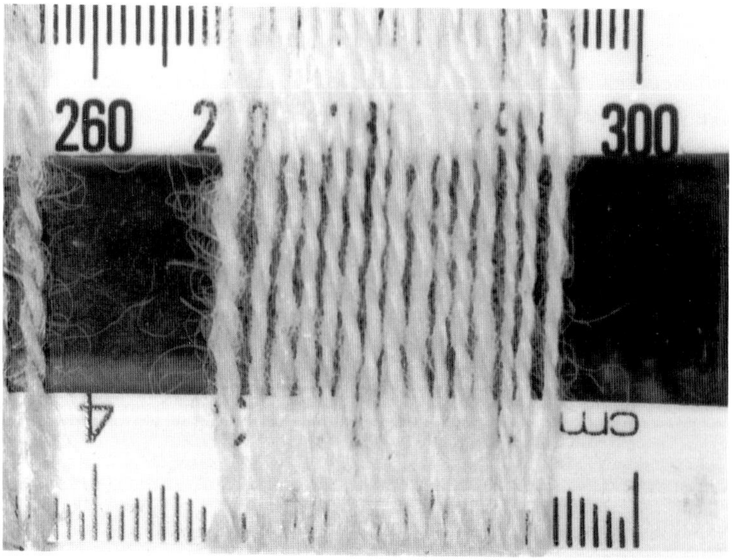

4.11 Measuring yarn size: wraps per cm (in)

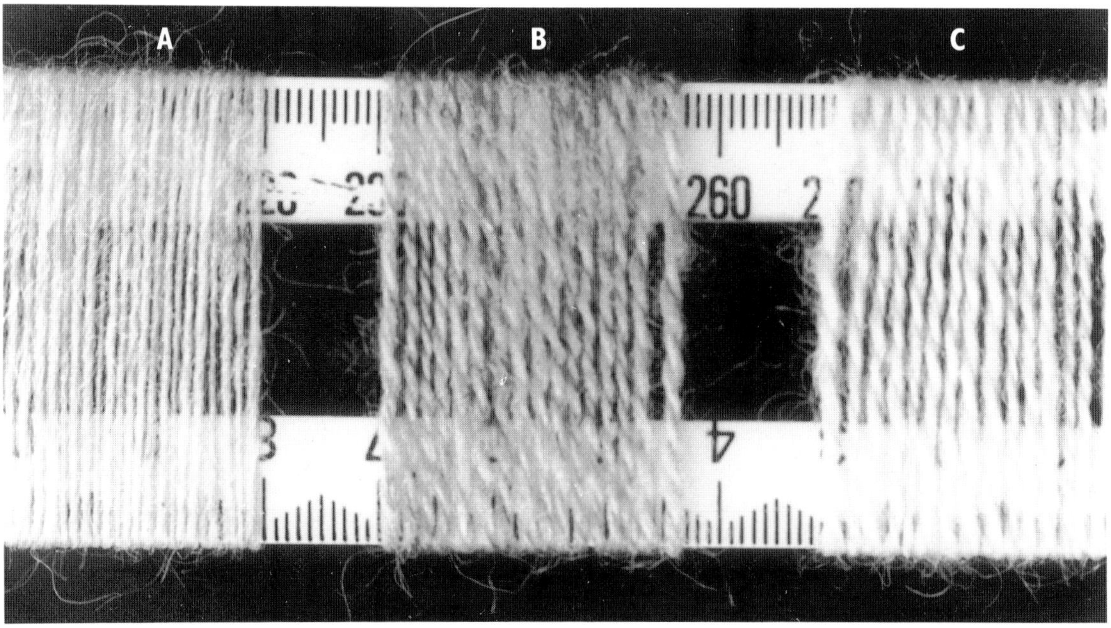

4.12 Comparative yarn sizes

Yarn sizes of singles and plied yarns

For weaving and knitting projects with handspun wool we are usually working with plied washed yarn. However, we start by spinning a single thread so it is helpful to know what size it will become when it is plied and washed. We also need to know the correct amount of twist for a particular size yarn.

Plied yarn is not double the thickness of single yarn, as you might expect, because the single yarns bed into each other as they twist together.

The single yarn (A) in the photo measures 23 wraps per 2.5cm (1in). When plied but unwashed (B), the same yarn measures 16 wraps 2.5cm (1in), and after washing, the same plied yarn (C) measures 15 wraps. These comparative measurements will vary, but you can expect about a 50 per cent increase from single to washed two-ply with most yarns.

An excellent method of judging the size of a plied yarn from the singles is to pull some of the single yarn off the bobbin while spinning and let it double back on itself (see Photo 4.3). This doubling back only happens when the yarn has just been spun. If the singles is left on the bobbin overnight or longer, the twist sets and it will not readily double back. This is why it is easier to ply singles that have been left overnight on the bobbins, as they do not kink up as you ply. If I need a single yarn for a project I always leave it on the bobbins to set before I skein it off.

Now the size of the yarn can be judged from the singles as we know it will increase in size approximately 50 per cent with plying and washing. Therefore, a single yarn of 18 wraps per 2.5cm (1in) will increase in size to about 12 wraps per 2.5cm (1in) with plying and washing. How many twists per 2.5cm (1in) should be put into a

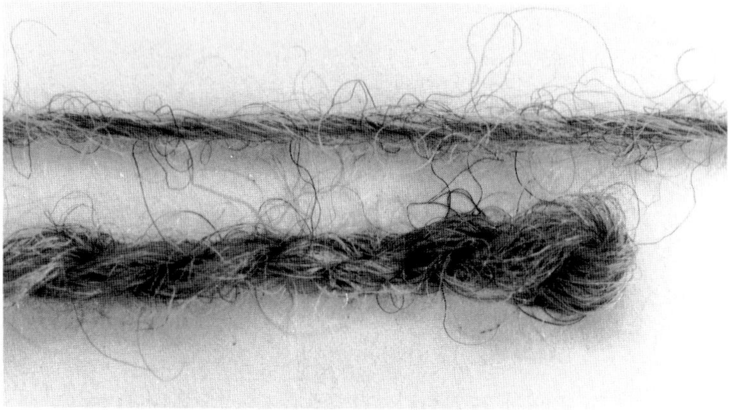

4.13 Single and doubled yarn

plied yarn of this size? In an average yarn, retaining the springiness and bounce of the original fleece, the wraps per 2.5cm (1in) should be approximately double the twists per 2.5cm (1in). So plied washed yarn with 12 wraps per 2.5cm (1in) should have about 6 twists per 2.5cm (1in). These calculations are on page 77, Figure 4.C.

Another example may help. If the single has 24 wraps per 2.5cm (1in), as in Figure 4.C, column C, the doubled yarn will have 16 wraps (column E), and the twist count in the doubled yarn should be 8 (column D).

Remember these are only guidelines and should be used as starting points for your own yarn design. Do not worry that you will spend all your time at the spinning wheel counting and measuring instead of enjoying the rhythm and relaxing hand-feet co-ordination that are the best parts of spinning. I do my measuring and counting at the beginning of a project, jot down a few figures (as my memory cannot be trusted) and then do a quick check now and then, usually each time I sit down to spin for that project. Once I have the treadle-to-hand movement rhythm I can keep it up for hours. A small length of single yarn taped to the wheel upright enables a quick visual check on the size, and a doubled length will give me a rough idea of how the plied yarn should look. It is as easy as that.

SAMPLE SKEINS

When you are planning a project, an hour spent on producing sample skeins can save several hours of wasted time later on. I use the information in this chapter as a starting point once I have chosen a certain fleece for a particular project. I usually spin a small skein or two, trying various spinning methods. I may try spinning one skein semi-worsted and one worsted, and then wash them both to see which has the correct handle for that project. Sometimes I vary the twist count slightly from the crimp count, to make a slightly harder or softer yarn, or I may ply with more or less than the usual two-thirds to make the plied yarn harder or softer. I have learnt from bitter experience to label these trials carefully as I go. It is infuriating to get a skein that is exactly what you want, only to find you cannot remember how you spun it! It is also important to wash these sample skeins before you make any decisions, as the change can be quite significant.

When you have chosen the sample you want for that project it is useful to mount the yarn on a card and file it in a plastic sleeve together with the relevant information. That card, with its notes on spinning method, size of singles, treadle to draft lengths when spinning and plying, and wraps per 2.5cm (1in) of finished plied yarn, can also be a useful resource and teaching aid. If you add a lock of the fleece and any other relevant information you will soon have a portfolio that is invaluable for teaching or showing to clients if you are in the business of selling your handspun wool.

If you add the sample tension swatches for a knitting or weaving project, this also adds to the information you have available next time you attempt a similar project. Some very well-organised spinners add photographs of the finished piece.

TWIST AND FLEECE CHARACTERISTICS

Now I want to take you back to relate what we have learnt in this chapter to Chapter Two on wool analysis. On page 30 I discussed matching the crimp pattern of wool with the twist. Look at sample Q. This wool had seven crimps to 2.5cm (1in), so I suggested it should be spun with 7 twists to 2.5cm (1in) in the finished washed sample. You are now in a position to do this.

Choose a drive ratio of 10:1 and spin two single yarns with 2 treadles to 10cm (2in) of draft, as outlined in Step 3. The singles should be about 21 wraps per 2.5cm (1in) in size. Ply these singles together with 7 twists per 2.5cm (1in). To change the twists from 10

MATCHING COMMERCIAL YARN SIZES

Many projects suitable for handspun yarn will be found in commercial pattern books and it is useful to know how to spin an equivalent yarn.

First wrap the commercial yarn around a ruler, as described on page 80, to find the wraps per 2.5cm (1in). Use Fig. 4.C, column E to find the equivalent two-ply handspun. For example, the commercial yarn may have 20 wraps. Following the chart across, it tells you that two singles of 30 wraps, each spun with 15 twists then plied with 10 twists, will give you an approximate equivalent.

This would give you a starting point only, as there are many variables. Spin a sample, compare it with the original and then make any necessary changes.

It does not matter if the commercial yarn is two-, three- or four-ply, as your handspun two-ply will be the same thickness. Note also that the twist count may be different from the commercial twist. Three-ply handspun yarn will usually be closer in appearance to commercial yarn than two-ply.

You will need to knit or weave sample swatches to test the tension first, as no two knitters or weavers have exactly the same tension. A good guide when deciding which size needle to use for knitting is to place the needle in the crimp wave of the staple of wool. When it fits neatly, this is the correct needle size.

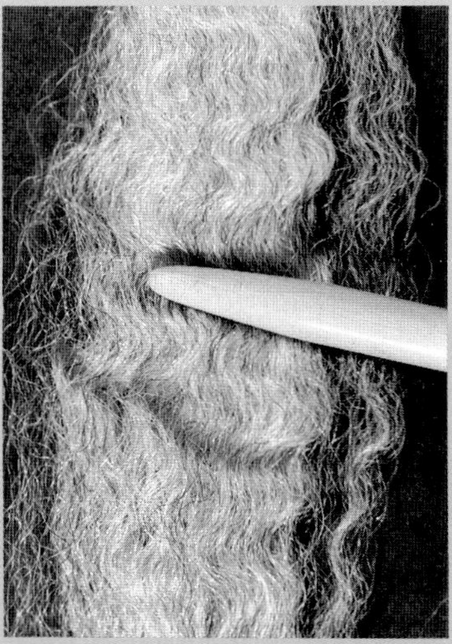

4.14 Needle and crimp size

in the singles to 7 in the plying, either change the amount fed in, as described on page 76, or change the whorl on your wheel if you have a variety to choose from.

Remember that the yarn will thicken with washing, even although this added bulk varies with different breeds and methods of spinning. Always spin with slightly *fewer* twists than required and slightly *more* wraps.

By matching the natural crimps of the fleece with the twists per 2.5cm (1in) in the finished yarn, any spinner can accurately spin yarn that is the correct size and twist for that particular fleece. The yarn will therefore retain the natural characteristics of the fleece. For example, a fine Merino fleece with 14 crimps per 2.5cm (1in), plied with 14 twists to 2.5cm (1in), will retain the lightness and softness we associate with that fleece type.

The best spinner I ever knew, the late Irene Firman, once showed me her samples. She had spun yarn from many different breeds and every skein reflected the characteristics of the breed it originated from. The skein from the Lincoln was thick, lustrous and strong. The Merino was fine and soft. The differences were apparent both in handling and to the eye. She was truly a master spinner.

Part Three

YARN DESIGN

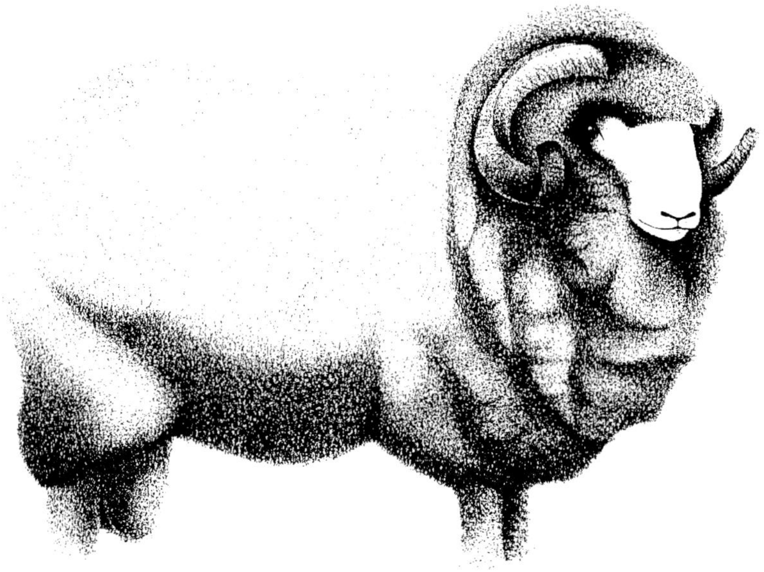

MERINO

5 Spinning Worsted and Semi-worsted Yarns

When I first began spinning, over 30 years ago, I learnt the short forward draft method (although I did not know its name), and I spun directly from the fleece with no wool preparation. I assumed this was the only way to spin. I learnt this way because the woman who taught me spun like that; we had no carders and New Zealand wool, being long in the staple, is suitable for that type of spinning.

Looking back, I am amazed that I could become a good spinner: all I had was a spinning wheel made out of a metal sewing-machine wheel, and my own hands. I knew nothing about drive ratio, carding, or worsted or woollen spinning. Yet I could produce a wide range of wools, in both size and twist count, from different types of fleeces. The fleece itself naturally seemed to dictate what type of yarn I produced, although I did not know how this happened. The fleece still dictates what I spin these days, but the difference is that I want to know how and why.

Even although I could change the size and twist count instinctively all those years ago, I could only spin a worsted-type yarn. One thing I have learnt over the years is the marked differences between worsted and woollen yarns in spinning method and end use.

Probably because I began as a worsted spinner, I find this the easiest spinning method to start beginners on. If you are an inexperienced spinner impatient to learn the craft and there is no other help available, I suggest you start by learning to spin worsted yarn as described on pages 93-95.

It is much easier to write for beginners because I can assume they know nothing about spinning and this is an easy starting point. This book is not intended for beginners, but I have written about each spinning technique in such detail here that you should be able to master the basic steps from these instructions. Most readers, however, will have the knowledge covered in my first spinning book, *The Ashford Book of Spinning*, and may find I have included information that they know already. If you are experienced, skim these sections briefly as you may still find helpful tips and hints.

> Spinners have been criticised for using the commercial terms 'worsted' or 'woollen' to describe their yarn, and it is true that we cannot produce yarns *exactly* the same as the manufactured counterpart. Personally, I cannot see why we would want to. Why spend all the effort spinning if the end result is exactly the same as the yarn you buy in a shop? However, we can produce handspun versions of worsted and woollen yarns and these yarns will widen the range of our end products. I will continue to use these terms because I believe they are applicable to handspun yarns.

QUALITIES OF HANDSPUN YARN

In an effort to spin yarn that looks 'handspun' and different from manufactured yarn, some spinners go for the rough look, producing wool that is uneven in size and twist. But this type of wool gives handspun wool a bad name because it will be hard in the overtwisted thin sections and fluffy and weak in the underspun sections. A garment knitted from this badly constructed wool will wear unevenly

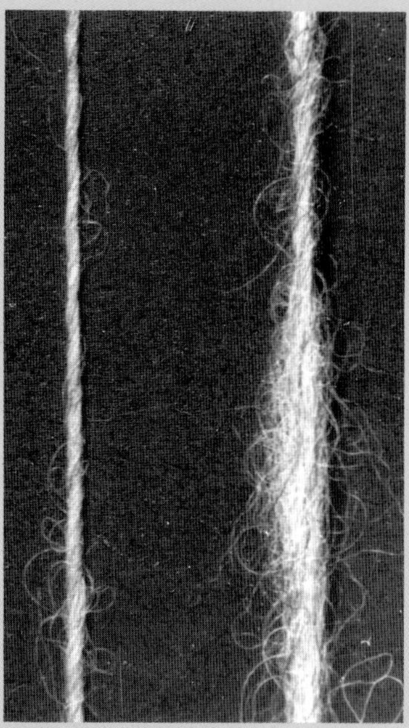

5.1 Worsted spun yarn (left) and woollen spun yarn (right)

WORSTED AND WOOLLEN YARNS: RECOGNISING THE DIFFERENCE

There are two basic processes in the making of yarn: the preparation of the wool and the spinning process. The difference between worsted and woollen yarns is quite apparent in both areas.

Worsted yarn

Preparation

Prior to spinning, the wool fibres are combed into a parallel arrangement. The fibres are from the long-staple wools, and the short fibres are removed during combing.

Spinning method

No air enters the parallel fibres of the wool as they are spun. The spinning method is such that no twist enters the drafting area. The resulting yarn is smooth, lustrous and hard-wearing.

Woollen yarn

Preparation

The wool is carded into a random mass with the fibres lying at different angles from each other. The fibres are of different lengths, with short pieces and noils included.

Spinning method

Air is trapped in the yarn as it is spun. The twist enters the drafting area and the resulting yarn is fluffy, soft and light.

Semi-worsted yarn has the preparation of a woollen and the spinning method of a worsted yarn. Semi-woollen yarn is the other way round.

PRACTISING DIFFERENT SPINNING METHODS

Some parts of the following instructions may be more familiar to you than others. You may have been spinning a worsted-type yarn for years but may have to practise more with woollen spinning, which is explained in Chapter Six.

Begin by spinning a skein using each of the four methods (worsted, semi-worsted, semi-woollen and woollen). The skeins should be a reasonable size – two quarter- or half-full bobbins of singles plied together – to allow enough practice in each method. For these smaller skeins, use a small niddy noddy or wind around two rather than four arms of your normal larger niddy noddy. This will keep tangling to a minimum while washing.

Identify each skein with a coloured tie as soon as you have skeined it to prevent confusion.

as it will have weak areas. (Weavers, however, may find this type of uneven yarn useful as a weft.)

A good spinner can produce a handspun yarn nearly as even as a manufactured yarn but with the unique qualities and the natural characteristics of the fleece retained, and with much of its liveliness and bounce carrying through to the finished garment.

By taking our spinning one step further and producing a wide range of worsted and woollen yarns, we are giving ourselves greater scope without losing that unique quality. Learning to spin these different types of yarn will add to your spinning skills and you will learn more about what your hands are actually doing during the drafting process. Although each spinner will be reading the same instructions, the yarn they produce will be slightly different. You may not be aware of the small individual changes you will make but they will be there. This is what makes spinning a craft.

It is important that the wool preparation is done correctly as this makes the spinning so much easier. I used to regard preparation time as wasted, as I was always impatient to get on with the spinning, but I now consider the time spent preparing as important as the actual spinning. Note that the wool is prepared differently for spinning worsted and woollen yarns correctly.

WORSTED SPINNING

Preparation: Flick carded or combed (parallel arrangement of fibres)
Spinning method: Short forward or backward draft

5.2 Wool combs

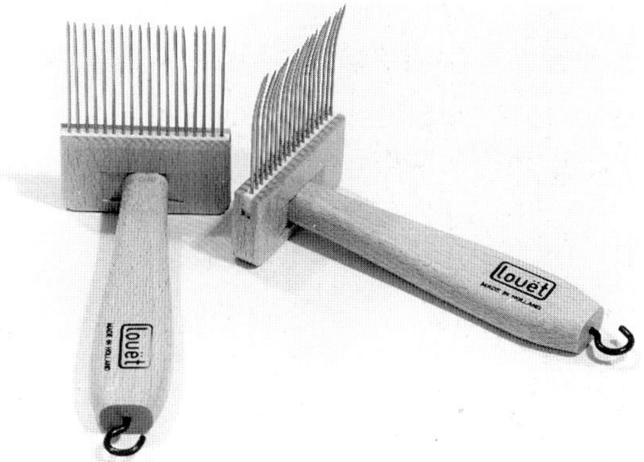

5.3 Mini wool combs

Preparation

For all four methods of preparation, select wool with a staple of at least 10cm (4in). Samples A, D and P would be ideal. These wools also have some lustre, which is desirable in worsted yarns. The wool should be combed or flick carded to remove all the short fibres, and to lay the wool out parallel. This can be done four ways:

1. Using purpose-built wool combs
2. Using mini-combs with only one row of tines
3. Using a flick carder
4. Using a comb similar to a dog comb

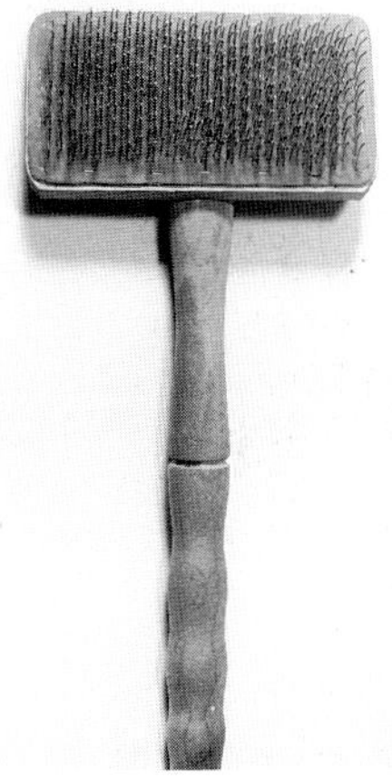

5.4 Flick carder

Wool combs

Wool combs are costly and the spinner needs to learn the skills required to use them. I will not cover the method here because it is explained so well in Peter Teal's book *Hand Woolcombing and Spinning*, an excellent reference book for all aspects of worsted spinning.

Using wool combs does produce the best parallel arrangement of fibres, but the other three methods are simpler and require less costly equipment.

Mini-combs

Mini-combs are easy to use and I produced well-combed wool at my first attempt. They are also a good stepping-stone for those who want to go on to buy the larger combs as they not only cost much less but also require less energy and muscle power.

Use wool no coarser than about 5-6 crimps per 2.5cm (1in). If the wool is too coarse the tines of these lightweight combs will bend out of alignment. Unless the wool is exceptionally clean, wash it before combing, but try not to disturb the staple formation while doing so.

5.5 Comb

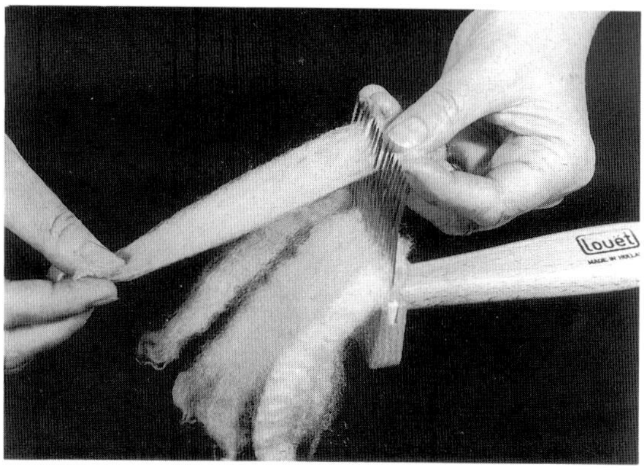

5.6 Mount the staples onto one of the combs, one staple at a time, with the butt or cut end attaching to the tines as shown.

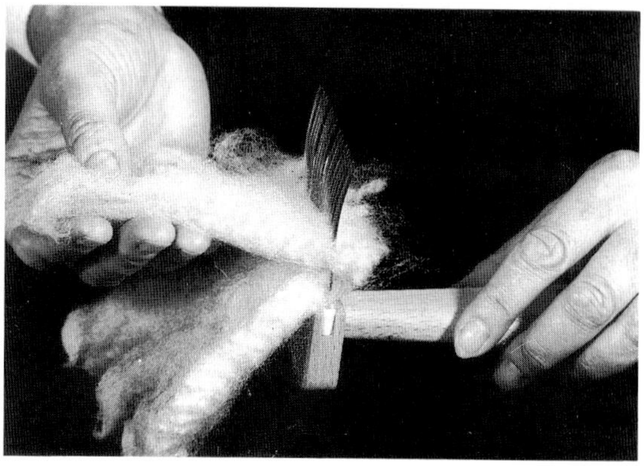

5.7 Two layers are enough so the comb is not overloaded.

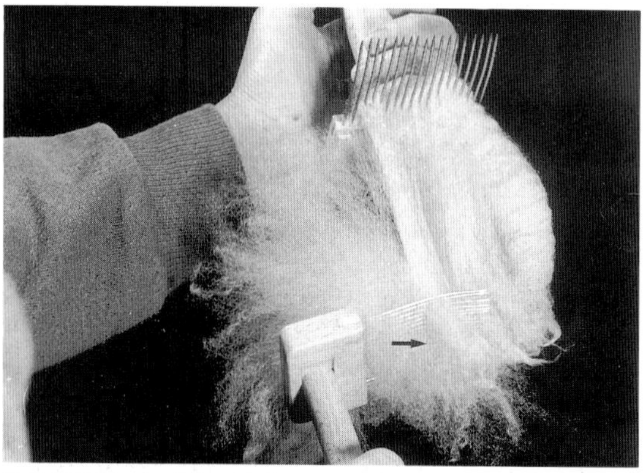

5.8 Hold the loaded comb in your left hand (reverse the directions if you are left-handed) and with the empty comb on its side and at right-angles to the left comb, make passes through the loaded comb in the direction of the arrow.

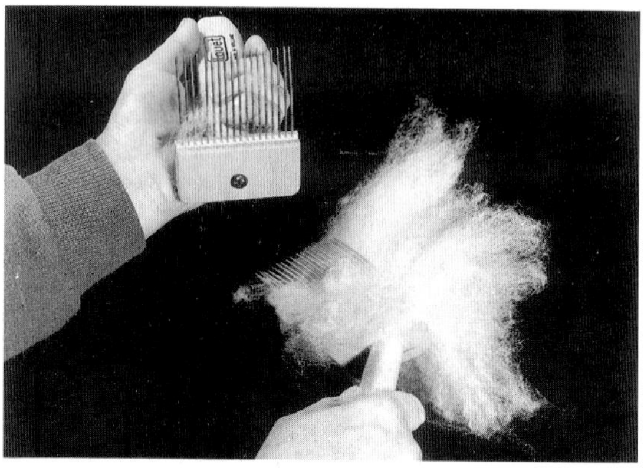

5.9 The first pass should just skim through the tips, the second goes deeper, and so on, until all the wool is transferred onto the comb in the right hand. The tines should not touch at all. There may be a few remaining scraps of wool left on the left-hand comb, which should be discarded.

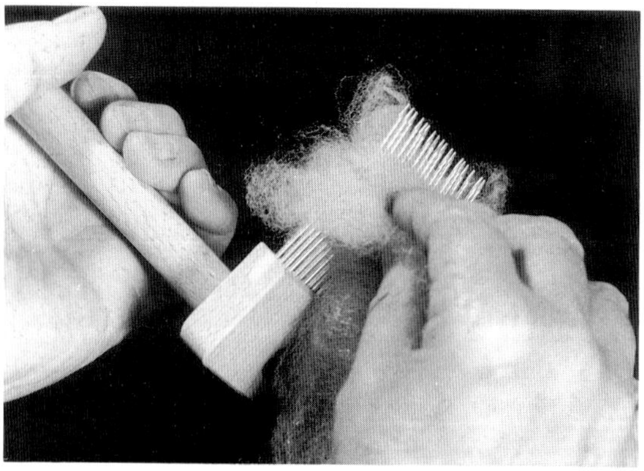

5.10 Transfer the loaded comb to the left hand. It will help the next combing if the wool is pushed slightly up the tines before combing begins again.

5.11 Place the empty comb in the right hand and repeat the action. Two or three transfers are usually enough to remove all the shorter fibres and make the wool parallel.

5.12 Pull and stroke the wool tips from the loaded comb into a point and draw them out towards you into a thin sliver of wool fibres. It helps if the comb is anchored during this process, as you can then use right and left hands alternately for this drafting.

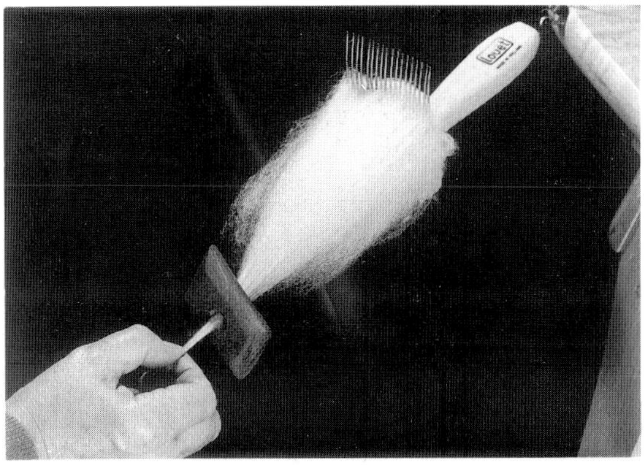

5.13 The wool can be drafted through a diz (a curved piece of plastic or bone or similar with a hole in the centre). The convex side of the diz should be facing you. Place the thumb and forefinger of one hand on the sliver about 2.5cm (1in) in front of the diz and pull the fibres towards you for 5-8cm (2-3in).

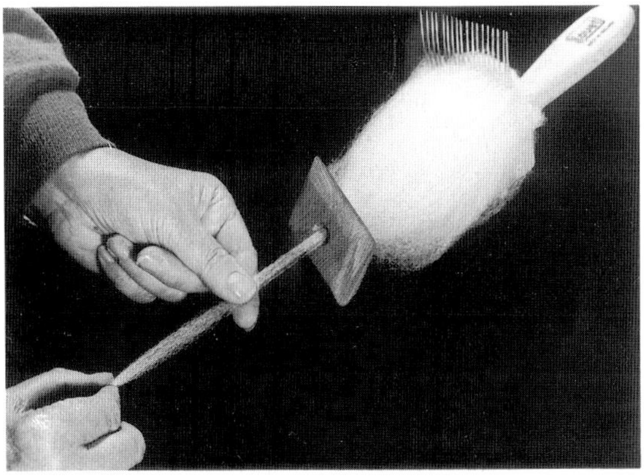

5.14 While this hand is still holding the sliver, place the other hand around the sliver, between the first hand and the diz. Push the diz back towards the comb, grasp another pinch of sliver and pull it out. This overhand motion continues, pulling an even amount of sliver through the diz each time. The sliver is left to lie in a heap on the floor.

5.15 Wind the sliver into a ball, giving the wool a slight twist as you do so by rotating the ball-winding hand. This will keep the sliver in one piece for spinning.

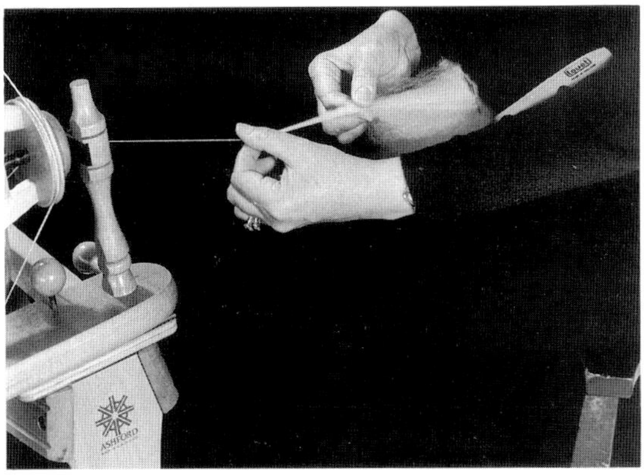

5.16 An alternative method of removing the wool from the combs is to attach the loaded comb to your belt by the hook and spin directly from the comb.

FLICK CARDING

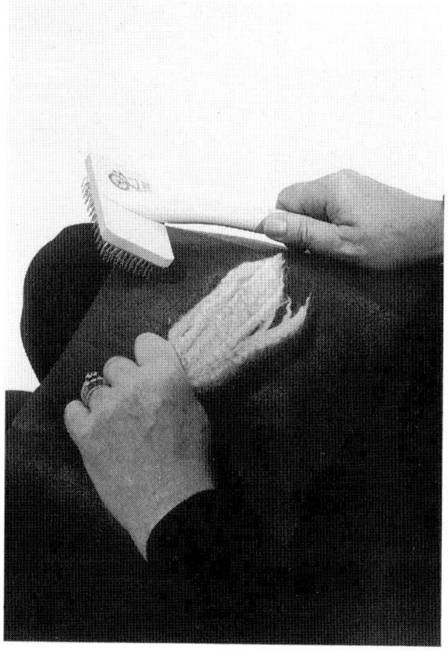

5.17 If the wool is clean it does not have to be washed prior to flick carding. Place a piece of leather or some firm fabric on one knee. Take a couple of staples out of the fleece cleanly, as described on page 14, as a tidy bunch of staples is easier to card than one with bits and pieces of wool hanging out.

Hold the staples tightly at the butt end with your left hand (if right-handed) against the leather. Take the flick carder in your right hand.

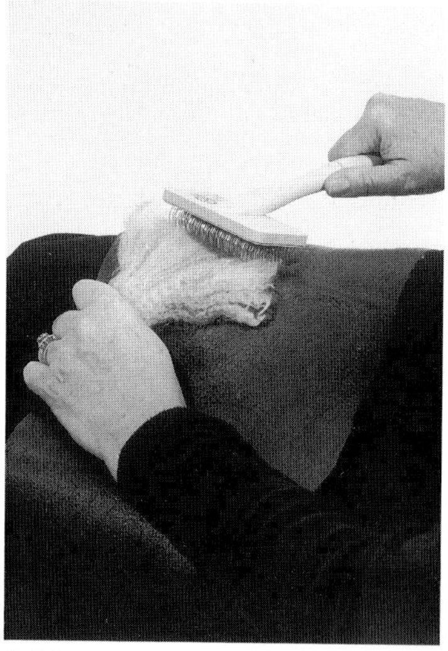

5.18 Hit the carder down onto the tips of the staples with a flick of your wrist. Keep tapping the wool, gradually working down towards the butt end, but do not card your left hand in the process. You can usually tell novice flick carders from the puncture marks on their left hand! Do not comb the wool as you would your hair (i.e. pull the carder through the wool) as this will result in a tangled mess.

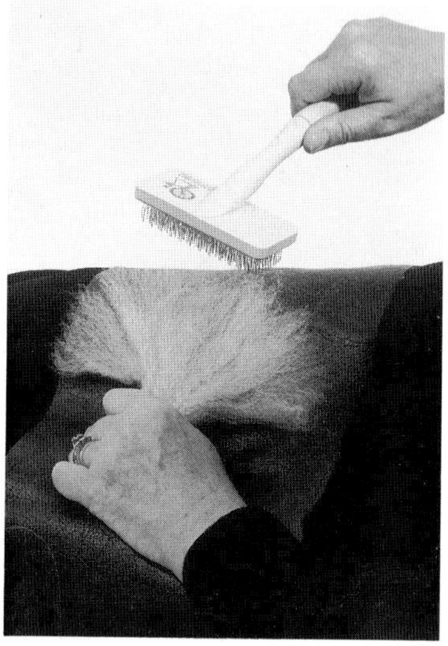

5.19 The staples should open out into a fan shape as you card. The tips of the staples, which are usually the dirtiest and where the grease collects, will need the most attention. After you have hit the wool with the carder, a small tug outwards is often necessary to loosen these tips.

Once one side is carded into a fan shape, turn the staple over and do the other side. Then give the butt ends a cursory flick to open them out and remove any second cuts.

COMBING

The wool does not have to be washed first if it is clean enough. You can buy special combs from spinning supply shops or use dog combs. The action is the same as that used in flick carding: hit down on the staples rather than actually combing the wool through. (**5.20**)

Do not card too much wool at once. If you end up with a tangle you are probably not holding the staples tightly enough in your left hand and they are pulling free. A flat carder about 10cm (4in) across is usually the right size and easy to manipulate.

The only wool left on the flick carder should be the short noils. Clean this off with an old comb before you start the next lot of wool. An experienced flicker can card quite short wool, but you will soon see how difficult it is to grasp and card a short staple without hitting your hand, and anyway short-staple wool is not suitable for worsted spinning.

Lay the carded staples neatly in a box or basket ready to begin spinning. Some spinners like to flick card all the wool for one project at once, others like to card as they spin. Whichever you do, the main thing to remember is that you have gone to some trouble to make the wool parallel so arrange it neatly and it will stay this way.

Once you have acquired the skill of flick carding it is a very quick method of preparing wool for worsted spinning. If you work mainly with fine wool choose a flick carder with fine teeth set closely together. For coarser wool, choose a coarse carder.

Spinning method

As discussed on page 88, the worsted spinning method excludes air from the yarn. It has been called the short forward or short backward draft, and has also been described as a slow method of spinning – even called the 'inchworm' method. It is neither, but simply the correct method of spinning a worsted yarn.

The results are exactly the same whether you use the forward or backward draft. Some spinners prefer one and some the other, so try both ways and see which one is easier. (One spinner told me spinners are divided into 'pushers' and 'pullers'!)

As I am a pusher, or a short forward drafter, I will describe this method first. I will not name your hands left and right but front and back, and as you may be either left- or right-handed. In the following photographs I have my left hand nearest to the orifice as my front hand, and my right hand is the back hand. I find this the most comfortable even though I am right-handed. I think this stems from my learning to spin all those years ago straight from the fleece, with uncarded wool, and using my more dexterous hand (the right) to keep the wool in order before it was drafted. It all goes to show that every spinner brings something individual to the craft.

You will probably already know your own hand preferences, but if you feel awkward in some movements, try changing hands to see if that makes it easier. And if you are not an experienced spinner, practise treadling so that the wheel moves in a clockwise direction as slowly as possible before you begin spinning.

Describing a spinning method in words makes it sound very jerky, but in reality it is a smooth, continuous movement, very rhythmical and soothing. As you draw out one draft of fibres, the wool scales cause the moving fibres to catch on and pull out adjacent fibres. If the wool is prepared correctly and flowing smoothly, the moving fibres will pull out approximately the same number of following fibres, ensuring an even yarn.

The length of the draft (the distance between your two hands) will depend on the length of the staple. If the fibres in your staple are 10cm (4in) long, the drafting area can extend to just under that length. Chapter Four explains the process of measuring the length of the draft to spin yarn with a certain twist count.

Tension

Before you start, make sure the tension is adjusted correctly. This is probably the most difficult part for beginners, as it is experience that tells a spinner the correct 'feel' of the tension. Pull the leader out from the orifice about 50cm (20in) and treadle slowly. Hold on to the leader, and if the tension is correctly adjusted you should feel it pulling slightly onto the bobbin. If the leader disappears in a great rush the tension is too tight; if the leader kinks and curls and will not pull on at all the tension is too loose. Directions on different tensioning systems and how to adjust them are given in Chapter Three.

I prefer to spin worsted yarn in the grease because it seems to keep the fibres smoother and they lie flatter. So if I have to wash the wool first I use the method described on page 26 that leaves the grease in the wool.

5.21 Before beginning spinning, position the wheel with the crank at the 1 o'clock position (see arrow) to enable the wheel to start turning with the first foot pressure.

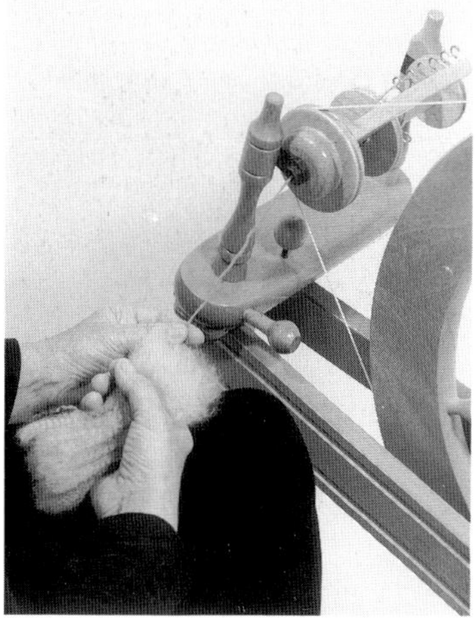

5.22 Have the leader extending from the bobbin, over the hooks and hanging out about 30cm (12in) from the orifice. Sit directly in front of the orifice and hold the bunch of parallel fibres in your back hand, with one end of the staple protruding about 5cm (2in) from that hand.

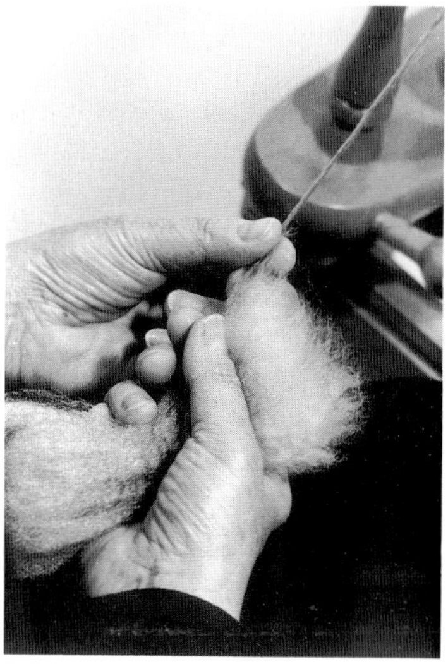

5.23 With the thumb and forefinger of the front hand pinch a small portion of the fibres against the end of the leader.

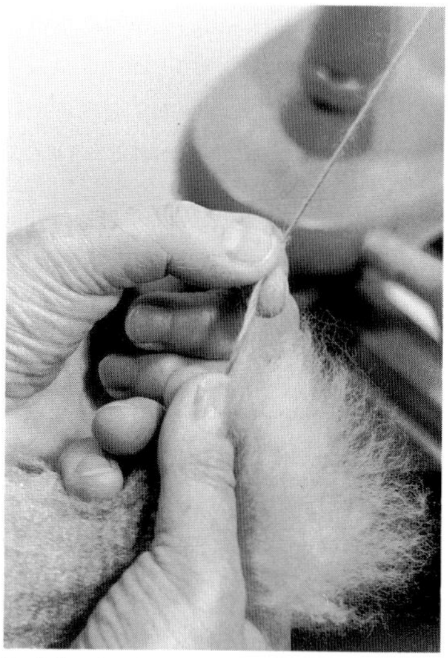

5.24 Begin treadling in a clockwise direction for Z twist wool (see Fig. 4.B, page 76), and treadle for three or four turns of the wheel until the leader and the wool are twisted together.

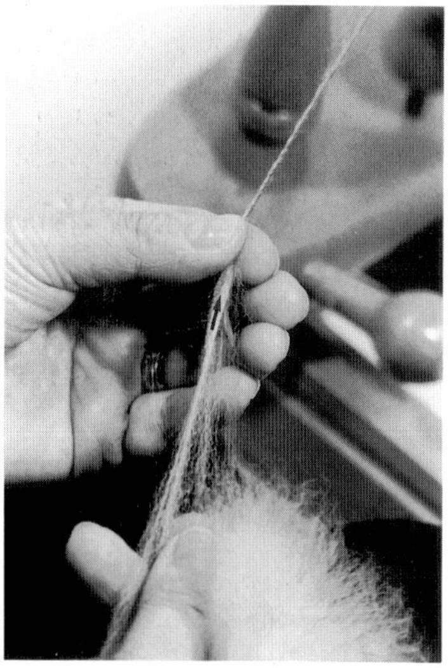

5.25 Move the front hand, still pinching hard, towards the orifice, taking with it some of the wool from the back hand. Hold the wool in the back hand just firmly enough to allow the wool to slip forward while still keeping the fibres parallel.

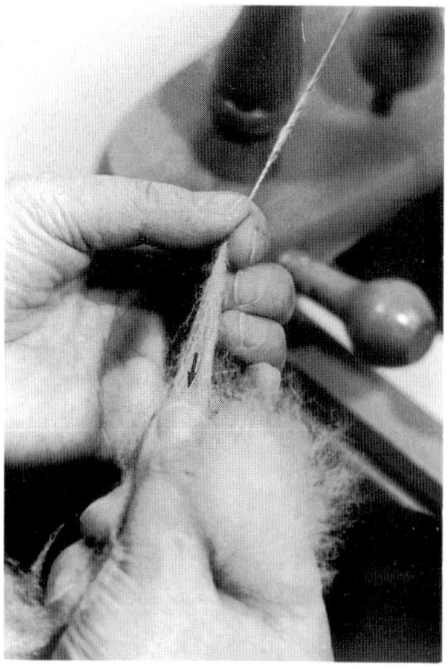

5.26 When the hands are 7-10cm (3-4in) apart, loosen the pinch and slide your front hand back down the wool, smoothing it flat and allowing the twist to follow the pinch down the yarn. Do not let the twisted yarn get through that pinch into the drafted area between the two hands.

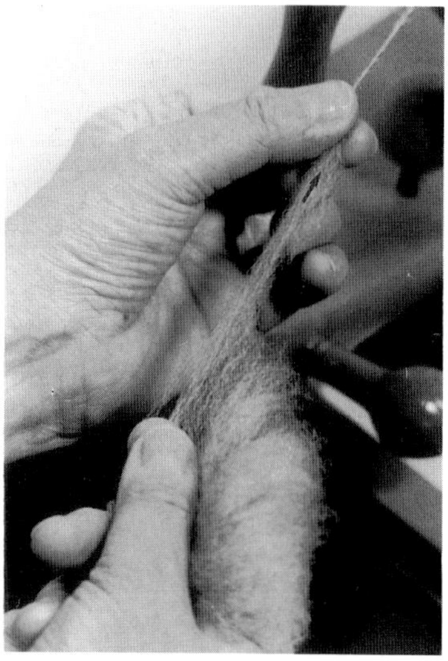

5.27 When the front and back hands are about 2.5cm (1in) apart, tighten the pinch again and move the front hand forward, repeating steps 5.25 and 5.26. The back hand stays still, resting on your knee if that is comfortable. Resting your hand is less tiring and also keeps it stable.

The function of the back hand is to keep the fibres parallel so you are always drawing the fibres from one end of the staple. Do not open and close the back hand as this can mess up the fibres. If the wool does not flow smoothly from the back hand you may be grasping the wool too tightly, or possibly the wool was not sufficiently combed or carded. If the wool does not flow smoothly the spun yarn will be uneven and lumpy. When you are spinning worsted yarn correctly, the drafted fibres should fan out from the back hand, narrowing to a point at the front hand, as in photo 5.26.

If you have to stop for any reason, such as to pick out seeds, the smooth flow is interrupted and the wool will be less worsted. Continue spinning until the supply of wool in the back hand is exhausted, then stop and repeat the process with another bunch of prepared wool.

The short backward draft spinning method is almost the same action as the forward draft, but the back hand does all the work. Begin spinning, and carry out the steps up to and including Photo 7:24. Then spin as follows:

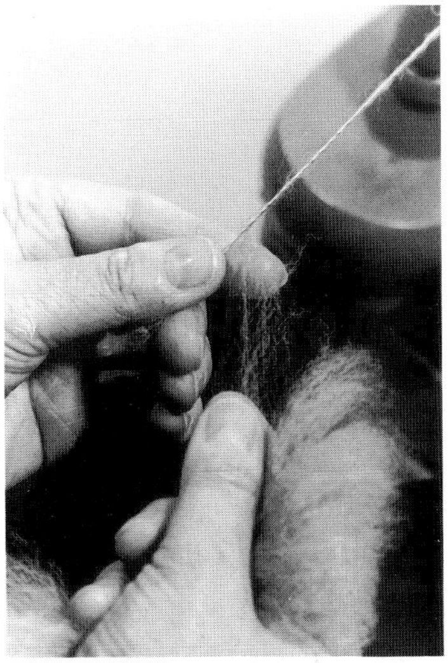

5.28 To join the new supply of wool onto the old, hold a few strands of wool in the pinch until they begin to twist together, as you did when joining onto the leader.

SHORT BACKWARD DRAFT

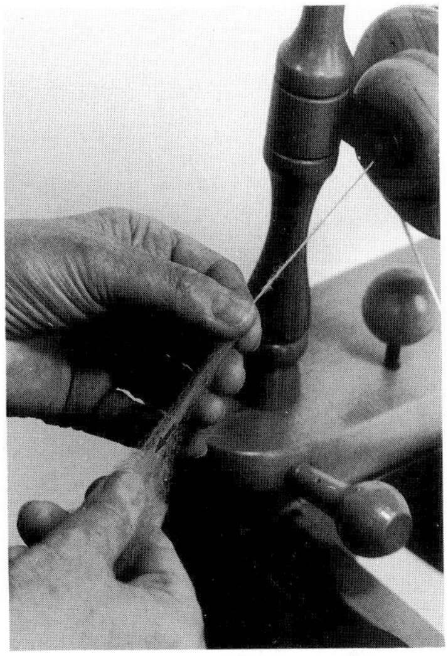

5.29 Still pinching firmly with the front hand, draw the back hand towards your body, drafting the wool back for about 7-10cm (3-4in).

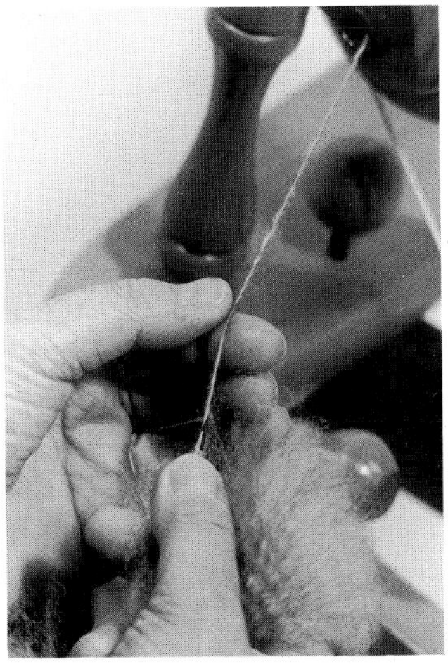

5.30 Release the pinch of the front hand to let the twist run into the drafted fibres. At the same time bring the back hand up, allowing the drafted and now twisted fibres to run onto the bobbin. Both thumbs and forefingers should be about 3cm (1in) apart at this stage.

The front hand remains still, pinching, then releasing the pinch just enough to let the wool run through the front hand, keeping pace with the twist so it never runs past the front hand.

Spinners often argue about whether they should spin from the tip or cut end of a staple when spinning worsted yarn. With flick-carded and combed wool you may find it hard to tell which end is which. I used to think the wool would flow more smoothly when spinning from the cut end, because you would be smoothing the scales down, but after some experimentation I can find no difference in the way the wool pulls out. The scales may be so minute that I cannot feel the difference, or my fingertips may not be sensitive enough.

Possible difficulties

Difficulties with these two methods of spinning are caused by:

1. Letting the twist get past the front hand into the drafting area. The wool fibres cannot slip past each other if this happens, and drafting stops. If this happens, release the wool in the back hand, let it untwist and start again.
2. Not pinching the wool at the correct place. The pinch should be exactly at the area where the twisted wool meets the untwisted wool.
3. Carelessly prepared wool that does not flow smoothly.

CORRECT AMOUNT OF TWIST

Chapter Four explains the twist in yarn in some detail, but for now a simple check will suffice. Take the plied yarn off the niddy noddy after skeining and let it hang loosely from one hand. If the skein hangs straight, the yarn has been spun and plied with the correct amount of twist. If the skein twists in a Z direction, as in Photo 7:31, there is too much twist in the plying compared with the spinning. If it twists in an S direction there is too much twist in the spinning compared with the plying.

5.31 Unbalanced plied yarn

Plying worsted yarn

Spin two half-full bobbins of single yarn, then ply the two together. If the yarn is left on the bobbins until the next day the plying will be easier as it will have stabilised and there will be fewer kinks and curls.

As we spun with a Z twist, the plying is done in the opposite direction, with a S twist – anti-clockwise. Plying equalises the twist and strengthens the yarn. A single yarn, unless it is very loosely spun, will twist and distort a knitted garment.

Because the wheel is rotating in the opposite direction, some of the twist is removed when plying two singles together. However, at the same time we are adding twist in the opposite direction. Plying should be done with two-thirds less twist than each single yarn. The way to achieve a balanced, plied yarn is described in Chapter Four.

Imagine you are squeezing the air out of the yarn as you smooth it back, keeping a constant light pressure on the two strands. Never let the twist past the front hand.

Results

A correctly spun worsted yarn will have the following qualities if spun from a medium/bulky lustrous fleece:

1. It will be smooth, solid and lustrous. If it is held up to the light, none should shine through the yarn.
2. It will be hard-wearing.
3. It should not pill. Pilling is the forming of small balls on the garment surface as small noils and short pieces work their way out, but there are no noils or short fibres in worsted yarn.
4. It will not change greatly with washing. It should not puff up and expand much, or full or mill easily. Fulling is the process of meshing the fibres together to form a firm stable fabric.
5. The twist will be clearly defined.
6. Little or no air will be trapped in the yarn.
7. There is little or no bulk or springiness in this yarn. If other breeds with different qualities (such as Sample K, page 47) are worsted spun the yarn characteristics will change. Yarn spun from this sample will be softer, springier and have more bulk.

Uses of worsted yarn

Knitting

As worsted yarn is hard-wearing it is suitable for outer garments, such as jackets and skirts, and is particularly suitable for guernseys. A guernsey is a hard-wearing jersey, traditionally navy blue and worn by fishermen (see Project 7). Garments made in worsted yarn have a slippery, silky feel. Some people find that worsted wool does not irritate their skin to the same extent as the fluffier woollen yarn.

Because it is a smooth yarn, patterns will show up clearly, so in complex aran and fairisle patterns each stitch will be distinct. As the yarn does not full you should use smaller needles, because the warmth will come from the closeness of the yarn rather than from the air trapped in it.

5.32 Change in sett with washing. As can be seen, the sett does not change much. Sample A, unwashed worsted yarn, has 15 wraps per 2.5cm (1in). Sample B, the same yarn but washed, has 14 wraps per 2.5cm (1in).

Weaving

This yarn makes an excellent warp yarn as it is smooth and strong (see Project 2). For hard-wearing outer garments, such as skirt and coat fabric, or for upholstery fabric, worsted yarn can be used for both the warp and weft. This will result in a smooth, flat lustrous fabric. For a softer fabric, use woollen-spun yarn for the weft.

Patterns such as leno and other lace weaves will be very clear and distinct. Sett the yarn closer than for woollen yarns because worsted yarns do not full or mesh together, meaning the warmth comes from the close sett.

SEMI-WORSTED SPINNING

Preparation: Drum or handcarded (random or non-parallel fibres)
Spinning method: Short forward or backward draft

For semi-worsted spinning the preparation changes but the spinning method remains the short forward or backward draft.

Preparation

Handcarders or drumcarders are used to prepare the wool into a random or non-parallel formation. Both methods leave short noils and fibres of uneven length in the wool. The fibres lie at different angles and this formation traps air when the fibres are spun together. If short-staple fleeces are chosen, the yarn will be softer, springier and less lustrous. With staples longer than 10-13cm (4-5in), fleeces will be difficult to handcard so a drumcarder is a better option. A practical guide is to measure the staple against the width of your handcarders. If the staple is longer, use a drumcarder.

A drumcarder is useful for carding large amounts of wool at once. It prepares the wool in the same manner as handcarders, but the wool comes off in one large batt. The wool can be washed first, as described on pages 26, to prevent the backing cloth from becoming soiled. If

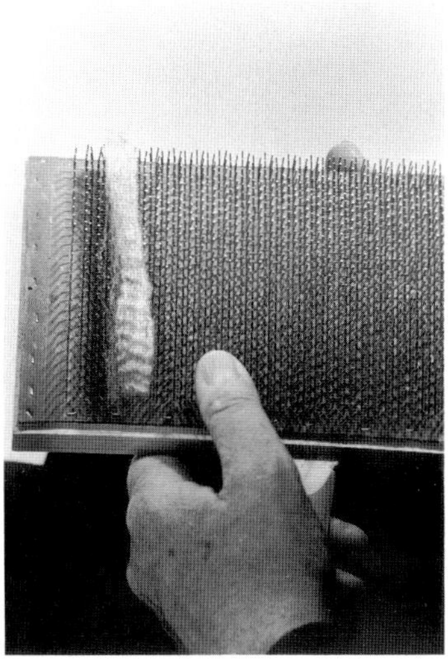

5.33 Width of hand carders relative to a staple of wool.

your drumcarder has a rubber backing, washing is not so important, but a leather backing cloth will soil quickly with dirty, greasy wool.

5.34 Drumcarder. In most drumcarders you can adjust the distance that separates the teeth of the two rollers. The teeth should be as close as possible *without* touching. Drumcarders can have fine or coarse teeth. If you use mainly fine wool your drumcarder should have fine teeth.

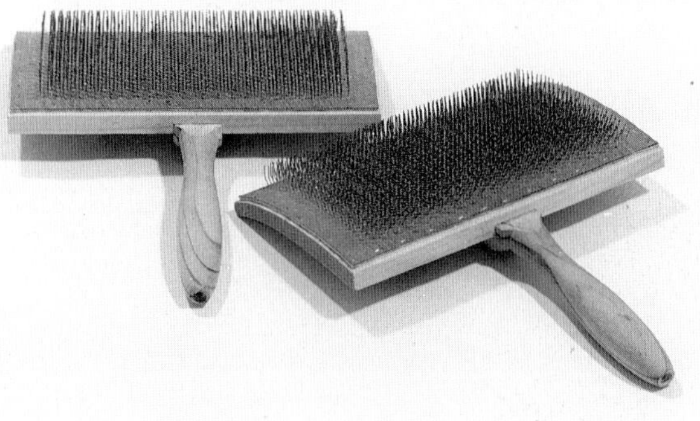

5.35 Hand carders. Most handcarders are either curved or straight. If you are using straight carders, brush them parallel to each other and all the surfaces will be covered. If the carders are curved, as in the following photographs, brush with a rocking motion to cover all the surfaces.

Handcarding

There are many different methods of handcarding so if you are an expert, continue with your tried and true method. If you have never carded before, here is one straightforward method that Mabel Ross has given me permission to describe.

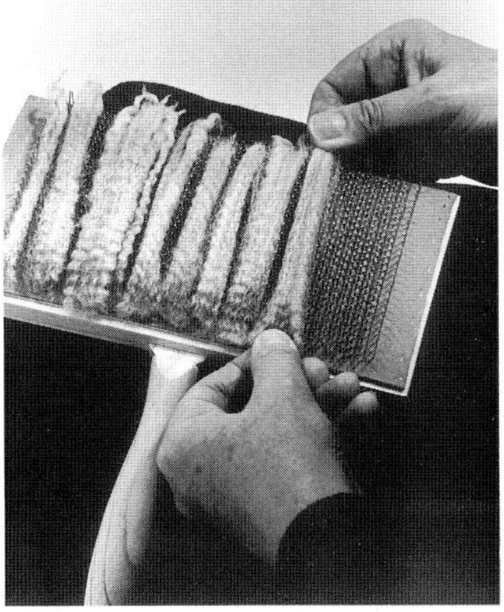

5.36 Place the left-hand carder on your lap, teeth up, with the handle pointing to the left, and fill it with staples of wool. Press the butt or cut end of each staple into the metal teeth, while pulling on the staple with the other hand. Do not overfill the carders – too little is much easier to card than too much.

5.37 The carders are held as shown. This allows you to turn the carders over without altering the grip, an important point. Brush the right carder lightly across the filled carder. The first stroke should allow the front one-third of each carder to overlap, the second stroke two-thirds, and the third stroke should cover completely. The teeth should barely touch, so if you can hear them scraping loudly against one another the carders are too close.

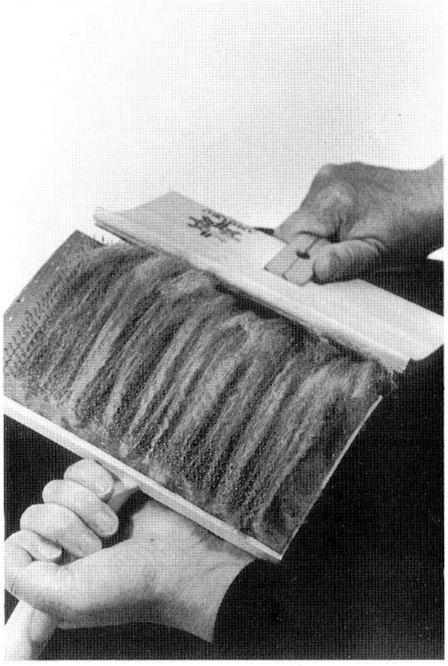

5.38 At the end of the last stroke, drop the right carder slightly to anchor the fringe. About half the wool should now be on each carder.

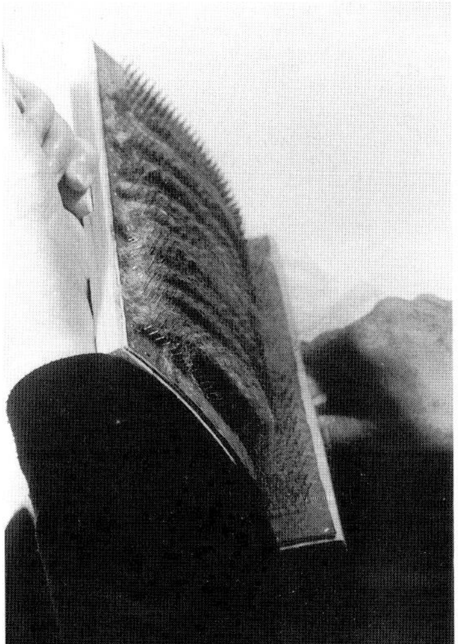

5.39 The remaining wool is now stripped off the left carder. Turn the right carder over with the teeth uppermost. Place the left carder at right angles to the right carder, with the fringe of wool hanging from the front of the left carder onto the back edge (near the handle) of the right.

5.40 Bring the handle of the left carder down towards the right handle and push the left carder away from you across the surface of the right.

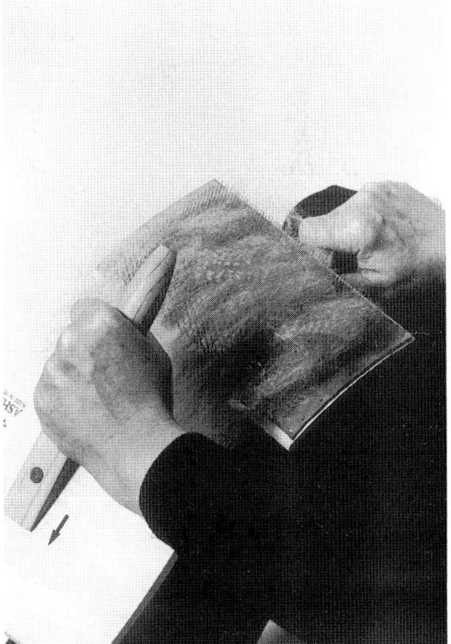

5.41 This leaves all the wool on the right carder.

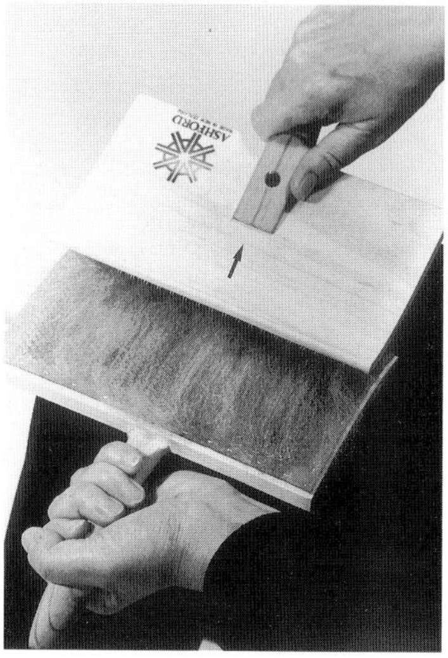

5.42 With the left carder back on your right knee, stroke it with the full right carder, again moving one-third, two-thirds, then completely over.

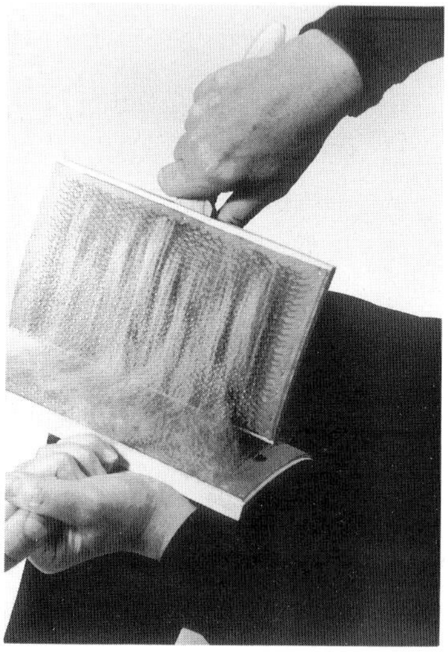

5.43 The remaining wool is now stripped off the right carder onto the left. Turn the right carder over with the teeth uppermost. Place it at right angles to the left, with the fringe hanging off the front of the right carder near the back edge of the left.

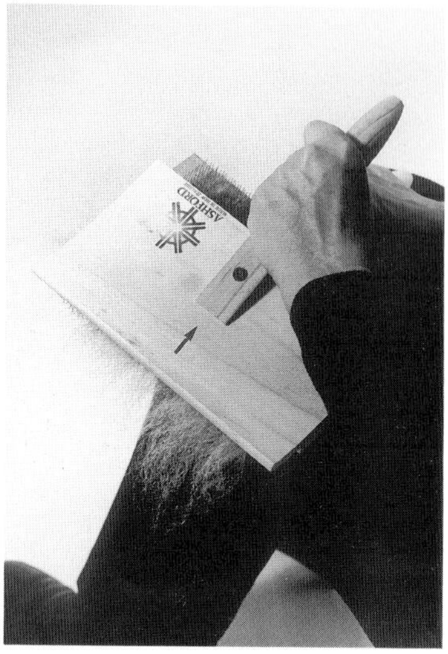

5.44 Bring the handle of the left carder close to the right carder and pull the left one towards you, stripping the right.

Stroke the right carder over the left three more times, as in Photo 5.37. Then strip the right carder onto the left carder as in Photos 5.43 and 5.44.

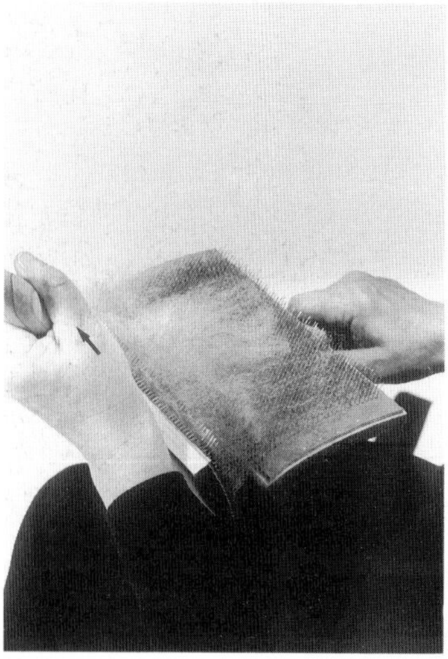

5.45 To remove the wool from the carder, place the front teeth of the right carder under the fringe of wool on the left with the teeth touching. Hold the carders at right angles and gently pull the right carder up, removing the wool from the left.

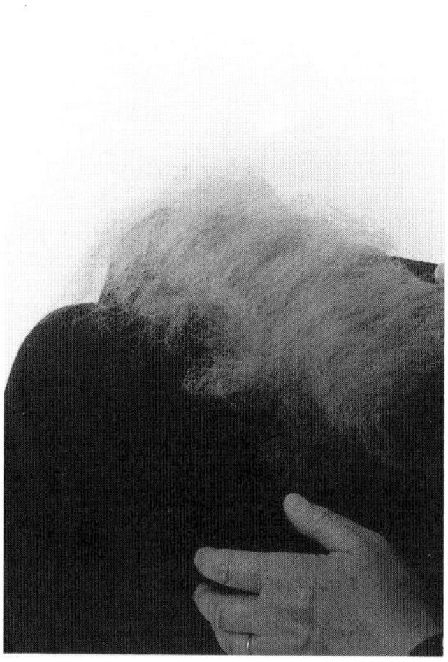

5.46 Lift all the wool carefully off the right carder with the left and lay the wool mass on your lap.

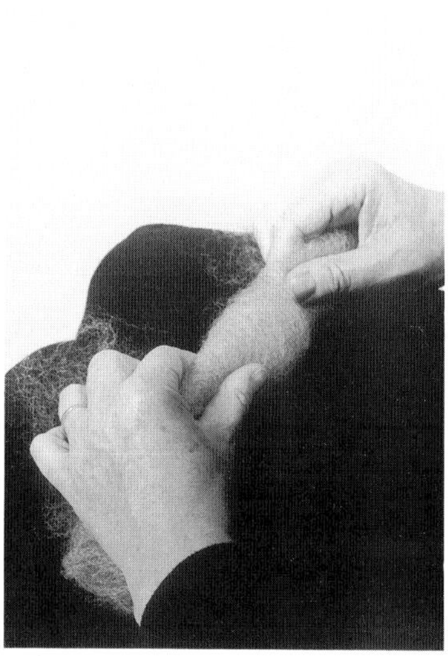

5.47 Make a rolag by rolling the wool into a tube. Give it a few extra rolls to keep this compact, cigar-like shape.

If you find the wool is not carding evenly, check the amount of wool of the carders. You may be trying to card too much at once.

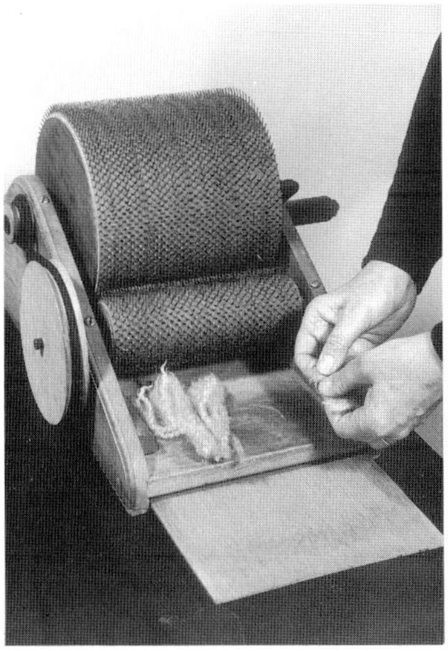

5.48 Tease the tips of the staple apart and place a few staples across the width of the feed tray.

5.49 Turn the handle to draw the fibres under the small roller. Do not hold these fibres back as this causes them to catch around the small roller.

5.50 Continue turning the handle until all these fibres are lying smoothly on the large roller.

5.51 Process another lot of teased fibres and continue until the large roller is evenly filled with wool to the top of the teeth.

5.52 Remove the batt from the teeth by inserting a metal awl under the batt at the point where there is a break in the carding cloth. This break is usually covered by a metal bar. Pull the awl up to break the batt at this point.

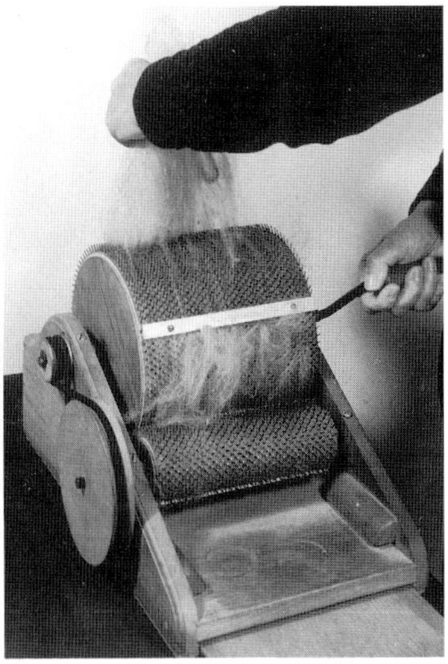

5.53 Rotate the handle in the opposite direction and peel the batt off. Most fleeces require two turns through the drumcarder to make a smooth, even batt.

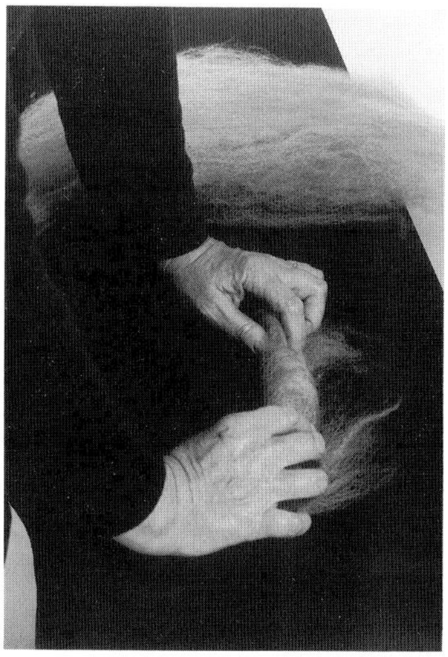

5.54 For semi-worsted spinning, break the batt into portions across the width and roll these portions into rolags ready for spinning.

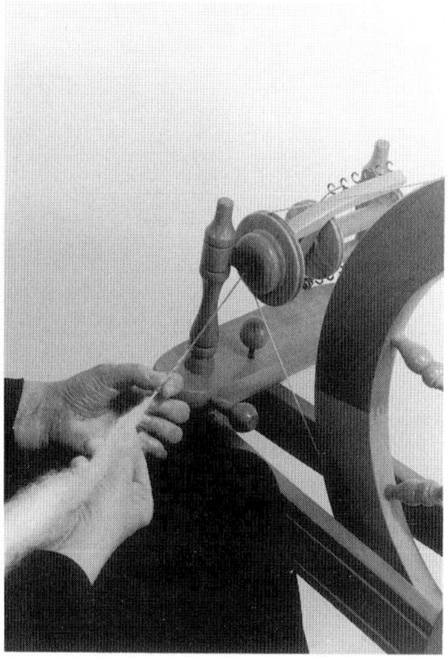

5.55 Semi-worsted spinning

Spinning method

The spinning method for a semi-worsted yarn is the short forward or short backward draft described on pages 94-95. But with semi-worsted yarn, the fibres are drafted from a rolag, not an arrangement of parallel fibres. The back hand should keep the rolag as close to its original formation as possible.

Use the same plying method as described on page 96 for worsted yarn.

Results

A correctly spun semi-worsted yarn will have the following characteristics:

1. It will be less solid and not as smooth and lustrous as the worsted yarn, but will still have some of these qualities.
2. It will be reasonably hard-wearing.
3. It will pill slightly as the short pieces and noils in the yarn work their way to the surface with wear.
4. The yarn will full or mill slightly, i.e. it will mesh together with washing.
5. The twist will be less defined than in worsted yarn.
6. A little air will be trapped in the yarn because the fibres were spun in a random arrangement.
7. There will be slightly more bulk in this yarn.

Uses of semi-worsted yarn

Knitting

This yarn is suitable for outdoor garments, hats, mittens, socks, sweaters and jerseys. Because some air is trapped in the yarn it will mesh slightly with washing, so use slightly larger needles than when knitting with worsted yarn. Patterns will show up but will not be as distinct as with the worsted yarn.

Weaving

This yarn will be slightly softer than worsted but it is still suitable for a warp. It has more bulk and would be suitable for jacket and coat fabrics, cushions and hard-wearing blankets. Do not sett the warp as close as you would a worsted yarn as the fabric is capable of fulling slightly and closing the gaps between threads when washed.

6 Spinning Woollen and Semi-woollen Yarns

Woollen spinning produces a softer, bulkier, more rounded and less hard-wearing yarn (see Photo 5.1). Fleeces chosen for woollen spinning are usually shorter in the staple than for worsted spinning; even fleeces such as Sample G in Chapter Four can be spun woollen.

It is no surprise that in New Zealand, where the most common wools are Romney or other similar long-wool breeds, worsted spinning is the most popular method of spinning. In countries where the common everyday fleeces are short in staple, woollen spinning is predominant. Many years ago a spinner from the Shetland Islands gave a demonstration in New Zealand on woollen spinning from a rolag. I was intrigued but could not see how our long-staple wools could be spun that way as a 15-18cm (6-7in) staple does not fit on a handcarder, and drumcarders for handspinners were not available then. The Shetland Island spinner was spinning the correct way for her fleeces, and we were spinning the correct way for our fleeces. Neither of us knew enough about other wools or methods of spinning to understand what the other was doing.

It is important to remember that the wool is prepared into the correct formation before spinning begins. Then spinning is just a matter of drafting the fibres out to let the twist form to make yarn. In worsted spinning the fibres are parallel and even in length before spinning begins. In woollen spinning the fibres are not parallel but randomly arranged, with short and long fibres mixed up together.

The other difference between worsted and woollen spinning is the amount of air in the finished yarn. Woollen spinning allows much more air to become trapped in the fibres as they are drafted and twisted.

WOOLLEN SPINNING

For woollen yarn, both the preparation and spinning method differ from those used to make worsted yarn. We use wool from the short-staple sheep, such as Samples G, K and M in Chapter Two, which is springy with high bulk, adding to the softness and bounce of woollen-spun yarn.

Preparation: Hand- or drumcarded (random arrangement of fibres)
Spinning method: Medium draft or long draw

Preparation

The wool should be prepared as shown on pages 99-101 in Chapter Five, with drumcarders or handcarders. If drumcarders are used on wool that is reasonably long in the staple the fibres tend to straighten out during carding and spinning and the yarn becomes slightly less 'woollen'.

If you are using a drumcarder, break the batt into portions across the width, and roll these portions into rolags as shown in Chapter Five, Photo 5.54.

With worsted spinning, most spinners can control the speed of draw-on with their hands. I can watch television and spin with the short forward or backward draft quite easily as my fingers are always in contact with the yarn and I can spin by touch rather than sight. With the medium draft and long draw I have to look at the yarn as I spin to judge when it is the right size and has enough twist, because my hands have less contact with the yarn.

Spinning methods

To retain the air in the yarn as it is spun use the medium draft or the long draw. Both methods let the twist past the front hand into the drafting area, trapping air in the yarn, which will therefore be softer and bouncier. If you have never used these spinning methods, try both to see which is easier.

With both methods it is important that the tension of the wheel is adjusted correctly to let the wool pull on at the correct speed. The tension and treadling speed control the rate of draw-on, so you may need to make small corrections in both until you have it right for you.

MEDIUM DRAFT

This method of spinning is an extension of the short backward draft but the twist is allowed to move behind the front hand and into the drafting area.

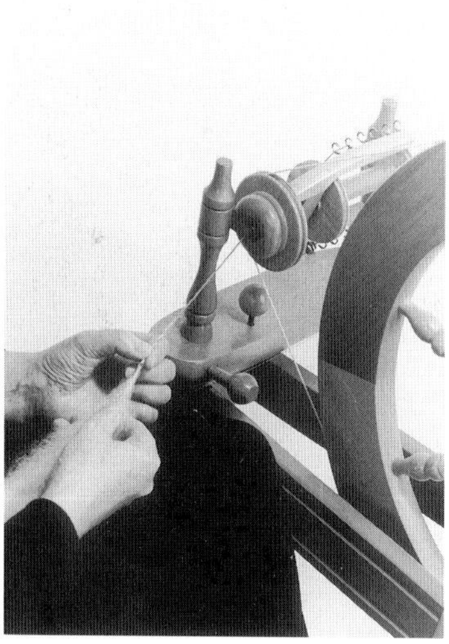

6.1 Hold the rolag of wool in the back hand against the leader. With the thumb and forefinger of the front hand pinch some fibres onto the leader and treadle for a few turns until the fibres have caught.

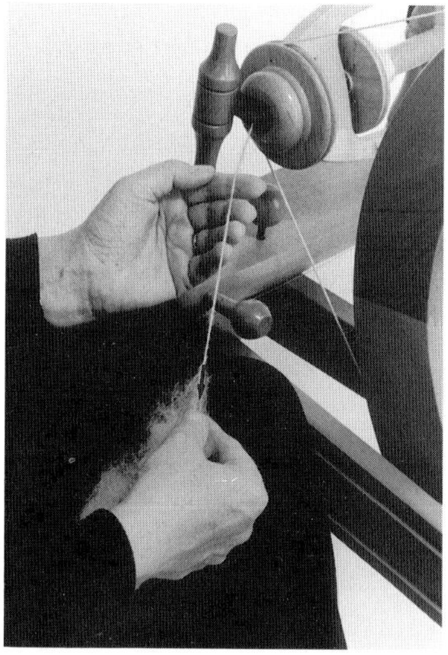

6.2 Draft back with the back hand, at the same time releasing the pinch of the front hand to let the twist past it into the drafting area. The front hand remains stationary: all it does is support the yarn, occasionally pinching if the back hand needs something firm to pull against. Try to pinch as little as possible as this flattens the air out of the yarn. If the wool is correctly prepared and running smoothly the front hand has very little to do and is sometimes superfluous.

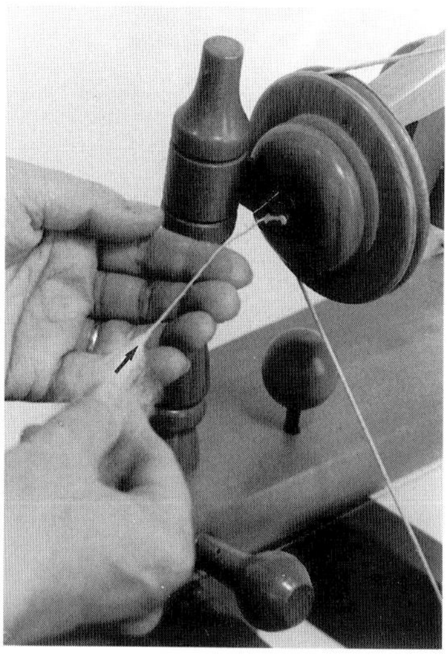

6.3 The back hand does all the work, drafting the wool just ahead of the twist. Open and close this hand to let just the right amount of wool into the drafting area. When the wool is the correct size and twist, the back hand moves forward to allow the wool to wind onto the bobbin.

There are many variations on this method. Some spinners like to draft a long length, the full extent of their arm, before they run the yarn onto the bobbin. Some prefer to work with shorter movements closer to the spinning wheel. The main difference between this and the long draw is that in the medium draft, a moving supply of wool is being fed into the drafting area. With the long draw, a fixed amount is fed into the drafting area.

Difficulties

Difficulties with this spinning method are usually caused by:

1. The back hand holding too tightly onto the rolag and preventing the wool from flowing forward.
2. Too much twist being allowed into the drafting area so the fibres cannot pull out. The fibres should be just *beginning* to twist as they are drafted.
3. The wool not being well prepared enough. Good preparation is essential because any hiccup in the smooth supply of the wool will cause unevenness in the yarn and possibly overtwisting in places.

SPINNING WITH DIFFERENT WHEELS

The spinning methods differ slightly according to the type of wheel used. If you are spinning on a double-drive-band wheel the yarn will continue twisting as it is fed onto the bobbin. So when the drafting is complete, and the back hand allows the yarn to feed onto the bobbin, the yarn should be slightly undertwisted. If you are using a single-drive wheel no extra twist is added as the yarn is pulled onto the bobbin so the yarn should have the correct amount of twist beforehand.

LONG DRAW

Hold the wool against the leader as in Photo 6.1 and join the wool onto the leader. The front hand holds the wool about 13cm (5in) from the orifice and remains in this position throughout the drafting process.

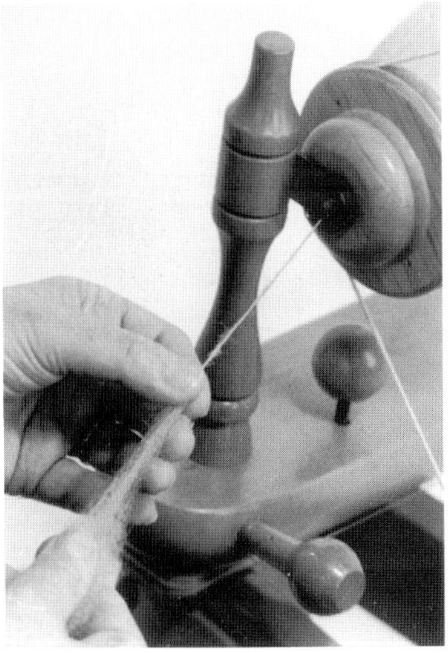

6.4 Pinch with the front hand to prevent any twist going past and treadle about five times.

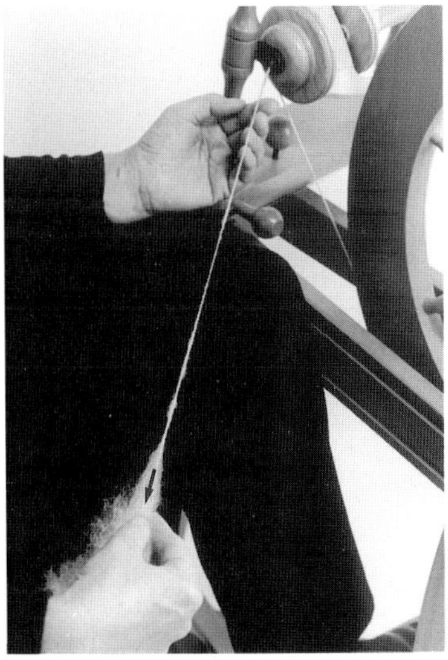

6.5 The back hand holds the rolag, with about 3-5cm of it extending from the fingers. Still treadling, release the pinch of the front hand to allow the twist into the area between the two hands, and pull the back hand towards you and slightly to one side until it is about level with your hip. As you gently pull back, the twist runs up into this drafting area. Do not open and close the back hand because only a fixed amount of the rolag is allowed into the drafting area at one time.

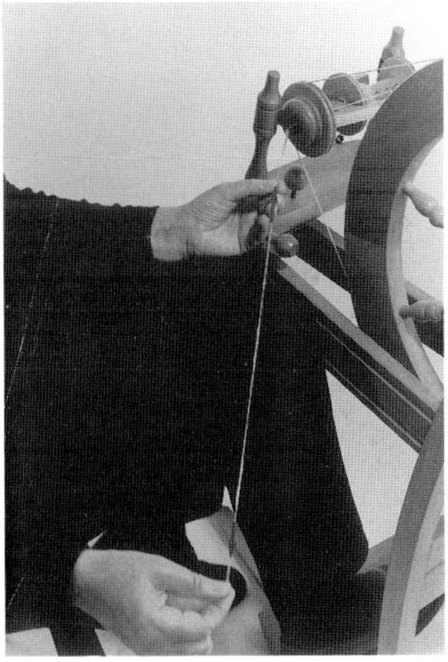

6.6 When the length of yarn between the two hands has roughly the correct twist and size, look for thicker unspun areas. These can be removed by continuing to pull out the yarn with the back hand while pinching with the front hand. Because the thicker areas have less twist, they will slide apart until they are the same as the rest of the yarn, equalising the twist in that length. Do not let any more wool into the drafting area from the rolag while this equalising is taking place.

6.7 When the full length of yarn has the correct size and twist, bring the back hand quickly up to the front hand and allow the yarn to wind onto the bobbin. The process will again differ between single- and double-drive wheels (see page 66).

Many spinners think they are doing the long draw because their back hand is moving out to its full length when spinning, but there is more to the long draw than that. The front hand remains about 13cm (5in) from the orifice, alternately pinching and opening to let twist into the drafting area for the whole operation.

This is much easier to demonstrate than write about. The secret is knowing when to stop the drafting process and begin equalising. Because you are continuing to add twist by treadling during equalising it is best to stop the drafting just before the yarn is 'finished'.

Difficulties

Difficulties with this method of spinning are caused by:

1. Carelessly prepared wool that will not flow smoothly from the rolag.
2. Overtwisting the yarn before equalising begins so the yarn will not slide apart to even out. If this happens, let go of the rolag and it will untwist, then you can pick it up and start again.
3. Letting more wool in from the rolag as equalising takes place.
4. The front hand gravitating towards the back hand.

Plying method

Use the plying method shown in Chapter Four, page 78 but instead of smoothing the yarn with the forefinger and thumb of your front hand to squeeze out the air, just support the yarn with the front hand.

Results

A correctly spun woollen yarn should have the following qualities:

1. It will be fluffy, soft, light and rounded. If it is held up, light should shine through it.
2. It will not be as hard-wearing as other yarns.
3. It will pill because it contains short fibres and noils.
4. It will full or mill well, and there will be more shrinkage with this yarn than with worsted types.
5. The twist will be less defined than in the other yarns.
6. There will be a lot of air trapped in the yarn.
7. It will be lofty and bulky.

Uses of woollen yarn

Knitting

Use for shawls, scarves, and stoles, i.e. garments that will not be washed frequently as this may cause matting. Lightweight fluffy sweaters can be knitted on larger needles than with worsted yarns, as the wool will mesh together and the air trapped in the fibres will provide warmth. Handwash these garments with care to prevent matting and shrinkage.

Because of the yarn's fluffy appearance, patterns such as fairisle and cable will not show up clearly.

Weaving

Again, use for shawls, scarves and stoles but sett the yarn further apart than for worsted yarns as the yarns will full well. Also, the fluffy texture of this yarn will cause the warp ends to stick together. This yarn can be used as a warp if the sett is correct. With open weaves as such leno and canvas weave the finished article will full and shrink so much that the pattern may be obscured after washing.

A woollen yarn is ideal for the pattern weft in such weaves as overshots or surface weaves.

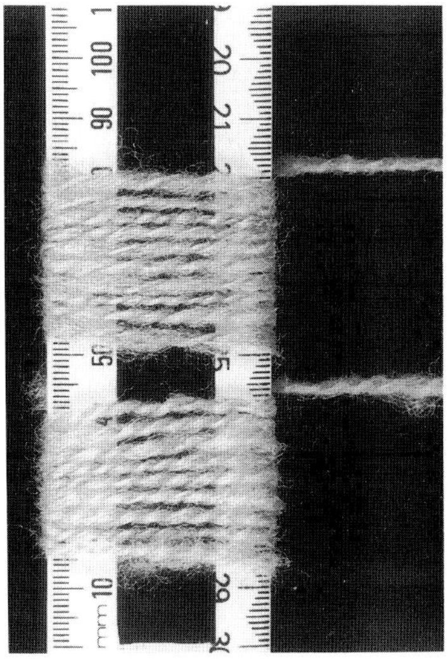

6.8 Change in sett with washing woollen yarn

SEMI-WOOLLEN SPINNING

Preparation

The factor that changes for semi-woollen spinning is the preparation. For this method the wool should be long-staple because this is easier to flick card or comb. This resulting yarn will be smoother, more lustrous and more hardwearing than woollen-spun yarn.

Prepare the wool by flick carding or combing as described on pages 90-92 in Chapter Five.

Spinning methods

Spin with the medium-draft or long-draw method described on pages 104-105.

Results

A correctly spun semi-woollen yarn will have the following qualities:

1. It will be reasonably smooth because the fibres are parallel, but will be lighter and bouncier than the semi-worsted yarn.
2. It will be more hard-wearing than a woollen yarn but less so than a semi-worsted yarn.
3. It should not pill because all the short fibres and noils have been removed by flick carding or combing.
4. It will full or mill reasonably well as the fibres have more room to move in this less solid yarn.
5. The twist will not be as well defined as in the worsted yarns.
6. Some air will be trapped in the yarn because of the spinning method.
7. It will not be flattened but will have a rounded bulky appearance.

Uses of semi-woollen yarn

Knitting

This yarn is suitable for wearing next to the skin and can be used for scarves, shawls and lighter, softer less hard-wearing jerseys and sweaters. Because the fibres lie parallel and the yarn is smooth, it is an ideal yarn for people who do not like the prickly feel of wool next to their skin.

Weaving

Use this yarn for scarves, stoles, shawls and garments such as cocoon jackets that require a soft drape. It is ideal for the pattern weft in an overshot weave as it has the required bulk and softness, or for the pattern weft on a surface weave.

SPINNING FROM THE FOLD

This is an excellent method if you find it difficult to keep the fibres in the back hand parallel when spinning with the medium draft. Spinning from the fold is also a good basic skill for beginners as it provides constant control of the wool supply.

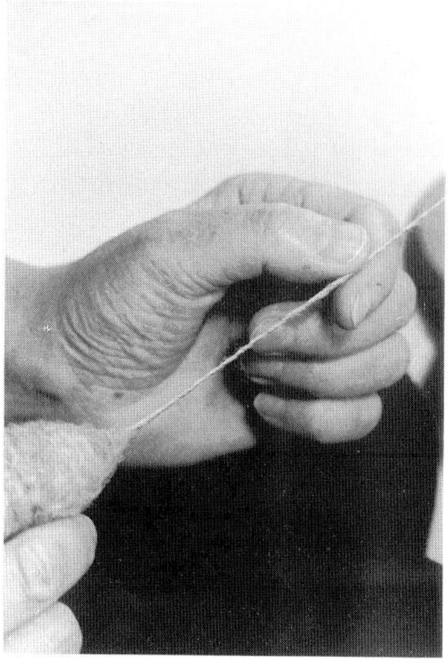

6.9 Fold the flick-carded or combed fibres over the forefinger of the back hand and spin with the wool drafting out from this fold.

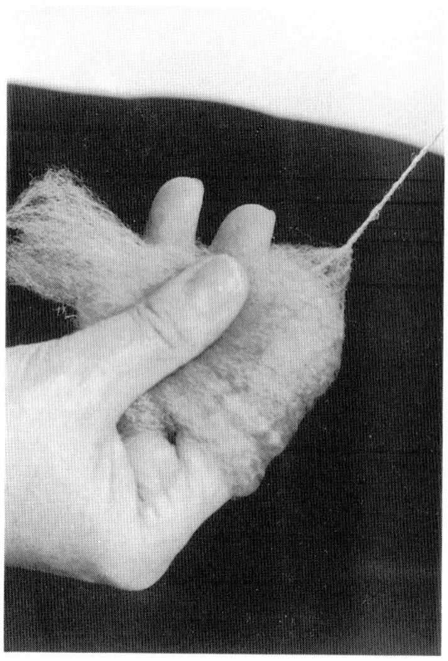

6.10 The thumb and second finger, by opening and closing, control the amount of wool pulled into the draft.

Results

Because the fibres are folded over they are not parallel, so the resulting yarn will probably be slightly softer and hairier than a true semi-woollen yarn. This method of holding the yarn can also be utilised with the short forward or backward draft to produce worsted yarn.

COMPARING DIFFERENT SKEINS

Wash the skeins in warm soapy water, rinse and dry in the open air, then lay them out close together to analyse the differences. Look at each skein and compare it with the checklist of results I have given in the last two chapters. Are your skeins the same as mine or are there differences? Try to see why any differences may have occurred. Was it the quality of the fleece? If a long-wool, lustrous fleece was chosen for the worsted skein, the worsted qualities will be enhanced. If a short-staple wool was spun, these qualities will be less evident.

Differences can also be due to your individual spinning skills. If you are a proficient worsted spinner your worsted skein will be fine but your woollen skein may be a bit peculiar. It takes some time to become proficient in all areas: practice is the only answer.

I often find when teaching that the most experienced spinners can produce four quite distinctive skeins. They are not only proficient in the spinning and preparation of their wool but are also fully conversant with the different wool types discussed in Chapter Two. This knowledge helps them to choose the correct type of wool for each spinning method and project.

Because handspun wool can be used in a wide variety of ways, the suggested uses for each type of yarn cover only a few garments in order to demonstrate the strong link between the yarn characteristics and the end product.

Of course, spinning does not end with these four yarn types: a huge variety is possible. For example, try spinning a worsted yarn from the fold, as described on page 108. This will result in a slightly softer worsted yarn. Experiment for yourself and see what types of yarn you can spin.

7 Spinning Bulky to Fine Yarn

A good spinner can spin any yarn size but there is much more to it than just changing the amount of wool fed into the drafting zone. When the yarn diameter changes so should the fleece type and the amount of twist. If you have read this book from the start you will know what I am talking about. However, in case you are, like me, a reader who dips into chapters seeking particular snippets of knowledge, I will bring all these factors together in this chapter.

There are two tables that will supply all the information you need to spin to a required size. Table 4.C, page 77, gives information on comparative spinning and plying twists to size of yarn. Appendix D will help you calculate the amount of yarn to feed into the orifice for each treadle. Your spinning rhythm will be easier if you spin with double this amount for two treadles. For example, if your fleece has 4 crimps per 2.5cm (1in), the singles should be spun with 6 twists per 2.5cm (1in). With a drive ratio of 7:1, you will see that the figures in Appendix D require you to feed in 3cm (1.25in) for each treadle or 6cm (2.5in) for two treadles.

Using the information in Chapter Four as a guide, spin about 5 metres (yards) of single yarn as a sample. Check the twists per 2.5cm (1in) as you spin by counting the twists on a doubled length, as in Photo 4.3. For the example in the previous paragraph you should be spinning with 6 twists per 2.5cm (1in). If not, change the drafting length slightly until it is correct. Remember that the doubled yarn untwists slightly as it twists back on itself, so if the doubled yarn gives about 5 twists you are correct. Less experienced spinners may need to spin more than 5m (5yd) to get this right.

Once you have the correct twist, check on the size of the yarn. Wrap the single around a ruler for 2.5cm (1in) and count the wraps: there should be approximately 12 in the above example. It is better to *under-estimate* the twists per cm (in) and *over-estimate* the wraps to allow for the bulk that will be added when washing.

All these figures can be a great help but it is your eye and plans for the yarn that are the most important. If you think the wool looks and feels too soft for the end use, add some more twist. If the yarn is too hard, reduce the twists. If it is too thin, add more wool into the drafting area. Your judgment is all-important.

If I am spinning yarn for a small project for which absolute accuracy is not essential I just plough ahead, spinning the singles, plying it with a third less twist and washing it. For large projects where I need absolute accuracy I spin and ply a small sample skein, wash it, and then decide if it is correct for what I had in mind.

SPINNING BULKY YARN

Bulky yarn is defined as having three or fewer twists per 2.5cm (1in) in the finished yarn (Chapter Two, page 31). Medium/bulky yarn has 4-6 twists per 2.5cm (1in) and should be lightweight. Although bulky yarn has very few twists, its long fibres of up to 18cm (7in) make it very strong.

Wool

Choose a fleece with 2-6 crimps per 2.5cm (1in). Samples A, E, I, J, L, P, R and T (in Chapter Two) are good examples.

Wheel

The drive ratio on your wheel should be in the range of 3:1 - 6:1. The orifice should be reasonably large in diameter: from 15mm (5/8 in) to 23mm (7/8 in) would be suitable. Some manufacturers have accessories such as a large flyer that can be placed on your spinning wheel to give this larger orifice and lower drive ratio, or there may be a choice of whorls.

The drive band should be thick enough to give you plenty of traction. If the groove on the wheel is wide enough, replace a fine band with a thicker one. The weight of the large bobbin and flyer common to most wheels with a low drive ratio requires this extra traction.

Spinning

Choose whichever spinning method is suitable for the end project as described in Chapters Five and Six. Jot down the number of crimps per 2.5cm (1in) in your fleece. Remember, you will be spinning the singles with two-thirds more twist than the crimps per 2.5cm (1in), so if you have a choice of drive ratios choose one as close to this twist count as possible.

SPINNING MEDIUM YARN

This yarn has 7-9 twists and 14-18 wraps per 2.5cm (1in) in the finished yarn. This is the most common yarn range, which is why many spinning wheels have at least one drive ratio in this range.

Wool

Choose a fleece that has 7-9 crimps to 2.5cm (1in), such as Samples B, K and N.

Wheel

Your wheel should have a drive ratio of between 6:1 and 10:1 and the orifice size should be 10-12mm (3/8-1/2in). The drive band should be of a medium thickness, which is the size usually supplied with the wheel.

Spinning

Again, choose the method suitable for the end use of the finished yarn. Set the drive ratio as close to the number of twists in the singles as possible. For example, in Sample B the crimp count is 7, so the singles should be spun with about 10 twists per 2.5cm (1in) and the drive ratio should be close to 10:1. The wraps per 2.5cm (1in) of the singles should be about 21. Check the twist and size of the yarn, then ply with two-thirds less twist – in this example this would be 7.

SPINNING FINE YARN

Medium/fine yarn has 10-12 twists and 20-24 wraps per 2.5cm (1in), and fine yarn more than 13 twists and 25 wraps per 2.5cm (1in).

Wool

Choose a fleece with more than 10 crimps per 2.5cm (1in), such as Sample C, G, M and S.

Wheel

Your wheel should have a drive ratio of 9:1 upwards and the orifice size should be 10-12 mm (3/8-1/2in). Have a fine drive band, and on a double-band wheel keep the tension light. If you have a single-drive flyer-lead wheel, have the brake band around the bobbin under a very light tension also. On a single-drive bobbin-lead wheel the brake band (often a leather strap) should be very loose and can usually be removed altogether. Spinning onto a half-filled bobbin will also help.

Spinning

Set the drive ratio as close to the number of twists in the singles as possible. For Sample C, with 15 crimps per 2.5cm (1in), this would be 22:1. The wraps per 2.5cm (1in) in this single yarn should be about 45. This is very fine and as not many wheels have this high a ratio so you will probably be using a wheel with a lower ratio and treadling fast while feeding in the yarn very slowly. To do this, your wheel needs to be running very smoothly and easily.

Check the twist and size of the yarn and spin a sample length as described earlier. Since many of the finer wools have very high bulk, as in Sample G, and will double in size with washing, it is wise to spin a small sample skein and wash it before spinning larger amounts.

Fine yarn can tangle when washing, so use only two arms of your niddy noddy when plying, or use a smaller niddy noddy to make smaller skeins.

> **VERY FINE YARN**
>
> Very fine yarns such as Merino need extra preparation (see Chapter One. page 27) and different spinning techniques. Again I would like to refer you to Margaret Stove's book, *Merino: Handspinning, Dyeing and Working with Merino and Superfine Wools*, where she describes in detail how to prepare and spin fine wools. She has allowed me to pass on a tip for spinning fine wool. She has found that because fine wools are spun with a very light tension, the crimp becomes trapped in the spun yarn. To prevent this, Margaret spins worsted yarn with the wool under tension as it enters the drafting zone.

MEASURING YARN LENGTH

It is very useful to know how much yarn you have spun and nothing is more frustrating then running out of yarn before a project is finished. Going back and spinning the extra amount months later can result in marked differences in size and twist.

Use your niddy noddy to measure the amount of wool. Run a length of wool around the niddy noddy to find out how much it holds with each turn. Remember to allow about 5 per cent extra for the contraction that will take place when you remove the skein from the niddy noddy if you want complete accuracy. My niddy noddy holds 182cm (2 yd) each turn, so 100 turns gives me 182 metres (200 yards). This measurement was essential when I was spinning the warp and weft yarn for Project Two. As I was dyeing part of the warp I also needed to know how much to dye, and having skeins of 182m (200yd) made the sums easy.

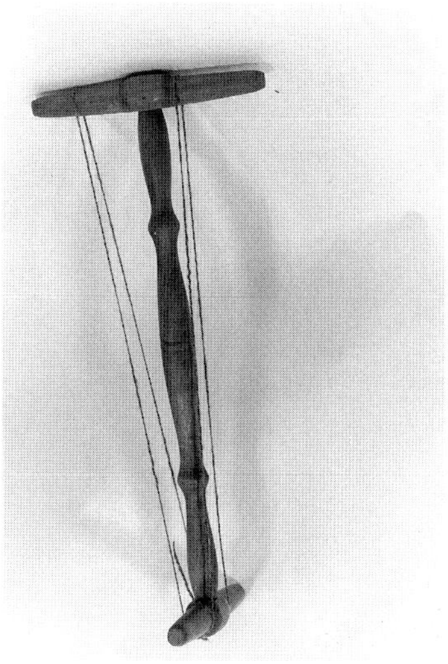

7.1 Using the niddy noddy to measure spun yarn

CONSISTENT SPINNING

Now you know how to spin with a pre-determined amount of twist and the correct size for that twist count, it is a simple step to learn to spin consistently. It is almost impossible to spin enough for one project in one spinning session – it can in fact take months or even years. Now you can learn to spin yarn of the same quality every time you pick it up and whatever your mood.

Find the correct size and twist of the yarn you want for a particular project. (Well-organised spinners have notebooks and files for all this information.) Make a note of the number of treadles and the length of the draft for both singles and plied yarn. For example, it could be 5cm (2in) to two treadles for the singles, and 8cm (3in) to two treadles for the plying. Then make a note of the amount of wool fed into each draft. This can be done by taping a short piece of the spun singles to a card (of contrasting colour), making sure the yarn cannot untwist. To be more accurate, a sample of the singles and plied yarn can be wound around a ruler for 2.5cm (1in). A doubled piece of the singles, knotted or taped to prevent untwisting, can also be kept as a guide.

Each time you sit at the wheel to spin that particular yarn, spend the first five minutes comparing the new yarn to your notes and samples and adjust your spinning until they match. After five minutes, spinning to that twist and size becomes second nature.

This is also a great help if you need to go back several months later to match a piece of yarn for mending, or to repeat a yarn for another project.

FELTING IN SKEINED YARN

If you find the yarn is felting, even with gentle washing, check the twist/yarn size ratio. The yarn may have the wrong number of twists to the thickness of the yarn. For example, if a fine Merino with 15 crimps to 2.5cm (1in) is spun into a thick yarn with 7 twists per 2.5cm (1in) the resulting yarn will not have enough twist and may well felt in the washing stages. If you use this yarn in a sweater or jersey the felting and shrinkage will continue with wear and further washing. If this Merino had been spun with 15 twists in the finished yarn there would be no felting.

PROJECTS FOR YOUR HANDSPUN YARN

The projects that follow, both woven and knitted, are designed to give you a wide range of articles to make with your fleece and yarn. Choose the ones that use the most common type of fleece for your area, and then branch out and try different types to extend your spinning range. Spinning the quantities needed for these projects will give you the practice needed to improve your techniques and you will also have some interesting articles to show for your efforts.

Part Four
PROJECTS

PERENDALE

1 Woven Fleece Rug

This rug is woven with two different fleeces, one dark brown and one white, with the colours merging in the centre. It could also be woven on one colour. The strong textural quality of this rug favours a strong simple design.

It should be woven on a strong counter-march or counter-balance floor loom, 102cm (40in) or more in width.

Materials

Warp: Linen rug warp, about 10-12 wraps to 2.5cm (1in).
Weft: Wool with a long staple and 2-4 crimps per 2.5cm (1in). Samples E, J, and R are good examples of this type of wool. The wool should be lustrous and strong. English Leicester, Border Leicester and Lincoln are some suitable breed types. See instructions below for washing this fleece.
Binder weft: Two-ply rug wool in a matching colour
Sett: 4 ends per 2.5cm (1in)

Dimensions

Width:

Finished rug:	100cm	(39in)
Add draw-in:	2cm	(1in)
Total width of warp:	**102cm**	**(40in)**

Length:

Finished rug:	150cm	(59in)
Warp take-up:	15cm	(6in)
Fringe allowance:	30cm	(12in)
Loom wastage:	61cm	(24in)
Total length of warp:	**256cm**	**(101in**

Total number of warp ends: 160 + 4 selvedge = 164
Threading: Straight draw: 1, 2, 3, 4
Sley: With an eight dent reed, sley one end in every second dent
Selvedge: Double the outside two ends on each side
Weight of finished rug: 5kg (12lb)

Washing the fleeces

Fleeces should be washed first. This rug usually takes two fleeces weighing 2-3kg (4$^1/_2$-6$^1/_2$lb) each. Divide the fleeces into smaller portions of about 1kg (2$^1/_4$lb) and soak each portion in warm water for at least an hour. A really dirty fleece may need soaking for up to 12 hours with one or two changes of water to loosen the worst of the dirt. Then dissolve about half a cup of cleansing agent in enough

Fleece rug designed and woven by Anne Field

hot water to cover the wool. I use a liquid floor cleaner that contains ammonia.

Soak the fleece in this solution for about an hour, then rinse two or three times until the fleece is clean and the water clear. Do not move the fleece around in the hot water as this will cause felting.

Put the wool in bags in the spin cycle of your washing machine to remove most of the water. Then lay it on netting or a slatted table outside to dry. Do not dry the wool in a tumble-dryer or it will tangle and felt.

Drying the wool outside on hot sunny days is best, but in the winter I sometimes use a rack over a slow storage-type heater. The house does smell rather woolly but is better than waiting weeks for a fine day. A mothproofing agent can be added to the last rinse.

Even in warm weather it can take two or three days to wash and dry two fleeces. I now wash them when the weather is right and store them ready for weaving. This way I can begin the weaving part regardless of the weather.

Putting on the warp

The linen warp is strong and inelastic and requires a special technique. All the ends must be wound under tension or the warp will become uneven and sag during weaving.

Wind the warp with one cross, attach the crossed end of the warp to the warp roller, put cross sticks in the warp and place the ends in the raddle. Lay the rest of the warp over the breast beam and onto the floor in front of the loom.

The cross sticks are attached to the loom to prevent them from winding onto the warp roller with the warp. Wind the warp through the cross sticks for one complete turn of the warp roller, without any tension on the warp. Then each bout of the warp is tightened (a bout is a group of about eight warp ends). Stand at the front of the loom, take these eight ends and wind them around a metal rod two or three times. Grasp this rod firmly and lean back, tipping all your body weight onto your heels to tighten those eight warp ends. Note how they tighten all the way around the warp roller.

Repeat this tensioning, pulling each bout in turn across the warp width. Because the weight pulling on each bout, your total body weight, remains constant, each bout is given exactly the same tension. Wind another complete turn of the warp roller and repeat the process. Place slats of wood or metal between the warp layers.

Weaving

Weave a narrow heading and place a stick across the warp to give you something to beat against. Place the washed fleece in baskets or boxes beside the loom. Fill a rug shuttle with the rug wool in a matching colour, and weave a heading for 10 picks. This heading should be woven as a correct weft-face weave; i.e. let the weft lie loosely in the shed, bubble it, change sheds and beat, in plain weave. Finish with this binder weft at the right side. Do not hemstitch the end. The warp tension should be very tight.

First fleece pick

Take a handful of fleece wool, pull it out to the required thickness and lay it in the next shed from left to right. You may need to experiment with the amount of wool required. Each length of wool is overlapped with the next. Halfway across the rug, change to the other fleece colour

Do not try to smooth out the staples or lay them parallel, but allow the wool to retain its natural springiness. Lay in the wool across the entire warp width, leaving about 5cm (2in) protruding at each selvedge, change sheds and beat hard with two or three sharp beats. Take the protruding ends, twist them between the thumb and forefinger and insert them back into the shed. This twisting gives the rug a firm edge.

On the right side carry the binder weft up the selvedge by taking the twisted fleece around the binder.

Second pick

Lay the next fleece pick into the shed in the same manner, from right to left, overlapping the fleece on the right side with the twisted ends from the previous pick. Let the fleece protrude from the left selvedge, change sheds and beat heavily.

Laying in the wool

Twisting the selvedge ends

Beating

Third pick

Twist the fleece protruding from the left selvedge back into the new shed and overlap it with the next fleece pick, which is laid in from left to right. Leave the fleece protruding from the right selvedge, change sheds and beat heavily.

Fourth pick

Repeat from right to left, remembering to carry up the binder weft on the right side. Each fleece pick is overlapped with the twisted wool on one side and protrudes on the other.

Fifth and sixth picks

Weave these picks with the binder weft, remembering to bubble the weft to prevent the rug edges from pulling in. Close the shed and beat very heavily two or three times.

Now beat with the weighted rug-beater. The woven portion will immediately reduce to about half its size, just when you thought you were progressing so well. The weft binder does not strengthen the rug in any way; it simply holds the fleece wool in place while you use the rug beater. Remove the stick between the heading and the beginning of the warp.

This is the technique for the entire rug. You will find the loom moving towards you with the heavy beating and it may help to anchor it in some way. Because the heavy beating is tiring, I usually weave a rug in three or four sessions and it takes me a total of about five or six hours.

The end of the rug is finished with the same narrow heading as the beginning of the rug. Remove the rug from the loom.

Finishing the fringes

There are many ways of finishing the fringes. It is important that the linen warp is strengthened in some way and I usually finish the ends with a double Damascus edge, as shown in Peter Collingwood's *Technique of Rug Weaving*, and then plait or twist the ends before finishing the raw ends with an overhand knot.

If you are a tidy weaver the rug surface will not need trimming but long fleece ends should be cut off. I recommend that the rug be turned once a week to give equal wear on both sides and allow the flattened ends to spring back up.

Test the rug for firmness by trying to poke your finger through the weave. It should meet with quite a lot of resistance.

2 Woven Skirt Fabric

The aim here was to weave a hard-wearing worsted material that looked handspun. To keep the slight colour irregularities that are a feature of handspinning I mixed up the fleece colours as I spun and did not blend the yarn before flick carding. This mixing gave the blue dyed areas slight irregularities in colour also.

Skirt fabric designed, spun and woven by Anne Field

It is exciting to design a fabric to match a garment design. This fabric was produced with the gored skirt in mind and was planned with the stripes becoming the vertical, herringbone patterns in the finished skirt.

The fabric is woven in plain weave and could be done on a four-shaft loom. It was woven to a width of 118cm (46½in) but a smaller loom could be used as the gores are not very wide. I used handspun for both warp and weft but you could also use a millspun warp and handspun weft.

Materials

Yarn size: 12 wraps to 2.5cm (1in) unwashed or 10 wraps per 2.5cm (1in) washed.

Fleece: Grey Romney fleece (sample A, page 37). This fleece has 4 crimps per 2.5cm (1in). To make a hard-wearing solid yarn, spin worsted (see pages 89-97), with 9 twists to 2.5cm (1in) in the finished yarn. This is slightly more than twice the number of twists a spinner would normally put into a fleece with this crimp measurement.

Warp spinning

1975m (2160yd) are needed for the warp, so allow for shrinkage and spin 2195m (2400yd).

The shrinkage rate is low (about 4%), as the yarn is spun worsted. Use the niddy noddy to measure the length, as described on page 113. This accuracy is necessary particularly for the dyeing. The yarn should be washed (see page 26), dried, then dyed.

Dyeing the warp

Five hanks measuring 183cm (200yd) each are dyed medium blue (I used Earth Palette cold water dyes). Because each hank is the same length you can measure out an equal amount of dye for each hank. One hank is dyed dark blue. The other six are left undyed.

Weft spinning

1609m (1760yd) are spun for the weft which is not dyed

***Warp sett*:** 10 ends per 2.5cm (1in)

Width: 118cm (46 1/2in)

***Length*:** Total warp length: 4.2m (4 1/2yds). This allows for a shrinkage and take-up of between 8 per cent and 10 per cent

***Threading*:** Straight draw, 1, 2, 3, 4

***Winding the warp with stripes*:** 14 ends grey, one end dark blue, 14 medium blue, one dark blue. This repeat is continued across the warp, ending with a grey stripe (4cm (1 1/2in) stripes). The colours are joined at either the beginning or end of the warp to avoid knots.

As this is a wide warp it should be wound in two sections and with two crosses to prevent any rubbing of the warp as it is put onto the loom.

Weaving

Weave a heading, then begin with the grey weft yarn. Concentrate on a balanced weave in these first picks, with 10 picks to 2.5cm (1in). Stop and measure with a tape measure until you have the correct beat. I wound the weft yarn onto six pirns, one from each hank, and mixed these pirns as I wove to further mix the colours.

Weave the complete warp, putting a tie at the selvedge every 50cm (18in) to mark your progress. Every now and then stop and measure the picks to 2.5cm (1in) to make sure you are beating consistently.

If the warp is spread out over four shafts it should not stick together, but change sheds when the beater is at the fell of the cloth to clear the shed.

When the complete length is woven, hem stitch or oversew the end to prevent fraying, then cut the weaving from the loom, leaving a short fringe.

Finishing the cloth

There is a particular way to finish worsted cloth and if you do not do it correctly all that careful spinning will be wasted. Mend any mistakes, such as skipped threads, then press *before* washing. Use a steam iron but do not rub the iron over the fabric: press then lift the iron over the entire fabric. Wash the fabric in a bath of hot soapy water, keeping it under tension throughout. I did this by stapling each end of the fabric, near the hemstitching, onto a roller. Most of the fabric was wound onto one roller.

Washing the fabric is a two-person job. We placed the rollers under the hot, soapy water in the bath, and rolled the fabric several times from one roller to another, trying to keep some tension on the fabric. This is only an approximation of the commercial finishing process for finishing worsted fabric, but the end result was satisfactory – apart from the sore knees.

The fabric is then rolled around a slatted drying roller and you should carefully smooth out any wrinkles or they will be permanent. Re-roll the fabric a couple of times, reversing the length, while it is drying. Press the fabric again. It should feel smooth and silky.

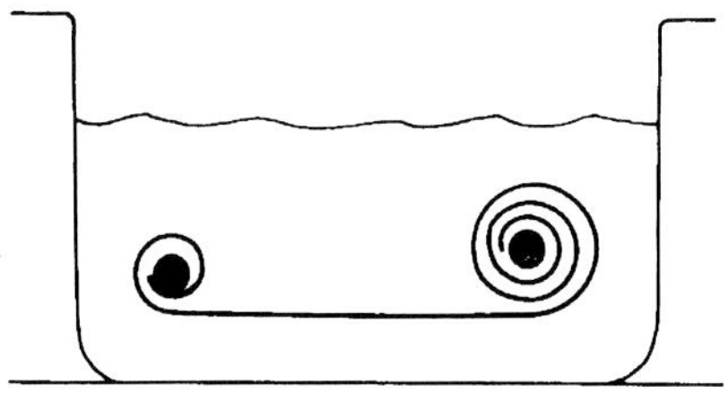

Washing worsted fabric under tension

Making up the skirt

A six-gored skirt pattern was chosen for this fabric so the stripes would appear as large, vertical, herringbone patterns. The pattern is not included but you can buy it. Remember to weave more fabric than stated on the pattern because matching the stripes uses up extra. The skirt is lined with a half-lining to prevent bagginess. The raw edges should be overlocked or zig-zagged to prevent fraying.

3 Woven Waistcoat

This waistcoat has a striped yoke and integral striped front edgings; the whole article being woven and made up in one piece. Handspun wool is used in the weft and millspun in the warp. The jacket is woven sideways, with the warp running horizontally across the jacket width.

Woven waistcoat designed, spun and woven by Ann Mulley

Materials

Warp and weft: 250g (9oz) Pure Colonial millspun Wool, 9500m per kg (4722yd per lb)
Weft: 100g (3.6oz) handspun, Sample K, page 47
1 reel black 40s sewing cotton
Cotton/polyester for lining

Spinning for weft
Finished yarn size: 18 wraps per 2.5cm (1in)
Twist: 10 twists per 2.5cm (1in)
Amount: 100g (3.6oz) handspun from Jacob X Suffolk shearling fleece
Spinning method: Semi-worsted singles, spun from rovings
Millspun weft: 100g (3.6oz) of the millspun was used for the edging

Warp

Amount: 150g (5.4oz) two-ply Pure Colonial millspun for the warp stripes. Three ends of the yarn were used as one in the stripes that form the design of the yoke. 250g (9oz) for the body of the waistcoat. Two ends of two-ply brown millspun were used as one in the remaining warp.

Width:	Warp stripes	27cm	(10½in)
	Body of waistcoat	50cm	(19½in)
	Total width	**77cm**	**(30in)**

Sett: In a 50/10 reed (50 dents to 10cm, 12 dents per inch), sett the warp stripes at three ends in each dent to make the yoke slightly heavier than the body of the waistcoat, that is 36 ends per 2.5cm (1in). The body of the waistcoat is sett at two ends in each dent, that is 24 ends per 2.5cm (1in).

Length: 2.3m (2½yd)

Winding the warp

The colour order in the pictured waistcoat is as follows:12 brown, 12 maroon, 6 orange/red, 12 red, 24 dark red. This is repeated five times. Remember the stripes, when threaded through the heddles and reed, will have three ends together counting as one warp end. Make the first brown stripe at the selvedge triple the width of the others (36 ends) for the seam allowance.

The remaining warp, for the body of the waistcoat, is wound in the brown millspun, for 50cm (19½in). Wind 24 ends for each 2.5cm (1in) and this will be doubled in the heddles and reed.

Weaving

Weave 1.5cm (½in) in black 40s sewing cotton in a firm plain weave for turnings at centre edge. This will prevent a bulky seam.

Weave the stripes for 3cm (1¼in), in 2/2 twill, using the millspun wool in its original two-ply. Follow the same colour sequence as in the warp stripes but without the brown. Beat this well to form a firm, weft-face edging braid for the centre front of the waistcoat.

Weave 127cm (50in) of plain weave, using the handspun wool at 9 picks per 2.5cm (1in). Then repeat the weft-face border, reversing the colour sequence of the first braid.

Weave the final 1.5cm (½in) in the sewing cotton, in plain weave, well beaten as previously.

Finishing

Remove the fabric from the loom and machine stitch along both cotton edges. Press the fabric with a hot dry iron between a wet towel and a damp muslin cloth. Dry lying flat. The finished size should be 71cm x 115cm (28in x 45in). It is best to machine zig-zag the fabric before cutting. Using the pattern on p.126 as a guide, mark the neck, shoulder lines and armholes. Cut out the lining to match the waistcoat before assembling the garment.

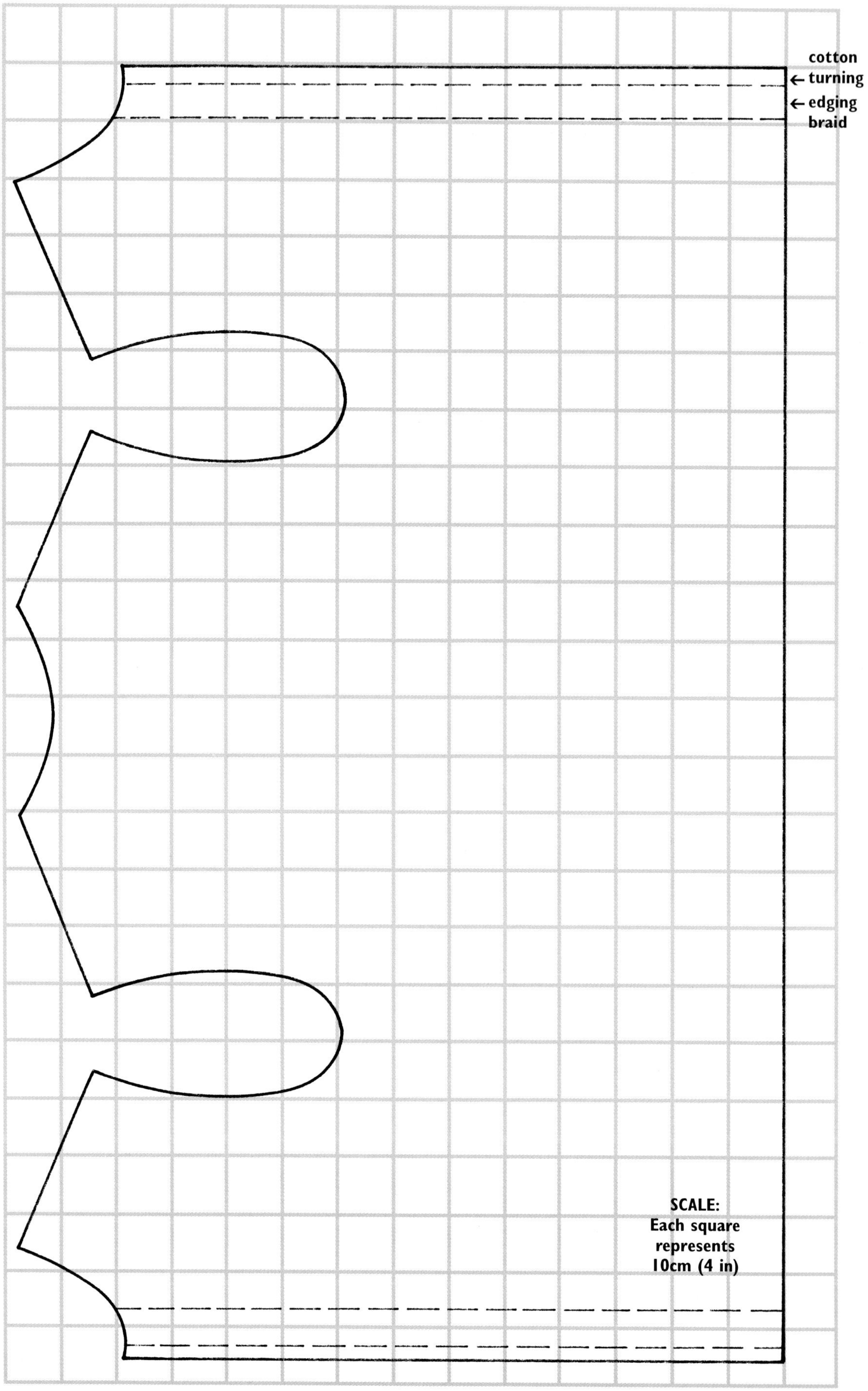
cotton
turning
edging
braid
SCALE:
Each square
represents
10cm (4 in)

4 KNITTED MITTENS

This mitten pattern has a long history. New Zealander Meg Anderson adapted the pattern from one she saw in a Norwegian magazine. Then Marion Valentine adapted Meg's pattern and it was published in the *Web* in June 1991. The mittens were further adapted and spun and knitted by Beth Halliburton.

The cap is very useful. It can be buttoned down out of the way to free your fingers, and then pulled over the fingers for added warmth. Try your own adaptations. Each finger can be knitted a different colour! The mittens are designed to fit an average size adult hand.

Materials

50g (2oz) semi-worsted or semi-woollen spun yarn with 14-16 wraps and 7-8 twists per 2.5cm (1in)
Small amounts of a different-coloured yarn for the fingers
4 needles size 3.25mm (metric), 10 (English), 3 (American)
4 needles size 3.5mm (metric), 9 (English), 4 (American)
2 buttons

Pattern

With main colour and 3.25mm needles, cast on 48 stitches. Divide evenly onto three needles and rib for 8cm (3in). Change to 3.5mm needles and knit 2cm (3/4in) in stocking stitch.

Increase for thumb

Knit 2 sts and put in marker, increase 1 st, knit 1, increase 1 and put in another marker. Complete round. Thereafter, increase at each marker every third round until there are 15 sts between markers. Transfer these 15 sts to a helping thread that will be removed later when the thumb is knitted. Knit a further 3cm (1 1/4in) on remaining 48 sts. Transfer these 48 sts onto a contrasting holding thread with the gap at the thumb end.

First finger (index)

Knit the first 6 sts from the holding thread, cast on 2, knit the last 6 sts from the holding thread. Divide these 14 sts on three needles and change colour. Knit in a small circle until the work reaches the first finger joint (about 8 rounds). Cast off.

Second finger (long)

Using main colour, pick up 2 sts from the base of first finger, knit 7 sts off the holding thread. Cast on 2, knit 7 sts off the other end of holding thread. Divide these 18 sts on three needles, change colour and knit in a small circle to the length of the second finger joint (about 10 rounds). Cast off.

Third finger (ring):
Using main colour, pick up 2 sts from the base of the 2nd finger, knit 6 sts off holding thread, cast on 2, knit 6 off the other end of the holding thread. Divide these 16 sts on three needles. Change colour and knit in a small circle to the length of the third finger joint (about 8 rounds). Cast off.

Fourth finger (little):
Using main colour, pick up 2 sts from the base of the third finger, knit 10 sts off holding thread. Divide these 12 sts on three needles, change colour and knit in a small circle to length of finger joint (about 6 rounds). Cast off.

Thumb:
Using main colour, pick up the 15 sts on the thumb holding thread, pick up 2 sts from the base of the thumb, twisting them to avoid a hole. Divide these 17 sts on three needles and knit until the thumb measures about 6cm (2^{1}/4ins), (12-14 rounds). Decrease each row by knitting 2, knitting 2 together for 2 rounds. Break of wool, thread through stitches, draw up and finish off.

Glove cap:
Using main colour and three 2.5mm needles, cast on 28 sts and rib for 2cm (^{3}/4in). Change to stocking stitch and 3.5mm needles and pick up 28 sts across the back of hand where the fingers begin. Divide these 56 sts onto three needles and knit in the round until the cap covers the little finger (15 rounds). Decrease 4 sts evenly spaced every following round until 8 sts remain. Break off wool, leaving a 46cm (18in) end. Thread this through the last 8 sts and crochet a small loop for the button.

Finishing*:*
No sewing is needed. Fasten all threads, sew cap ribbing to each side of mitten and sew button firmly to back of mitten to hold the cap down when not in use.

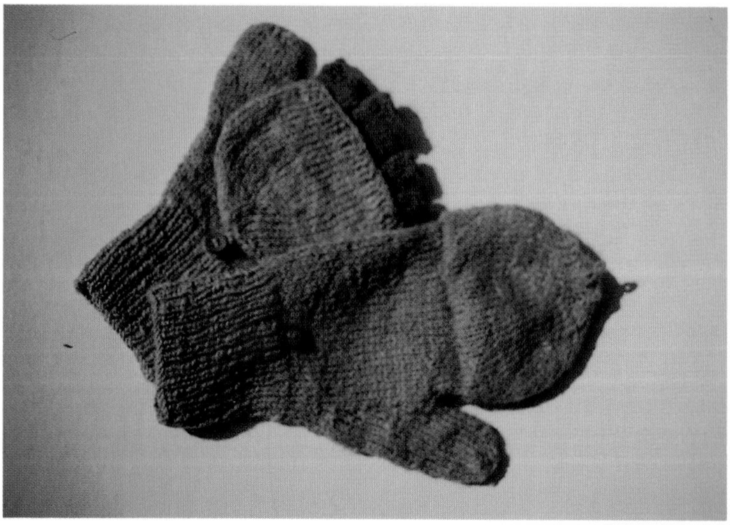

5 Child's Handwoven Jacket

This is a light, attractive, warm jacket made from handspun yarn which is hard-wearing and not too bulky for the small frame of a young person. The weave structure is a textured surface weave that allows the handspun yarn to remain on the surface, with a strong binder thread making a firm but light fabric. As this cloth is only 46cm (18in) wide, it can be woven on a narrow table loom.

A child's handwoven jacket featuring handspun yarn, which was designed, spun and woven by Alison Graham

Size

80cm (32in) chest
36cm (14in) underarm seam
61cm (24in) centre back seam

Materials

Warp:

Fine millspun 110T/2 (2/16) 100% wool dyed teal (A, below right)

Weft:

Binder: same as warp

Pattern yarn:

500m (545yd) approximately 150g (6oz), handspun from a commercially dyed and blended fleece wool, similar to and from the same source as Sample O, page 51. This handspun singles (B, below right) is spun into a bead yarn (D) on a millspun bouclé (C).

Spinning for the weft

Fleece:

Romney/Dorset hogget fleece with 7 crimps per 2.5cm (1in). The average staple length is 9cm ($3^1/2$in).

Finished yarn size

12 wraps and 8 twists per 2.5cm (1in), Z twist

Spinning method

Semi-worsted or woollen spinning. To create a soft, textured yarn that is both thick and light, spin a bead yarn (D, right). The fine millspun bouclé is dyed a deep burgundy colour, but only the woollen core of the millspun takes the dye, leaving the loops of synthetic yarn white.

To make a bead yarn, hold the core yarn tightly and coming straight out from the orifice of the spinning wheel. Allow the handspun yarn to spiral itself gently onto the core yarn from a right angle so it wraps itself around the core, creating a bobble effect. Try to be consistent with the number of wraps of handspun over the core

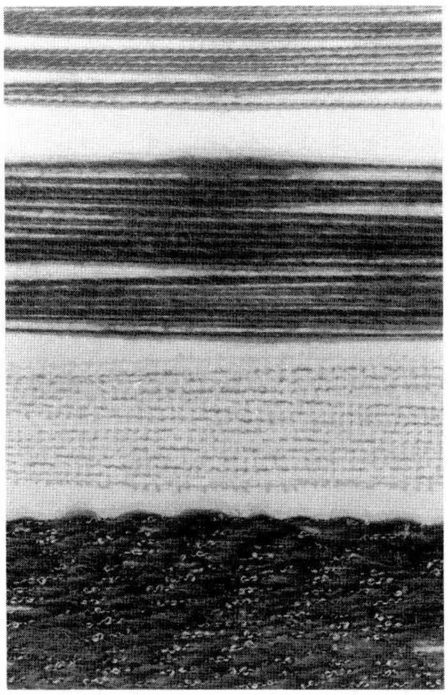

Samples of yarn used

per 2.5cm (1in). Three is ideal. The finished yarn is left to set before washing and weaving.

Dyeing

Warp: 100g (3.6oz), 1128m (1225yd)
Binder: 60g (2.1oz)
Knitted bands: 60g (2.1oz)
Dye this 220g (8oz) of the millspun yarn teal blue

Weaving

Warp: Sett: 18 ends per 2.5cm (1in)
Width: 46cm (18in)

Length

Finished fabric:	2.4m	(94in)
10% shrinkage and waste:	25cm	(10in)
Loom waste:	75cm	(30in)
Total warp length:	**3.4m**	**(134in)**

Weaving draft

The tabby binder in this pattern, woven in the same yarn as the warp, is on shafts 2, and 1 & 3.
Weft: Bead yarn

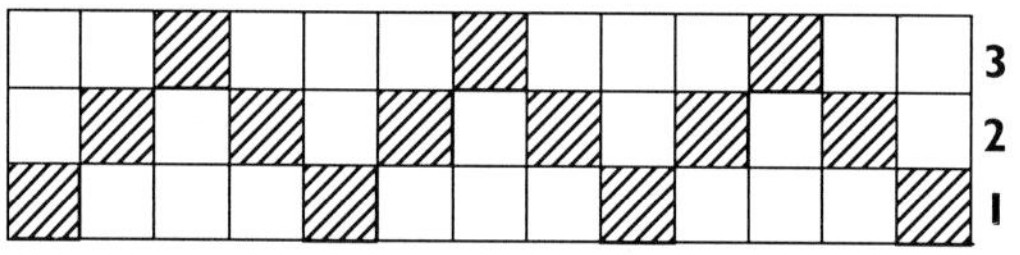

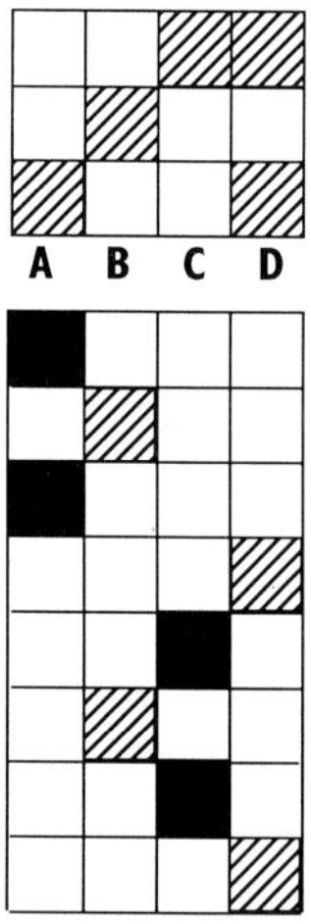

Fine yarn

Bead yarn

Binder: Same as warp

Weave a 5cm (2in) heading, then begin weaving, following the draft and checking that there are 18 picks per 2.5cm (1in). Mark the edge every 50cm (18in) to check your progress.

Finishing the cloth

After cutting the cloth from the loom, wash it on a gentle cycle in the washing machine for about five minutes. Rinse and spin dry, then dry around a slatted roller or over several lines of a clothesline. Do not press the fabric or you will flatten the texture, but take it to a dry cleaner for steaming.

Making up

This ethnic-style pattern is very suitable for children as it is easy to wear and to get out of in a hurry. The style works well in many sizes, and the proportions remain constant.

Fold the body piece in half to find the centre back and mark with a pin. Now fold the fronts to the centre to meet the centre back mark. Mark your side 'seams'. Fold the sleeve length in half lengthwise and measure it to find the centre point. Carefully cut *one layer of fabric only* up this centre line to the fold. This is the rest of the front opening.

To make the front neck shape, measure 6cm (2 1/2in) out either side of the cut along the folded edge and also 6cm (2 1/2in) down the cut. Now carefully cut a curve between the two points. You may like to make a paper cut-out first, 12cm (5in) across the top and 6cm (2 1/2in) deep, and copy this onto the fabric.

Cut the back neck between the two points only 1cm (1/2in) below the fold line. At this point it is advisable to overlock or zig-zag all cut edges to prevent fraying. Attach sleeves to body piece, making sure the sleeves join at the side 'seams'. Join hood top and shape through a slight curve for a better fit.

Knitted bands

These can be knitted by machine or by hand. The lower band should measure 60cm (23in) long (it may be necessary to have this made in segments) and 14cm (5 1/2in) deep. The cuffs are 26cm (10in) long, and 14cm (5 1/2in) deep. A narrow strip 1cm (1/2in) wide and 100cm (39in) long is used for neatening the hood edge and covering the centre seam in the hood.

Cover the hood seam and neaten the front edge with the knitted strip. Attach the hood and bind the edge, or attach it with a flat french seam. Sew the front fobs onto the knitted band and then machine sew the lower band onto the jacket, gently stretching it evenly around the hemline. Insert the zip and hand neaten. Machine-sew on the cuffs and hand-neaten.

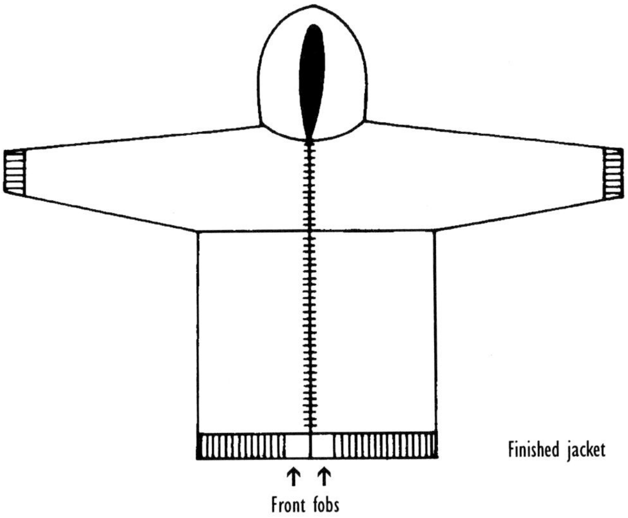

Finished jacket

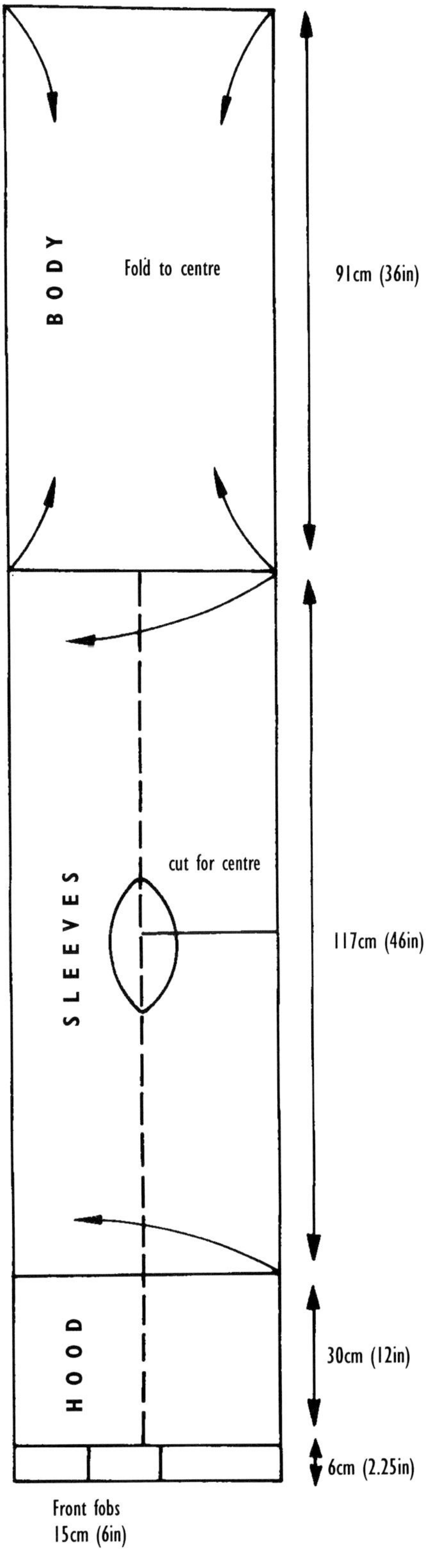

Cutting layout

6 Knitted Hood

A knitted hood spun by Anne Field and knitted by Alice McElroy

This knitted hood, wimple or snood (it has lots of names) is very warm and flattering. It would fit an average-size head.

Materials

150g (6oz) yarn, spun woollen. The 2-ply yarn measures 11-12 wraps and 5 twists per 2.5cm. It was spun from a Romney/Dorset fleece, Sample O, page 51.
Circular needle, size 4.00mm (metric), 8 (English), 5 (American).

Knitting

Cast on 136 sts, taking care not to twist cast-on edge. Tie first stitch with contrasting thread to mark beginning of each round. Knit 2, purl 2, repeat to end of round. Continue in 2/2 rib for 50cm (20in). Cast off loosely in rib.

Variations

There are many variations possible with this pattern. The hood can be knitted in stripes. If the tube (which is all it is) is knitted as a mobius strip (with a twist), it sits very well under the chin as a neat pleat forms. The twist can be done as you cast on, or the hood can be knitted on two needles and the twist put in as you sew the join together.

Another possibility is for the tube to be knitted in two sections, half the stitches in each portion on two needles each, for 12cm (5in). Then complete the hood on the circular needle. This leaves a slit in the tube and when the hood is worn, with the slit under the chin, the two edges from a collar, which also sits well.

7 Knitted New Zealand Guernsey

This worsted guernsey uses the traditional patterns of 'trees and bars', 'anchor', 'rope' and 'rigs and furs' (ridges and furrows). The colour is dark grey rather than the more common navy.

A New Zealand guernsey, spun, knitted and designed by Pat Atwell

Size

Chest: 92cm (36in)
Length from back neck: 56cm (22in)
Sleeve length, from underarm: 48cm (19in)
For larger or smaller sizes adjust the number of moss sts either side of 'seam' sts.

Materials

Circular needle size 2.25mm (metric), 13 (English), 0 (American)
Set of 4 needles size 2.25mm (metric), 13 (English), 0 (American)
600g (22oz) worsted-spun yarn from a grey Romney fleece, with three crimps per 2.5cm (1in) The yarn was spun with 14 wraps and 5 twists per 2.5cm (1in)

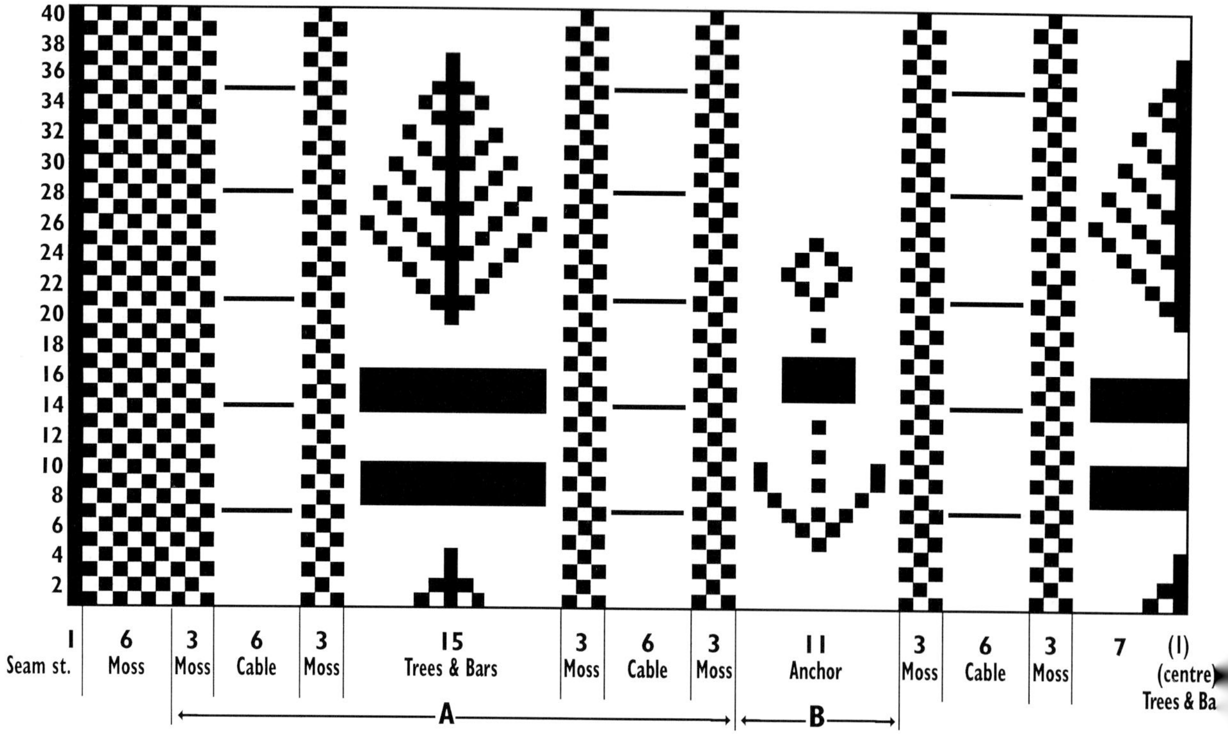

Pattern continues across pages.

■ = 1 purl stitch
——— = cross cables

Casting on and off in traditional guernseys is often done with doubled wool for strength; this is optional, as are side vents at the bottom of the body.

Tension

8 sts to 2.5cm (1in)

Abbreviations

K = knit; P = purl; M = moss st; R = round or row; st = stitch; stst = stocking stitch; cc = cross cable; decr = decrease; incr = increase; tog = together; RSF = right side facing.

Front and back

Cast on 304 sts on the circular needle.
First round rib: *K2, P2, repeat from * to end.
Repeat R 1 for 5.5cm (2 1/4in) or as required. K 4 rounds stst having one P st as a seam st each side. Place initials in P sts if required in the next 9 rounds. K 6 rounds.

Begin pattern as follows:

Round 1: M6 sts beg with P1, *P1, K1, P1, K6, P1, K1, P1, K5, (P1, K1) twice, P1, K5, P1, K1, P1, K6, P1, K1, P1, K11. Repeat from * until 7 sts short of halfway, M6 (beg with P1), P1 (seam st). Work other half of round as above.
Round 2: M6, *P1, K1, P1, K6, P3, (K6, M3) twice, K11. Repeat from * to 7 sts short of halfway, M6, P1. Work other half of round the same.
Round 3: M6, *M3, K6, M3, K7, P1, K7, M3, K6, M3, K11. Repeat from * to 7 sts short of halfway, M6, P1. Work other half of round the same.
Round 4: As R3.
Round 5: M6 (Side border);
*M3, K6, M3, K15, M3, K6, M3 (Trees and Bars (A))
K5, P1, K5 (Anchors (B)). Repeat from * etc.

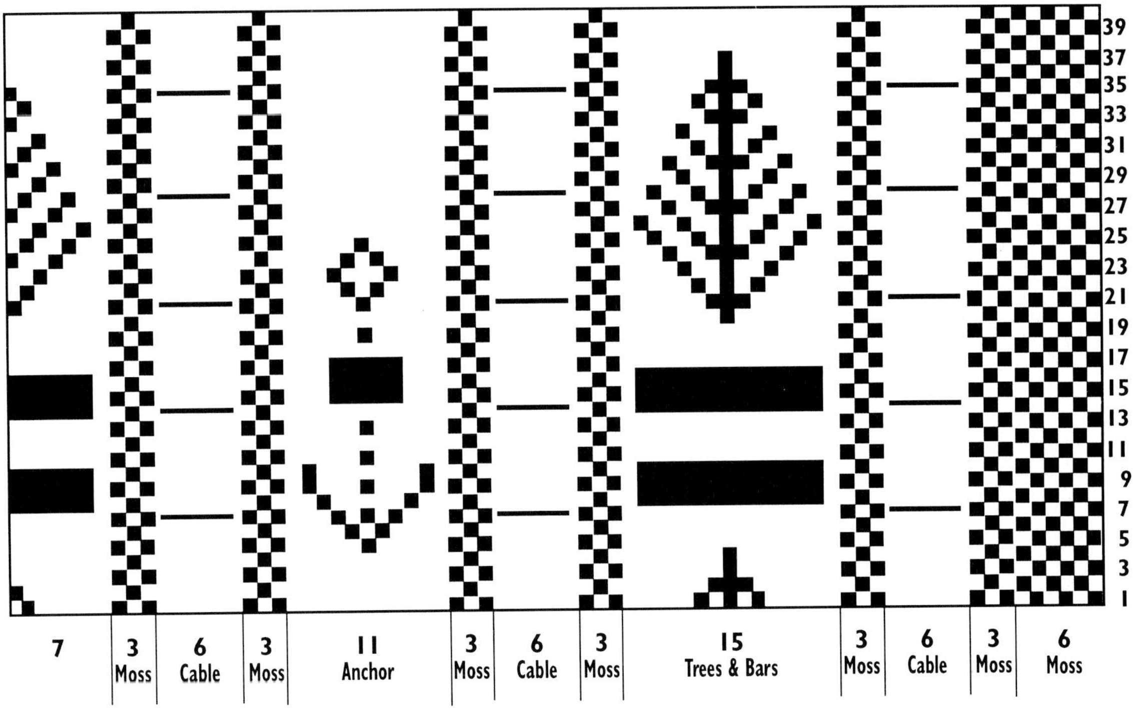

Continue working side borders, Trees & Bars (A), Anchors (B), and seam sts as in diagram until Round 63, 23-24cm (9-9 1/2in), beg of underarm gussets; CC every 7th round and maintaining the M borders as follows:

(Instructions now given for only A & B)

R6 A: as R5; B: K4, P1, K1, P1, K4.
R7 A: as R5 but CC; B: K3, P1, K1, P1, K1, P1, K3.
R8 A: M3, K6, M3; K1, P13, K1; M3, K6, M3; B: K2, P1, K5, P1, K2.
R9 A: as R8; B: K1, P1, K3, P1, K3, P1, K1.
R10 A: as R8; B: K1, P1, K7, P1, K1.
R11 A: M3, K6, M3; K15; M3, K6, M3; B: K5, P1, K5.
R12 A: as R11; B: K11.
R13 A: as R11; B: K5, P1, K5.
R14 A: M3, CC, M3; K1, P13, K1; M3, CC, M3; B: K11.
R15 A: as R14 (no CC); B: K3, P5, K3.
R16 A: as R15; B: K3, P5, K3.
R17 A: M3, K6, M3; K15; M3, K6, M3; B: K3, P5, K3.
R18 A: as R17; B: K11.
R19 A: as R17; B: K5, P1, K5.
R20 A: M3, K6, M3; K7, P1, K7; M3, K6, M3; B: K11.
R21 A: M3, CC, M3; K6, P3, K6; M3, CC, M3; B: K5, P1, K5.
R22 A: M3, K6, M3; K5, M5 (start P), K5; M3, K6, M3; B: K4, P1, K1, P1, K4.
R23 A: M3, K6, M3; K4, (P1, K2) twice, P1, K4; M3, K6, M3; B: K3, P1, K34 P1, K3.
R24 A: M3, K6, M3; K3, P1, K2, P3, K2, P1, K3; M3, K6, M3; B: K4, P1, K1, P1, K4
R25 A: M3, K6, M3; (K2, P1) twice, K1, P1, K1, (P1, K2) twice; M3, K6, M3; B: K5, P1, K5.
R26A: M3, K6, M3; K1, P1, (K2, P1) 4 times, K1; M3, K6, M3; B: K11 for 21 rounds (1)

R27 A: as R24; B: K11 for 21 rounds (2)
R28 A: as R25 but cc; B: K11 for 21 rounds (3)
R29 A: as R23; B: K11 for 21 rounds (4)
R30 A: as R27; B: K11 for 21 rounds (5)
R31 A: as R22; B: K11 for 21 rounds (6)
R32 A: as R23; B: K11 for 21 rounds (7)
R33 A: (M3, K6) twice, P3, (K6, M3) twice; B: K11 for 21 rounds (8)
R34 A: as R22; B: K11 for 21 rounds (9)
R35 A: as R33 but cc; B: K11 for 21 rounds (10)
R36 A: as R20; B: K11 for 21 rounds (11)
R37 A: as R20; B: K11 for 21 rounds (12)
R38 A: as R17; B: K11 for 21 rounds (13)
R39 A: as R17; B: K11 for 21 rounds (14)
R40 A: as R17; B: K11 for 21 rounds (15)

A: Repeat pattern from R8 (inclusive); (33 rounds to pattern);
B: Cont K11 until 21 rounds have been worked, then repeat from R5 to R46 (inclusive).
NOTE that A repeats every 33 rounds; B repeats every 42 rounds.

At **R63** begin u/arm gusset by incr 1 st each side of seam st, keeping seam st P, and every following 7th round up to armhole.
After **R141** or length to suit, begin armhole by putting gusset and seam sts on holders.**

Front armhole

Keeping pattern correct, without incr or decr, and working backwards and forwards, continue until neck shaping (**R239** or as required).

Neck shaping and shoulder strap

Right shoulder: **R239** (on 'wrong' side) K51, turn, P back. Continue in this manner in double garter st (2 rows P, 2 rows K, as seen from RSF), decr 1 st every other row 4 times, then 1 st every 3rd row twice. K 2 rows and leave sts on holder. Left shoulder: Work to match right shoulder, leaving centre sts on a holder.

Back armhole

Work as front from ** to Neck Shaping to match front, but working right across all rows and with *no* shaping. Work an extra 4 rows, then leave sts on a holder.

Shoulder seams

Cast off back and front shoulders tog on 'wrong' side, so that seam forms a 'furrow'.

Sleeves

(Knitted from the top)
Pick up 175 sts on a circular or set of 4 needles around armhole as follows (with the gusset and seam st included): RSF K last 12 gusset sts, pick up 75 sts to shoulder, 1 st on shoulder seam, 75 sts to gusset, K12 gusset sts, P1 (seam st). Proceed as follows to place patterns, remembering to 'read' them *downwards*, and *decreasing gusset* (from outer edges) every 2nd round until gone, then decr each side of stst every 3rd row to R66.
R1 A: as R40 (i.e. M9, K6, M3; K15; M3, K6, M3, K11; M3, K6, M3; K15; M3, K6, M3; K11; M3, K6,

M3; K15; M3, K6, M9; B: K11.

R2 A: as R39 (remember decr); B: K11.

R3 A: as R38; B: as R25 (K5,P1,K5).

R4 A: as R37 (remember decr); B: as R24.

R5 A: as R36 (CC); B: as R23.

Continue in this manner until 66 rounds have been worked.

R67 Knit, knitting 2 tog at centre of each cable (121 sts plus 1 seam st).

Continue in plain stst, decr each side of seam st on every 5th round from last decrease until 80 sts remain. Adjust length here as required.

Cuff

K2, P2 rib for 6.5cm (2 1/2in) or as required. Cast off loosely.

Knit other sleeve to match.

Neckband

RSF pick up sts down left side of neck, K sts from holder at front, pick up sts along right side of neck, K sts from holder at back (126 sts). Work 14 rounds in K2, P2 rib. Cast off loosely.

8 Machine Knitted Jersey

This jersey is evocative of a landscape of rolling hills. The garment in Photo 1.12, page 25, was also designed and knitted by Jenny Lineham in the same manner. This pattern is written for people with a reasonable amount of experience in partial knitting.

Materials

500g (18oz) semi-worsted yarn. The blue/green yarn was spun from a Romney/Dorset cross fleece, Sample O, page 51. The two greys were spun from unknown fleeces, probably Romney. The dark blue yarn is the lighter grey yarn dyed with chemical dyes (Earth Palette). All the yarn was spun with 12 wraps and 6 twists per 2.5cm (1in) in the finished yarn.
NOTE: The finished garment is made up with the purl side as the right side.
Machine used: Brother KH 830

Finished size

Body 114cm (45in)
Length underarm 37cm (14½in)
Total length 57cm (22½in)
Sleeve length 47cm (18½in)
If you want to lengthen garment add additional rows at the beginning after rib and first 2 rows of increasing sts.

Tension

13 sts to 5cm, 14 sts to 5cm
T. 10 Yarn has been fed in from floor. With handspun do not put through tension gauge.

Abbreviations

RC = row counter; MK = machine on K to knit all sts; PK = partial knit; HP = holding position for partial knit; WP = Working position to have sts back in knit position; *-* = repeat the last time *-* was mentioned: St (LH) or (RH) = needles as numbered on machine; LH = left-hand side of machine; RH = right-hand side of machine; CA = carriage.

In partial knitting the wool is looped around the last needle in HP before knitting back (avoiding leaving a hole).

Key

MC (main colour): light grey
CC1 (contrast 1): dark grey
CC2 (contrast 2): blue/green
CC3 (contrast 3): dark blue

Back

CC1 T.4.1 Cast on 133 sts, work 1x1 rib for 20 rows. Transfer to main bed.
RC 20, T.10, CC1, K 1 row. Transfer sts out evenly to 150 sts. K 1 row.
MC K to R40. CA LH side.
PK. Put 10 sts RH side in HP, K 2 rows.
Put next 10 sts in HP, K 2 rows. Repeat *-* 3 times.
Put next 5 sts on RH side in HP, K 2 rows. Repeat *-* 4 times.
*Put further 5 sts RH in HP, K 1 row.
Pull out 5 sts LH side in HP, K 1 row*. Repeat *-* 4 times. Break off wool and leave.
Put all sts in HP. CA on LH side. MK, CC3, K 1 row.
PK. Put all sts in HP except 10 RH side. RC off. CC2, K 2 rows.
Put next 10 sts in WP, K 2 rows. Repeat *-* 3 times.
Push next 5 sts in WP, K 2 rows. Repeat *-* 4 times.
MK, CC 2 RC on, K 2 rows (all sts). CA on RH side.
Put all sts to L of needle 0 HP, RC off, PK, K 1 row.
Pull out 6 sts RH side HP. K1 row. Pull out 3 sts LH side. K 1 row. Repeat *-* 4 times.
Put all sts HP. Break off wool.
CA on RH side. MK, CC3, RC on. K 1 row (CA LH side). Turn off RC.
PK. Leave first 5 sts in WP, rest in HP. CC1, K 2 rows.
Push next 5 sts into WP, K 2 rows. Repeat *-* 3 times.
MK, RC on, K 1 row to RH side. Leave first 6 sts in WP, put rest in HP. PK, RC off. K 2 rows.
Push next 6 sts into WP, K 2 rows. Repeat *-* 3 times.
Put all needles from RH side to st5 (LH), WP, K 1 row.
Pull out sts RH side of st 0 into HP. K 1 row. CA RH side.
Push back 5 sts LH side to WP, K 1 row. Push 3 sts RH side to WP, K 1 row. Repeat *-* 4 times.
CA RH side of working needles. RC on. Push all LH needles into WP, K 1 row.
MK, K 11 rows. CA RH side.
PK. Pull out needles from st30 (LH) to LH side and put in HP. K 2 rows on remaining sts.
Pull out 3 sts LH side into HP, K 2 rows. Repeat *-* 3 times.
Put 10 sts LH side in HP, K 2 rows. Repeat *-* 4 times.
MK, CC3, K 1 row. CC2, K 2 rows. Turn off RC.
MC, PK. Pull out sts RH side of st30 (LH) into HP. K 2 rows.
Put next 3 sts in WP, K 2 rows. Repeat *-* 3 times.
Put next 10 sts in WP, K 2 rows. Repeat *-* 4 times.
CA LH side. RC on MK, K 11 rows. CA RH side.
PK. *Put 20 needles LH side in HP, K 2 rows*. Repeat *-* once.
Put 3 sts on LH side in HP. K 2 rows. Repeat *-* twice.
MK, CC3, K 1 row.
PK, RC off. Put all needles in HP except 20 LH side. CC2, K 2 rows.
Put next 20 sts in WP, K 2 rows.
Push next 3 sts into WP, K 2 rows. Repeat *-* twice (rows now 132).
Put RC on R130. *Put marker in each side to mark armhole.*
MK, RC on. K 15 rows. CA on RH side.
Put all needles LH of st40 (LH) in HP. PK, K 2 rows.
Put next 3 sts in HP, K 2 rows. Repeat *-* 3 times.
MK, CC3, K 1 row. CC2, K 1 row (CA RH side).
PK. Pull all sts to LH of st 0 in HP, K 2 rows.
Pull out next 3 sts in HP, K 2 rows. Repeat *-* 4 times.

Pull out 6 sts on LH side, K 1 row. Pull out 6 sts RH side, K 1 row. Repeat *-* 3 times. Break off yarn.
All needles in HP, CA RH side. MK, CC1, K 1 row, RC off, MC.
PK. Put all sts to RH side of st40 (LH) into HP, K 2 rows.
Put next 3 sts in WP, K 2 rows. Repeat *-* 3 times.
Put needles L of st 0 in WP, K 2 rows.
Put next 3 sts in WP, K 2 rows. Repeat *-* 4 times.
Put next 6 sts LH in WP, K 2 rows. Repeat *-* 3 times.
MK, RC, on CC3, K 1 row. CC1, K 1 row.
Pull out all needles RH of st10 (LH) in HP, PK, K 2 rows.
Put next 3 sts in HP, K 2 rows. Repeat *-* 5 times.
MK, CC3, K 1 row. CC 2, K 5 rows. CC3, K 1 row.
CC2, PK, CA RH side. RC off. Pull out all needles except 6 RH side, K 2 rows.
Put next 6 sts RH side in WP, K 2 rows. Repeat *-* twice.
Put all needles RH side of st10 (LH) in WP, K 2 rows.
Put next 3 sts in WP, K 2 rows.
RC on, MK, CC3, K 1 row. MC, K 1 row (CA now RH side).
RC off, PK. Put out sts LH of st15 (LH) in HP, K 2 rows.
Put next 3 sts in WP, K 2 rows. Repeat *-* 3 times.
RC on, MK, MC, K 7 rows.
Cast off 50 sts. K 1 row. Cast off 50 sts. CC1, K 1 row.
Transfer sts to 1x1. T.4.1, rib 27 rows. Transfer to main bed. T.10 K 1 row loosely.
CAST OFF.

Front

CC1 T.4.1 Cast on 133 sts, work 1x1 rib for 20 rows. Transfer to main bed. RC 20, T.10, CC1, K 1 row.
Transfer sts out evenly to 150 sts, K 1 row. MC, K to R.40. CA RH side, PK. Put 10 sts LH side in HP, K 2 rows.
Put next 10 sts in HP, K 2 rows. Repeat *-* 3 times.
Put next 5 sts on LH side in HP, K 2 rows. Repeat *-* 4 times.
*Put further 5 sts LH side in HP, K 1 row.
Pull out 5 sts RH side in HP. K 1 row*. Repeat *-* 4 times. Break off wool and leave.
Put all sts in HP, CA RH side. MK, CC3, K 1 row.
PK. Put all sts in HP except 10 LH side, RC off. CC2, K 2 rows.
Put next 10 sts in WP, K 2 rows. Repeat *-* 3 times.
Push next 5 sts in WP, K 2 rows. Repeat *-* 4 times.
MK, CC2, RC on, K 2 rows (all sts). CA on LH side.
Put all sts to R of needle O HP, RC off. PK. K 1 row.
Pull out 6 sts LH side HP, K 1 row. Pull out 3 sts RH side HP, K 1 row. Repeat *-* 4 times.
Put all sts HP. Break off wool.
CA on LH side. MK, CC3, RC on, K 1 row (CA RH side). Turn off RC.
PK. Leave first 5 sts in WP, rest in HP. CC1, K 2 rows.
Push next 5 sts in WP, K 2 rows. Repeat *-* 3 times.
MK, RC on, K 1 row to LH side. Leave first 6 sts in WP, put rest in HP. PK, RC off, K 2 rows.
Push next 6 sts into WP, K 2 rows. Repeat *-* 3 times.
Put all needles from LH side to st5 (RH) WP, K 1 row.
Pull out sts LH side of st 0 into HP, K 1 row, CA LH side.
Push back 5 sts RH side to WP, K 1 row. Push 3 sts LH side to WP, K 1 row. Repeat *-* 4 times.
CA LH side of working needles. RC on. Push all RH needles into WP, K 1 row.

Wool spun and dyed by Anne Field, jersey designed and knitted by Jenny Lineham

MK, K 11 rows, CA LH side.
PK. Pull out needles from st30 (RH) to RH side and put in HP, K 2 rows on remaining sts.
Pull out 3 sts RH side into HP, K 2 rows. Repeat *-* 3 times.
Put 10 sts RH side in HP. K 2 rows. Repeat *-* 4 times.
MK, CC3, K 1 row. CC2, K 2 rows. Turn off RC.
MC, PK. Pull out sts LH side of st30 (RH) into HP, K 2 rows.
Put next 3 sts in WP, K 2 rows. Repeat *-* 3 times.
Put next 10 sts in WP, K 2 rows. Repeat *-* 4 times.
CA RH side, RC on MK, K 11 rows. CA LH side.
PK. *Put 20 needles RH side in HP., K 2 rows*. Repeat *-* once.
Put 3 sts on RH side in HP, K 2 rows. Repeat *-* twice.
MK, CC3, K 1 row.
PK, RC off. Put all needles in HP except 20 RH side. CC2, K 2 rows.
Put next 20 sts into WP, K 2 rows.
Push next 3 sts into WP, K 2 rows. Repeat *-* twice (rows now 132)).
Put RC on R130. *Put marker in each side to mark armhole.*
MK, RC on. CC2, K 16 rows. CA RH side, PK.
Put needles LH of st10 (RH) in HP, K 2 rows.
Put next 3 sts in HP, K 2 rows. Repeat *-* 3 times.
Put next 9 sts in HP, K 2 rows. Repeat *-* 4 times.
MK, CC3, K 1 row, RC off, PK, MC (CA LH side).
Put all sts in HP from st10 LH side to RH side. K 1 row.
Put 10 sts LH side in HP, K 1 row.
*Put 3 sts RH side in WP, K 1 row.
Put 10 sts LH side in HP, K 1 row. Repeat *-* 3 times.

CA LH side. *Put 9 sts on RH side in WP, K 1 row.
Put 12 sts on LH side in HP, K 1 row*. Repeat *-* 4 times.
Push remaining RH sts in WP, K 1 row to RH side, RC on.
*Put 3 sts LH side in HP, K 1 row.
Put 5 sts RH side in HP, K 1 row. Repeat *-* 3 times.
Put 3 sts LH side in HP, K 1 row, CA LH side.
Push RH needles in WP, K to RH side.
MK, CC3, K 1 row, RC off.
PK. CC1. Put all sts except 1st 10 LH side in HP, K 2 rows.
Put next 10 sts in WP, K 2 rows. Repeat *-* 3 times.
MK, RC on, K 1 row to RH side, PK, RC off.
Put all sts in HP except 5 RH side, K 2 rows.
Put next 5 sts in WP, K 2 rows. Repeat *-* twice.
MK, RC on, CC3, K 1 row. PK, RC off.
Put all sts from st12 (LH) to RH side HP. MC, K 2 rows.
Put next 12 sts in WP, K2 rows. Repeat *-* 3 times. RC on (R180).
Shape neck: PK (CA LH side). Put sts 10 (LH) to RH side in HP K 2 rows.
Put 5 on RH in HP, K 2 rows. Repeat *-* twice, the last time not putting wool around the needle. K to R212.
CAST OFF 50 sts.
MC, PK, RC R180, PK. Put sts 10 (RH) to st32 (RH) in WP. Carefully move carriage and thread across to first HP sts. MC, K 1 row.
Put 5 sts LH side HP, K 1 row.
Put 3 sts RH side in WP, K 1 row.
Put 5 sts LH side in HP, K 1 row.
Put 3 sts RH side in WP, K 1 row.
Put 5 sts LH side in HP, K 1 row. Do not put yarn around this needle.
Put 3 sts RH side in WP, K 2 rows. Repeat *-* once.
CA LH side. Put all remaining sts in WP, K to R212.
CAST OFF 50 sts.

Pick up neck: Stretch each side of neck out and pick up approx 100 sts altogether.
MC, K 1 row. CC1, K 1 row. Transfer to 1x1 rib. T.4.1, rib 27 rows. Transfer back to main bed. T.10, K 1 row loosely. *CAST OFF.*

Sleeve I

CC1, cast on 63 sts 1x1 rib. T.4.1, rib 20 rows. Transfer to main bed, (RC20), K 1 row.
Increase sts out evenly to 80 sts altog, K 5 rows.
Inc 1 st each end and every following 6 rows to R 80 (98 sts).
Inc 1 st each end of this and every following 8th row to R120 (108 sts).
Inc 1 st each end, PK. Put needles from 10 (RH) side in HP, K 2 rows.
Put further 10 sts RH into HP, K 2 rows. Repeat *-* 3 times.
Inc 1 st LH side.
Put further 10 sts in HP, K 2 rows. Repeat *-* once (R134).
Put all sts in HP. Break off wool.
CA RH side, RC off, MC, push st15 and all to RH side in HP. Inc 1 st RH side, K 2 rows.
Put next 4 sts into HP, K 2 rows. Repeat *-* 5 times. Break off wool.
Put all sts in HP, CA LH side. MK, RC on, CC3, K 2 rows, PK, RC off.

Put sts15 to RH side in HP. MC, K 1 row. Put st10 (RH) to LH side in HP, K 1 row.
*Push 4 RH sts back into WP, K 1 row.
Push 10 LH sts back into WP, K 1 row*. Repeat *-* 5 times.
RC on. Push all RH needles into WP, K 1 row.
Push all LH needles into WP, K 1 row.
Inc 1 st each end, K 10 rows.
Inc 1 st each end, K to R164 (116sts).
CC3, K 1 row. CC2, K 2 rows.

Join body to sleeve
With stock stitch side facing, attach shoulder of back to st 0 and put up sts to marker on LH side. Front SS facing, pick up shoulder on st0 out to RH side to marker. MK, CC1, K 1 row loosely. *CAST OFF.*

Sleeve 2
CC1, rib cuff as for sleeve 1.
RC on 20, K 1 row. Increase to 80 sts as for first sleeve. K 2 rows. CC3, K 1 row.
CC2, K 2 rows. MC, inc 1 st each end and every following 6th row to R80.
Inc 1 st each end every following 8th row twice.
CC1, K 2 rows, PK.
*Put 6 sts RH side on HP. K 1 row.
Put 6 sts LH side in HP, K 1 row*. Repeat *-* 7 times. Break off yarn.
CA LH side, RC on 98, MK, CC3, K 2 rows. (Note working on LH side inc 1 st LH side on rows 106 and 114.) Put all sts except first 6 in HP, RC off, PK, MC, K 2 rows.
Push next 6 sts into WP, K 2 rows, Repeat *-* 6 times. Break off yarn.
Put all needles in HP, RC off, CA RH side. RC on 100 (inc on rows 106 and 114).
Push 1 st into WP, K 2 rows.
Push next 6 sts into WP, K 2 rows. Repeat *-* 6 times.
CA on LH side,MK, CC3, K 3 rows.
CC1, K 3 rows, inc 1 st each end. K 2 rows (R124).
MC, K 6 rows, inc 1 st each end.
K 10 rows, inc 1 st each end. K to R155.
CC3, K 1 row. CC1, K 4 rows. CC3, K 1 row. CC2, K 2 rows.
Pick up body onto sleeve as for Sleeve 1 and cast off.

Finishing
Press with damp cloth. With purl side facing graft shoulders together. Next, graft front and back and sleeves. Neck is sewn down on the purl side of the jumper.

9 Triangular Shawl

Triangular shawl, spun and knitted by Joy Bryant

Materials

450m (500yd) 2ply handspun yarn, 10-12 wraps per 2.5cm (1in). This shawl was spun from a pale grey Perendale fleece, which gave added bulk to the shawl.
1 pair 10mm ($^3/_8$ in) needle

Pattern

Cast on 201 sts and mark the middle stitch (101) with a safety pin.
1st row: Knit
2nd row: K1, K2 tog through back of loops, K until centre 5 sts, K2 tog through back of loops, K1, K2 tog through back of loops. K to last 3 sts, K2 tog through back of loops, K1.
Repeat rows 1 and 2 until there are no stitches left. To add appeal, insert rows of *make 1, K2 tog, repeat from * to end. Remember to continue shaping throughout.

Making up

Do not be alarmed at the strange shape at this stage. Crochet along the cast-off edge, which becomes the neck edge, for strength and to make a good finish. Now wet the shawl thoroughly, hand squeeze, then shake out and peg on the line at each end of the neck edge only. It will miraculously fall into the right shape. When dry, knot a fringe right round the cast-on edge, which has now become the two sides of the triangle.

APPENDICES

ROMNEY

APPENDIX A

The address of the New Zealand Association of Black and Coloured Sheep Breeders is:

The Secretary
Leslie Jensen
40 Roberts Road
Masterton

New Zealand.

Write to this address for your local contact from the World Association of Black and Coloured Sheep Breeders.

APPENDIX B

Classification of New Zealand wools (all figures are averages). In the conversion from metrics to imperial, the figures have been rounded off.

Breed	Microns	Quality No	Staple length	Staple shape	Crimps per 2.5cm
Merino	19-23	60s-70s	75mm (3in)	flat tip	11
Polwarth	21-26	58s-64s	100mm (4in)	flat tip	7.5
Corriedale & Halfbred	26-33	50s-58s	108mm ($4^1/_2$)	almost flat	5
Perendale	28-35	48s-56s	125mm (5in)	slightly pointed	4.5
Borderdale	29-35	48s-54s	125mm (5in)	slightly pointed	4.5
Romney	31-38	44s-52s	146mm ($5^1/_2$in)	pointed tip	4
Coopworth	33-38	44s-50s	150mm (6in)	pointed tip	3.5
Border Leicester	37-38	44s-46s	175mm (7in)	pointed & curled tip	2.5
English Leicester	38-40	40s-44s	190mm ($7^1/_2$)	curled tip	2
Lincoln	38-42	36s-40s	230mm (9in)	pointed	1.5
Cheviot	28-33	50s-56s	100mm (4in)	slightly pointed	5
Southdown	21-26	58s-64s	50mm (2in)	square	n.a.*

*n.a.: not apparent

APPENDIX C

The wool analysis chart opposite may be photocopied and used as a guide for your own wool analysis.

SAMPLE:

Staple length

Staple shape

Crimp pattern

Fibre size

Colour

Lustre

Bulk

Cleanliness

Soundness

Suggestions for spinning

Suggested end uses

Breed

Source of wool

APPENDIX D

REQUIRED INCHES PER TREADLE FOR TWISTS PER INCH

Twists/inch	Drive ratio of your wheel																
	2	3	4	5	6	7	8	9	10	11	12	13	14	15	16	17	18
2	1	1.5	2	2.5	3	3.5	4	4.5	5	5.5	6	6.5	7	7.5	8	8.5	9
3	0.7	1	1.3	1.7	2	2.3	2.7	3	3.3	3.7	4	4.3	4.7	5	5.3	5.7	6
4	0.5	0.7	1	1.3	1.5	1.7	2	2.3	2.5	2.7	3	3.3	3.5	3.7	4	4.3	4.5
5	0.4	0.6	0.8	1	1.2	1.4	1.6	1.8	2	2.2	2.4	2.6	2.8	3	3.2	3.4	3.6
6	0.3	0.5	0.6	0.8	1	1.2	1.3	1.5	1.6	1.8	2	2.2	2.3	2.5	2.6	2.8	3
7	0.3	0.4	0.6	0.7	0.8	1	1.1	1.3	1.4	1.6	1.7	1.8	2	2.1	2.3	2.4	2.6
8	0.2	0.4	0.5	0.6	0.7	0.9	1	1.1	1.2	1.4	1.5	1.6	1.7	1.9	2	2.1	2.2
9	0.2	0.3	0.4	0.5	0.7	0.8	0.9	1	1.1	1.2	1.3	1.4	1.5	1.7	1.8	1.9	2
10	0.2	0.3	0.4	0.5	0.6	0.7	0.8	0.9	1	1.1	1.2	1.3	1.4	1.5	1.6	1.7	1.8
11	0.2	0.3	0.4	0.5	0.5	0.6	0.7	0.8	0.9	1	1.1	1.2	1.3	1.4	1.5	1.5	1.6
12	0.2	0.3	0.3	0.4	0.5	0.6	0.7	0.8	0.8	0.9	1	1.1	1.2	1.3	1.3	1.4	1.5
13	0.1	0.2	0.3	0.4	0.5	0.5	0.6	0.7	0.8	0.8	0.9	1	1.1	1.2	1.2	1.3	1.4
14	0.1	0.2	0.3	0.4	0.4	0.5	0.6	0.6	0.7	0.8	0.9	0.9	1	1.1	1.1	1.2	1.3
15	0.1	0.2	0.3	0.3	0.4	0.5	0.5	0.6	0.7	0.7	0.8	0.9	0.9	1	1.1	1.1	1.2

These figures have been rounded off. To convert to cm, multiply inches by by 2.5.

I have a concern about putting tables such as this in a book. They contain useful information but give a misleading picture of how accurate a spinner can be. Can you imagine spinning 0.2 of an inch of wool onto a bobbin for one treadle! It is impossible to be so accurate. However, if you take the information as a guide, such tables can be useful.

Bibliography

Amos, Alden *Spinning Wheel Primer*, Interweave Press, USA, 1989.

Aspin, Chris *The Woollen Industry*, Shire Publications Ltd, 1982.

Baines, Patricia *Spinning Wheels*, Batsford Ltd, Britain, 1977.

Chadwick, Eileen *The Craft of Handspinning*, Batsford Ltd, Britain, 1980.

Crockett, Candace *The Complete Spinning Book*, Watson-Guptill Publications, New York, 1977.

Fannin, Allen *Handspinning, Art & Technique*, Van Nostrand Reinhold Co, USA, 1970.

Field, Anne *The Ashford Book of Spinning*, Shoal Bay Press, New Zealand, 1986.

Jackson, Constance and Plowman, Judith *The New Zealand Woolcraft Book*, Collins, 1980.

Henderson, A.E. *Growing Better Wool*, A. H. & A.W. Reed, New Zealand, 1968.

Henderson, A.E. *Wool and Woolclassing*, A.H. & A.W. Reed, New Zealand, 1965.

Horne, Beverley *Fleece in Your Hands*, Revised edition published by Interweave Press, USA, 1979.

Raven, Lee *Hands on Spinning*, Interweave Press, USA, 1987.

Ross, Mabel *The Essentials of Handspinning*, published by the author, 1980.

Ross, Mabel *The Essentials of Yarn Design for Handspinners*, published by the author, 1983.

Ryder, M.L. and Stephenson, S.K. *Wool Growth*, Academic Press, London and New York, 1968.

Simmons, Paula *Spinning and Weaving with Wool*, Pacific Search Press, USA, 1978.

Stevens, P.G. *Sheep Part 2*, Whitcombe and Tombs Ltd, 1961.

Stove, Margaret. *Merino: Handspinning, Dyeing and Working With Merino and Superfine Wools in New Zealand*, Caxton Press, New Zealand, 1991.

Teal, Peter *Hand Woolcombing and Spinning*, Blandford Press, Britain, 1976.

Varney, Diane *Spinning Designer Yarns*, Interweave Press, USA, 1987.

Young, Joan *This Is Wool*, New Zealand Wool Board, 1965.

Coloured Sheep and Their Products, World Congress on Coloured Sheep, New Zealand, 1984.

Coloured Sheep and Wool, the proceedings of the World Congress on Coloured Sheep, USA, 1989, edited by Kent Erskine, Black Sheep Press, Oregon.

Dyeing for Fibres and Fabrics, edited by Janet De Boer, Kangaroo Press, 1989.

Index